ALICIA

PETER PURCHASE

From revolutionary Mexico to
contemporary Western Australia, a
remarkable young woman faces her
demons with courage, determination
and resilient independence

DUNE
PUBLISHING

Perth Western Australia

First published in Australia 2024 by Dune Publishing
Copyright © Peter Purchase 2024
www.peterpurchasebooks.com

The Truth And Reconciliation Trilogy
Book I   The Glass Cenotaph
Book II   The Life And Times Of Gerrit de Waal
Book III   Alicia

Cataloguing-in-Publication data is available from
The National Library of Australia

General acknowledgement is made to the following for permission
to reprint previously published material: Use of the Australian
Aboriginal Malgana language, permission courtesy of Ben Bellottie
of Denham, Shark Bay; Photographs of the *Zuytdorp* wreck site, ©
Fremantle Shipwrecks Museum, permission granted by photographer
Pat Baker, courtesy of Fremantle Shipwrecks Museum; Photographs
of Jandamarra's Rock and the *Zuytdorp* Cliffs © Adam Monk Art
Photography, courtesy of Adam Monk.

ISBN: 978-0-9756216-8-4 (paperback)
            978-0-9756216-9-1 (epub)

Cover photographs from Jack36 (Shutterstock) and VHStudio
(Shutterstock)

For those who died in the Tlatelolco massacre in Mexico City
on 2 October 1968, and for Australia's First Nations people
committed to eradicating racial injustice and social disadvantage
through a treaty, a voice to parliament and a process of truth
and reconciliation.

PROLOGUE

IT IS MID-JUNE, 1990, in Fremantle, Western Australia. Lennard and I are leaning across the railing on the back veranda of his house on Belleview Terrace, gazing over rooftops sloping down towards the city and the Indian Ocean beyond. The air is still and the blinding sun is arching down the cloudless sky towards the western horizon, but shade from the bullnose corrugated iron roof enables us to make out the distant pale blue haze of Rottnest Island across the undulating sea.

We can see Lennard's glass sculpting workshop from up here. It looks more like a primitive church than a workshop, with three tall arched windows, sandstone bricks and a high-pitched red corrugated iron roof. It sits on the grassy bank of Bathers Beach—down there, between the fishing harbour and the rocky causeway of the south mole.

We spent the morning there. Lennard showed me round the furnaces, the kilns, the sand-casting moulds and the annealing ovens. The processes he described left me mystified until he displayed the blueprints and photographs of glass sculptures he'd produced since his student days. Their unexpected beauty took my breath away. Their elegance and slender shapes, colours and sizes were eye-catching, especially those on show in London's Victoria and Albert and New York's Metropolitan and Corning Glass Museums. Many others complemented prominent buildings and landscapes in parks and gardens around the world.

Then he showed me the preliminary drawings for his next project, his most ambitious yet. It will be a gigantic, solid glass cenotaph designed to commemorate the First Nations warriors who died fighting in the Frontier Wars resisting the colonial invasion. Based on Jandamarra's Rock in Windjana Gorge in the Kimberley, it will stand two storeys high. Lennard imagines it as a dazzling iceberg refracting shades of blue from turquoise to ultramarine as the sun, arcing across the sky, lights it up.

* * *

I've been here now for a week.

Time to wrap my head around the radical change in my situation. Time to come to terms with such an unforeseen new direction.

It is hard to believe a 30-year-old part-indigenous Mexican woman with a PhD in Amerindian languages and linguistics suits the needs of Lennard Currie and his First Nations Malgana mob so perfectly. Especially the timing. With Annie Morgan's life hanging in the balance, we have no time to lose. She's the last fluent speaker of Malgana.

Lennard introduced us when we passed through Northampton on the way south to Perth. She was sitting with two friends on her front veranda beneath sprays of purple bougainvillea. Their animated conversation reached us when Lennard switched off his Harley motorbike and we dismounted. It sounded as though they were bickering and squabbling good-humouredly at the tops of their voices, bursts of laughter carrying to us as we approached.

They were silent as we climbed the steps. The whirring of their battered Panasonic tape recorder greeted our arrival, before one of them—Susie Kelly, I soon discovered—switched it off and the rollers squealed to a stop.

'Afternoon, Aunties,' Lennard said. 'Let me introduce Alicia Serrano.'

With an extended forefinger he pointed out Annie Morgan, Susie Kelly and Molly Sanderson in turn, before explaining, 'I picked Alicia up on the side of the road at Exmouth, hitch-hiking to Darwin—'

'*Darwin?*' Molly interrupted him. 'You lost your bearin's, sister? Aren't you headin' in the wrong direction?'

'No, Aunty Mol. I've convinced her to join us. This is where she belongs right now. Where she's needed. Alicia is the linguist we've been looking for.' He grinned. 'With a PhD.'

The three old ladies looked up at me bright-eyed, appreciation dawning in their collective, '*Aaaah...*'

'Just what the doctor ordered,' Annie Morgan said, patting the seat beside her. 'Never mind Darwin. Make yourself at home right here, 'Leesh. Next to me. Tell us all about yourself.'

Although her sunken eyes were bright and her strong, dark face appeared cheerful beneath a red-chequered scarf concealing her skull, her hacking cough told a different story.

We can't allow the Malgana language to die with her.

* * *

I had no intention of returning to Perth or Fremantle. It was the last thing on my mind. After my beloved Alain's death in West Africa in such tragic circumstances five months ago, I had to get away. Escaping north to Darwin seemed the sensible thing to do. To distance me from the trauma, ease the pain and enable me to reflect on what had happened. To give me time to heal and empower me to move on.

Yet here I am, such a short time later, back where I'd experienced the worst of it.

'Everything happens for a reason,' Lennard said the evening we arrived back in the city and were settling in. 'If you hadn't met me on your way up north, who knows where you'd have ended up?'

'It all depends on what you mean by reason,' I said. 'If you believe your life is somehow orchestrated for you, I have to disagree. It's random and unpredictable. Things happen by chance and coincidence. It's a matter of luck, one way or the other. Serendipity. And if they do work in your favour, it's by way of a happy accident, when you find yourself in the right place at the right time. As I did with you. Pure and simple.'

'Too right, Alicia, it all comes down to luck. Like right this minute when you've won the lottery, though you may not know it yet. From what you've told me, I reckon you've reached a character-defining moment, a rare opportunity. How you face the challenges will tell us who you are... how resilient, by crikey.'

How I face the challenges? I thought. *How resilient I am? That's always been at the heart of my story.*

As he spoke, the years fell away and I saw myself once again a terrified girl of eight, standing on the bloodstained paving stones of the Tlatelolco Plaza in Mexico City in October 1968. Deafened by the gunshots, I wound rapidly through the film in my grandfather's Leica camera and shot the scene, a witness to the horror, before sprinting to safety from the massacre through the labyrinth of the Aztec ruins below me. It was a defining moment when I'd held my ground, and it has never left me.

SURÉ

Aqui esta mi secreto. Es muy simple: soló con el corazón se puede ver correctamente; Lo que es esenciel es invisible a los ojos.
And now here is my secret. It's very simple: it's only with the heart that one can see rightly; what is essential is invisible to the eye.

Antoine de Saint-Exupéry
The Little Prince, April 1943

In Cerocahui, beside the Copper Canyon in North Western Mexico, May 1967

MY MOTHER, SURÉ, DIED on 10 May 1960, a month after I was born. Although I have no memory of her, I've spent my life trying to recall her particular smell, her comforting touch, the beating of her heart against my own.

I have a tinted photograph showing me feeding at her right breast, taken a week before she died. I carry it with me everywhere. She held me in her arms for those thirty days and I treasure every moment of our imagined closeness.

The day she died is Mother's Day, of all days. Can you believe it?

When I was growing up and missing her, my father, Victor, used to reassure me the date proved I was so special Mamá made it her purpose in life to give birth to me, despite the risks. She was forty years old. He'd take me in his arms and give me a consoling embrace, often cradling my face in his hands—but in the secret corner of my mind, I'd wish it was Mamá comforting me. I'd feel confused and even more upset, and guilty too, for hurting Papá if he ever suspected how I felt.

Every year without fail, we used to visit Mamá's older sister, my *Tía* Ariché, on the anniversary of Mamá's death. We'd spend a week at her *ranchería* in Cerocahui, deep in the

Sierra Madre Mountains among the canyons. We'd honour Mamá's memory, as though celebrating the *Día de los Muertos*, the Day of the Dead, six months early.

The first such visit I clearly remember occurred in May, 1967.

We drove up from our home in Saucillo the day before, in my Tarahumaran grandfather Cerrildo's 1956 Golden Hawk Studebaker. It was a seven-hour journey, with short stopovers in Cuauhtemoc and Creel.

My older brother Andrés let me win four games of checkers out of seven during the drive, 'Because you're still a beginner and learning the moves.'

I went through Andrés's latest comics between games, reading and rereading the adventures of my favourite superhero, Kalimán, and his eleven-year-old apprentice, Solín, until I was car sick—just the once and fortunately outside the car. Papá bent me over at the roadside, an arm around my waist and his free hand holding back my hair, urging me not to soil his shoes. I slept the rest of the trip stretched out on the back seat with my feet up on Andrés's lap.

The next morning I woke early and found my *Tía* Ariché sitting in silence on the chilly patio, looking out across her grapevines. Andrés was out on his early morning training run, and Papá and Abu Cerrildo were still asleep.

Tía's feisty white miniature Schnauzers, Zipi and Zape, lay alert beside her, their muzzles on their paws, their eyes scanning the vineyard for any marauding thick-billed green parrots or other birds daring to feed on the grapes.

When I sat down, Zape lifted his overhanging eyebrows and met my gaze, the glint of warning in his bright, dark eyes letting me know he'd nip me if I got too close. I promptly lifted my bare feet to the seat of my chair and rested my chin on my raised knees, wrapping my arms around them, and he dismissed me and resumed his surveillance.

The green and gold leaves of the vines gleamed as the sun rose behind us. Clouds of tiny midges shimmered here and there in particles of light above the ripening purple bunches. The sun's rays slanting towards the rim of the Urique Canyon warmed my back and shoulders, melting away my icy dread at the thought of confronting Tía with the question I'd asked Papá and Abu Cerrildo countless times.

'Tía, please tell me the truth this time.'

No one else will and I'm sick of asking. The frustrating thought ran through my mind.

'What truth, sweetheart?'

'What happened to Mamá? Why did she die?'

Until now, Papá and Abu Cerrildo have not replied to me directly. They've diverted my attention. You're too young to understand. You barely knew her, if at all. All in good time. As if the cause of her death is a secret or they're shielding me from the distress of discovering something unbearable in her passing.

Tía's shrewd black eyes stared thoughtfully into mine for several long moments as she rearranged a loose strand of her thick black hair streaked with grey back into the bun coiled on top of her head.

I took a deep, determined breath and held her narrow-eyed look, unsure what she was thinking or what was coming next. She slowly nodded, rocking her body from the waist up in her creaky wicker chair, the gold Aztec Tree of Life pendant on her necklace swinging like a hypnotic pendulum across her black, loose-fitting linen blouse.

'An infection took her, Alicia,' she said at last, her voice an unexpected hiss. 'Septicaemia. After an emergency caesarean to bring you into the world.'

To bring me into the world? Uncertain what she meant, the words struck me like an accusation and I ducked my head as though she'd slapped me.

After a long pause, relaxing back in her chair, she continued, 'You are seven years old, going on seventeen. It's time you knew yours was a complicated breech birth. It took so much longer than we expected. It was never-ending and extremely painful for her. *Pero ella era estoica*, but she was stoical.'

Bewildered, I looked up and stared at her with hesitant defiance as she gathered her thoughts. Then my stubbornness gave way and I nodded, pretending with a thoughtful look that I understood her. She reached across with a calloused hand to pat my shoulder as though acknowledging my confusion.

'You arrived feet first. We couldn't turn you round,' she said, her voice now reassuring and matter-of-fact. She raised her eyebrows and showed her strong white teeth in a smile I guessed was sympathetic, 'as if you couldn't wait to meet the ground running. *Como la pequeña cabra montañosa*, like the little mountain goat you've become. But Suré had just turned forty. Very dangerous. Especially for a *mukí* of the Tarahumaran *Rarámuri*. And even though the pregnancy was unplanned, she didn't listen to our advice. As usual. *Ya mero, pero no*. Almost, but no. No. She was having none of it.' She gave a quick shake of her head. 'She was determined to have you, *mijita*. She always was the pig-headed one. Just like you. And the prettiest. How else did she snare your father from under my nose when we were young, while I was her *acompañante*, her chaperone?'

She leaned forward, wrapped her arms around me and squeezed before I could wriggle away, her smell earthy and her voice rasping as she spoke beside my ear. 'We wouldn't have it any other way, honey. She did us all a favour. You, especially you.'

When I broke free and ran, I heard her call out. 'Relax, *nenita*, relax, child. Now her spirit is *kiri-i-kiri huko*. At peace.'

9

She cackled as if to emphasise the Tarahumaran phrase she'd shouted. One of the working mules in the paddock beside the house brayed in response, both silenced as the door slammed shut behind me.

The words she yelled again were faint, 'At peace, compared to the rest of us… me and you both.'

It took me many years to come to terms with the realisation that I was partly responsible for Mamá's agonising death and understand that she'd considered an abortion early in her pregnancy but decided against it. Even Tía Ariché, who hadn't realised she'd be fostering me when Mamá died, advised her to abort me.

Almost, but not quite. My life in exchange for hers.

Was that to be my ongoing story?

* * *

When I opened the curtains an hour later, Tía still sat alone, sunlight now igniting the blood-red climbing roses blooming on the trellis above her head.

A pine-scented breeze brushed across the vineyard, its minty fragrance reaching me through the open window, and there, beyond the nearby shadows of the canyons and the mauve silhouettes of distant mountains, a pale three-quarter moon hung like a fingernail in the brightening sky.

'What colour would you paint it, Mamá?' I whispered, picturing us standing together at the window admiring the landscape, just as I'd fantasised about us doing at home in Saucillo, allowing her to share with me the experiences she'd missed. *'Oh, something golden, mijita, with the sun coming up,'* I imagined her saying. *'Something golden would be perfect.'*

The fact that I was speaking on her behalf did not diminish the authenticity of the shared moment. It seemed to me to add to it.

Before rejoining Tía, I took out Mamá's treasured brown

leather beret from my chest of drawers. Papá gave it to me a month ago on my latest birthday, along with another two of her favourite things—a silver butterfly brooch embedded with garnet stones green as emeralds and a fringed sky-blue silk rebozo shawl he assured me she'd used as a child.

He explained that before she died, she'd insisted I should have them when old enough. She didn't want them buried with her in the coffin.

I hadn't yet worn any of them. I'd been afraid to. And now I wasn't sure I deserved to, but I braced myself, put both hands inside the beret, held it open and placed it over my head. I tugged at my ponytail to adjust the beret there before tightening the leather thong running around the rim so it fitted me perfectly.

I stood for several minutes facing the mirror, arranging the beret with the bright green oak tree emblem on it front and centre. *It's shaped like Tía's Tree of Life*, I thought. *This is how Mamá must have worn it, checking her reflection as she adjusted it, just as I am.*

I felt uncannily connected to Mamá at that moment. I could not remember her, but now perhaps could get to know her by piecing together everything I was told about her and allowing my imagination to do the rest.

Perhaps.

It was a start.

What I wanted then more than anything was to have used the superpowers I'd learned from Kalimán and done a somersault in Mamá's womb seven years ago before moving headfirst down her birth canal, leaving us both intact and alive when I was born.

A surge of relief, almost of happiness, ran through me as the painful, unsettling sense of isolation and loneliness I usually experienced when I asked or thought about her fell away. I beamed at my image, as though her eyes were looking into mine and mine hers—and the unexpected idea flashed across my mind—*This is how I'd feel if Mamá was giving me the unconditional love I need to give myself.*

On my way out through the dining room, I surprised myself by using my fingertips to transfer a kiss to Mamá's charcoal portrait. Sketched when she was young, so long before she became my mamá, I'd always considered hers the face of a stranger. For the first time, however, I recognised myself in her. The high cheekbones with their shadows, though mine were not yet as pronounced. The wide-set eyes. The hint of creases at the edges of her smile.

The picture was propped up on the temporary *ofrenda* altar the maid Ofelia and I helped Tía construct, with a glass of water and bowl of Mamá's favourite salted cashews and peanuts, and five melting candles and incense sticks Ofelia had lit earlier for the day. The brightly coloured mandala of crepe paper flowers we'd made matched the two vases of brilliant orange and yellow *cempasúchil* marigolds I'd picked from the rows bordering the vegetable garden. Their distinct musky scent was designed to guide Mamá's spirit on her journey home to protect us, or away to the other world awaiting her.

Surrounding the offerings, Ofelia laid a semi-circle of her magic stones and crystals—a miniature dry-stone wall designed to protect Mamá from evil spirits and other *diablitos* who might want to cause her harm. The centrepiece was a small white *calavera* sugar skull Ofelia made. She decorated it with rainbow-coloured icing and sequins.

By way of contrast, a copy of Filippino Lippi's *Adoration of the Magi* was hanging on the wall beside the altar. One of Tía Ariché's favourite religious illustrations, she believed its presence guaranteed Mamá good fortune in the afterlife.

When I walked out, Tía Ariché adjusted the empty wicker chair beside her without facing me. She patted the seat. 'Are you hungry, *mijita?*' she asked. 'After *desayuno* why don't we ride the horses down to Urique and leave some flowers on your mamá's grave like we did last year? Would you like that?'

Then she looked at me with her eyebrows raised and waited for me to nod.

'I know Suré would,' she went on. '*Nada mas segura*, nothing surer. What do you say? Some sunflowers again? Her favourites. Why don't you go and pick some? We can stay there overnight and come back up tomorrow. Oh, I like your beret. It suits you. You look as striking in it as your mamá did.'

I looked away as a warm glow rushed through me at her compliment and her mention of my similarity to Mamá.

When I stood to get the clippers, Andrés appeared on the path leading to the canyon edge. He'd removed his t-shirt and wrapped it around his head against the sun. The dark skin of his lithe torso gleamed above his faded blue running shorts.

His black mixed-breed Calupoh dog, Geronimo, sleek as a greyhound with a white flash down his chest, bounded past him, his long tongue extended, his tail a runaway metronome when he recognised me. He slurped at his water bowl before slumping with a heavy sigh beneath the table, where he stretched out, panting, just beyond kicking distance of Tía's sandalled feet and a respectable distance from Zipi and Zape, who acknowledged his arrival with a combined warning growl.

Andrés glided up to us, barely panting and looking as though he hadn't raised a sweat. He placed his metre-long snake-catching pole on the table and pressed the button on the stopwatch he wore on his left wrist. Ten years older

13

than me at seventeen, I worshipped the ground he ran on, joining him for short stretches whenever he'd allow me to. Despite our teasing, he insisted he'd been training for the 1968 Olympics in Mexico City all his life. The Games were now a year away.

'*Una hora y veinte*, an hour and twenty,' he said. 'Same as yesterday. Halfway down to Lorenzo's lookout and back.' He glanced at me. 'You should have joined me, *floja*.' Then he noticed the beret. 'Or should I call you Che? All you need is his red star… and his beard.'

'I'm not a lazybones and I'm not Che, I'm *me*. Come with us to Urique after breakfast and I'll show you who can run.'

'I'll have a shower and breakfast first before we find out who shows who.'

As he walked away, I was reminded how much we looked alike, how closely we shared our looks with Mamá. A thrill ran through me. It gave me a new sense of belonging, a deep connection I was craving to offset the aloneness I sometimes experienced when I was mixing with girls my age who had their mothers.

* * *

Hours later, we laid the sunflowers across Mamá's horizontal ochre-painted grave in the Urique cemetery in the scanty shade of an alder tree.

'*Los girasoles simbolizan la adoración*,' Tía said. 'Sunflowers symbolise adoration, as I told you last time.' She squinted up through the leaves at the pale blue sun-scorched afternoon sky. 'They may not last long in this heat but our adoration will.' She hesitated, before adding, '*Mientras Dios esté feliz de sonreírnos*. For as long as God is happy to smile down on us.'

We paid our respects and left offerings of food and drink Tía had prepared, which we arranged on the grave.

We stood with bowed heads for a minute before Tía

murmured her consent and Andrés and I chased each other in and out of the white-trunked sycamore trees encircling the cemetery—trees so pale and ghostly Andrés partly convinced me as we ran that they came out of the ground at the full moon and danced among the tombstones on their roots to the hooting of the giant owl roosting in their branches.

'That owl is La Lechuza,' he said as we ran, catching me unawares and giving me goosebumps. I knew the myth. She was the shape-shifting wicked old witch who swooped down, talons drawn, to seize unsuspecting children at night, ripping them apart with her beak and taking revenge on people who'd wronged her.

The goosebumps eased when he suggested Mamá was running unseen beside us. He said she'd loved to do so with him when she was alive, and suddenly I could sense her there, the eerie rustling of the breeze among the sycamore leaves no longer the beating of a giant owl's wings but the whisper of Mamá's breathing—a sound so soothing in that moment it struck me that Mamá was not dead to us. In a sudden rush of emotion I took his hand and squeezed it, aware he must be missing Mamá as much as I was. He allowed me to hold it for several privileged moments before releasing mine to sprint the last few metres to the gravesite.

Later, we sat for some time in the nearby sanctuary of Our Lady of Guadalupe, the cool, calm silence of the chapel occasionally shattered by the expanding corrugated iron roof cracking like a starter's pistol.

Tía reminded us to make the sign of the cross and kneel when we entered. As I did so, I looked up at the mural of the dark-skinned *la Virgen* on the wall behind the altar. She still wore the bright purple eyepatch someone crudely painted over her right eye during the Easter celebrations last year, protecting her from witnessing the suffering of her son on the cross, but allowing her to watch through her left eye the destruction and burning in hell of the papier mâché effigy of Judas—the climax to the ceremonies.

Before she settled into a pew, Tía Ariché adjusted her favourite cotton rebozo shawl embroidered in olive-green and gold snakeskin diamonds over her head and shoulders. Next, she removed my beret, replaced it with Mamá's rebozo and assured me I looked as fresh and untouched as la Virgen Purísima herself wearing it.

'So did your mamá when she was your age and as innocent,' she added as she adjusted it, before leaning forward with a meaningful glance. '*Pero sin tu rebeldía*, Alicia. But without your rebelliousness.'

My rebelliousness? How dare you? You're not my mother. You never will be! I forced a smile and bit my tongue, but my eyes gave me away and for a brief second I sent her a spark of defiance, quickly extinguished by the respect and fear I held for her uncertain temper.

'Oh, look at you, *mijita*. So fiery. So headstrong.' She shook her head. 'What are we to do with you?' Her expression softened and her voice changed as she reminded us as always that Mamá was far from dead and we should pray for her. Still alive in that other place, with spiritual access to our world, she was doubtless watching over us. '*Un milagro gracias a Dios, nada mas*,' she said.

A miracle? Thanks be to God? Nothing more?

Part of me wanted to believe her, and did, but in the following silence, perplexing questions flooded my mind. *Has Mamá forgiven me without me asking her to because she loves me and is my mother? Am I worthy of her sacrifice? Does she miss me as much as I miss her? Can I ever make it up to her?* And the question tormenting me above all: *If giving me life meant she'd died in accordance with some miraculous purpose, as Papá*

had suggested, what does it mean for my future? A future I was
destined to spend without her.

'*Un milagro?*' I asked.

'*Un milagro sin lugar a dudas, como tú.*' She patted my knee.
'A miracle for certain, just as you are.' She gave me her familiar
enigmatic smile and contradictory look. 'On the other hand,
only God truly knows.'

'And if God has his doubts, then we keep guessing—'
Andrés broke in.

'Sssssssssssst! Not in this place,' Tía Ariché admonished
him. She stretched across my back and delivered a sharp slap
to the back of his head. 'You leave your scepticism at the
door, and any other doubts you've got floating around in your
empty skull, Andrés. In this place, our faith keeps hope alive,
not questioned by your so-called logic and reason.'

I suppressed a laugh when I heard him grumble as he
flinched, '*Sí. Sí.* Okay, Tía.' He made a face and I saw him
mouth under his breath, '*Pero no*, but no,' as he often did,
reasserting his seventeen-year-old machismo Mexicano.

When we left the chapel, Andrés asked if we could race
along the thousand-metre sandy circuit cleared of rocks beside
the river. 'We don't have time,' Tía replied. 'It's getting late.'

Impulsively ignoring her, I took off my riding boots
and laced on my made-to-measure huaraches. They'd been
designed for running—with car tyre soles.

'Race you up the hill!' I shouted, and with a head start,
I sprinted with Andrés and Geronimo over the rocks and
slippery gravel up the slope to the tethered horses. I punched
him several times on the arm when he said he'd let me win.

'Tía's right about your running.' He gazed intently at me,
his dark brown eyes alight. 'You are a little mountain goat—
and you look like one.'

'That makes two of us,' my tongue surprised me by replying before I'd thought of an answer. 'And you're ten years older so you're twice as ugly.'

My quick response caught him off-guard.

'*Tienes razón*. Touché!' he said, and we both laughed till the tears came, Andrés tickling my ribs with the bony fingers of his left hand while he held my upper arm with his right, careful to protect the long fingernails he'd grown for Papá and his good friend Tío Guillermo, who were teaching him to play new flamenco techniques on his guitar. Of course I'd grown mine as well, and when Andrés was practising after his lessons, he allowed me to sit beside him, joyfully tinkering with the child-size guitar Papá gave me when I'd complained about being left out.

Tía Ariché, beaming, struggled up the hill towards us. I could see her wondering what the fuss was all about. The two rebozos lay across her shoulders and in her right hand she held the little *hielera* cooler with our Lulú drinks on ice. When she lifted the lid, she surprised us with an unexpected extra treat—a slice of her homemade *mazapan de cacahuate*, her peanut marzipan, left over from the plateful of pieces she'd placed on Mamá's grave, along with the paper cup of her favourite drink—crushed-ice mango licuado.

Before she handed us our rewards, she held out her arms, as always. '*Abrázame*, hug me,' she said. And I did, just as I'd have hugged Mamá if she'd lived. The smoky smell of sweat and camphor lingered when she let me go and I asked myself achingly, *Did Mamá feel and smell the same?*

* * *

Looking back on it now, when I was seated between Tía Ariché and Andrés in the chapel, her dark Rarámuri skin and his deep mestizo tan so distinctly contrasted to my paler fawn, I felt different—in some way blessed—and yet the same, and sensed emotions stirring within me I didn't yet understand. For the first time, I feared living in a mystifying world where I suspected my destiny was no longer of my choosing or my will, but more a matter of chance.

I learned on that Mother's Day that the world, for all its magic and mesmerising beauty, can turn and strike you quicker than a homeless cat you're stroking in the street when it rubs against your leg. Shocked and bleeding, you stifle your scream and wonder, *Did I deserve the vicious clawing and the unexpected bite? And if so, why?*

Either way, you carry the scars as a lifelong reminder of your questions and the lessons you learn, and the confusing thought struck me, *If my relationship with Mamá—the most important of my life—lasted no longer than a month, are all my relationships only temporary and destined to end quickly?*

When we returned to Cerocahui the next day, Tía took me out to one of the ramshackle garden sheds. It was dark inside, the single cobwebbed window grimy. She reached up to a shelf where there was a row of lidded jars.

'Cup your hands together,' she said.

She shook the jar, unscrewed the rusty lid with some effort and poured a handful of small white sunflower seeds into my open palms. 'Now go, *mijita*. You know where to plant them. The early ones will be ready for you next year.'

Since then, I've taken a handful of seeds to plant in whatever flowerbeds are available wherever I am so that I'll have a bunch of sunflowers in full bloom on the following Mother's Day.

Caring for them as they grow, watching their buds develop and listening to stories told about Mamá over the years, have extended the one unremembered month we shared into decades, giving me a comforting, imaginary sense of bonding with the mother I never knew.

In ten short years, I'll be as old as she was when she died. It gives me an intense, uneasy awareness of my mortality, as if I'm living on borrowed time, and it reminds me—just as the growing sunflowers do each year—that mourning for her will never end.

What I learned that day I spent with Tía Ariché I've never forgotten. And although the memory can be mysteriously selective, fragmented and unreliable, I've often returned to those moments for insights into my own story, my coming of age and my quest for self-awareness, to better understand who I am and accept the person I've become.

There I am, my eager younger self, thrilled Tía has confirmed I looked so much like Mamá when she was younger, wearing her beret and rebozo and listening for further revelations to add to my growing picture of her. She took her stories with her when she died, but listening to Tía enabled me to imagine her retelling them.

There are times when I can still hear Tía describe the challenges Mamá dealt with during my birth and explain how she faced her demons with the courage, determination and resolute independence I like to think I've inherited.

VICTOR

In Saucillo, Northern Mexico, April 1968

ANOTHER MEANINGFUL MEMORY OCCURRED when Papá showed us his blue reinforced cardboard suitcase for the first time. I had just turned eight years old. I clearly recall him revealing the contents to us as he explained how he travelled from Spain to Mexico during the Spanish Civil War when he was twelve, and met Mamá by chance seven years later.

Andrés and I found him that day relaxed in his black leather armchair in the lounge. He was reading, his legs outstretched on a footstool, when we burst in from the garden. We'd been sprinting around the circuit in the backyard of Papá's house in Saucillo under Abu Cerrildo's coaching supervision and we were heading to the kitchen for a drink.

Andrés skidded to a halt beside him. 'Papá, *por favor*, please tell us how you and Mamá met,' he said.

Papá looked up. He closed his book and retrieved his distance glasses from his forehead. He put them on, sat motionless for a second, then raised his eyebrows.

'*Again?*' he asked.

'Yes, again. *Por favor.*'

'I've told you before. We met on the cathedral steps in Chihuahua City. We were both nineteen and members of the Children's Cultural Army. Teaching illiterate kids and adults to read and write.'

He rubbed his forehead as if to clear the horizontal furrows and allowed me to lift his feet from the footstool. I made myself comfortable on it and looked up at his long, thin sunburned face with its bony cheeks, Grecian profile and straight, high-bridged nose. I considered him more handsome than any *vaquero* in a Western on TV, especially considering his remarkable eyes. They were the same amber colour as mine, though in his, you could detect flecks of gold around the pupils. I leant forward with my elbows on my knees, my chin on my hands and stared into them.

'I joined Mamá's group that day,' he went on, before frowning for a moment as if collecting his thoughts. 'Later, we played chess during the breaks at school. We used a set Abu Cerrildo carved for her.'

'Like he does now? Using crystals from the Cave of Swords at the Naica mine?' I asked.

'The same.'

'And you liked her when you both played chess?'

'Yes, I did. We fell in love. You want me to go on?'

'That's not what I asked,' Andrés said. 'I want to know what happened *before* you came to Mexico. Before you met her. You've never told us the story. Not in full, anyway.'

'Because it's such a long one.'

'I want to know everything. Not just the bits and pieces you've told us so far.'

'Every detail?' He pointed at Andrés and shook his forefinger. 'You don't know what you're asking.'

'Yes, I do. It's our story too, don't forget.' Persistent as always, Andrés held both hands out, palms up. 'Your story will help Alicia and me understand.'

'Understand?'

'What you were like as a boy. How you came to *be* in Chihuahua City. Besides...' he seemed to search for the words, 'we want to know where *we* belong in the story. At least, I do.'

'Me too,' I said at once, supporting him as usual, but uncertain what he meant.

'Ah, I see.' Papá nodded, frowning. He rose abruptly to his feet and placed his open book face down on his chair. 'Very well. Come with me.'

We followed his tall, angular frame to the privacy of his darkened bedroom, where he pulled aside the curtains. Blazing sunlight filled the room as he lifted down a blue suitcase I'd never seen before, concealed on top of his wardrobe. He placed it on the bed, dusted it off with the back of his hand, flicked aside the rusty locks and slowly opened it, as though disclosing a mystery to us.

I was excited as he revealed the contents. It seemed he was bringing his past into our present at last, introducing us to the magic of his treasured boyhood memories lying in wait for us all our lives. Peering over his shoulder, I wondered what surprising stories each item held in store. I glimpsed a plastic bag of chipped, multicoloured glass marbles and steel ball bearings, a pair of battered yoyos, and a chess set in a net bag, its pieces intricately carved in light and dark wood. I saw crayons and several sketching pads, and a pair of black leather running shoes, cracked and twisted out of shape, their long spikes rusty. Two large, beige celluloid Philip Morris cigar boxes stood out beside a handful of comics and magazines, and beside them a photo album.

He took out the album, placed it on his lap, moved the open suitcase to one side and invited us to sit beside him.

'My papá Xavier, your other grandfather, was a professional photographer in Spain,' he said, opening the cover. 'He became a freelance photojournalist when the civil war broke out in 1936, over thirty years ago. He sold his pictures to the highest bidder or took assignments from the newspapers when they paid him enough to feed the family. Which wasn't often. Most of the pictures in here are his.'

He held the album open at the third page, his hand covering the right-hand page, fingers splayed. At the top of the left-hand page, written in neat white cursive, I read the words *Gernika—antes*, Guernica—before. Beneath it the date—26 April 1937.

It showed the peaceful scene of a small rural town in black and white that could be anywhere in Spain or parts of Mexico, taken at street level. Two and three-storey buildings with roman-tiled roofs, some inset with dormer attics. Arched front doors and whitewashed walls. Wooden windows framed with dark bricks and decorative cast iron grills. White-paved cobbled streets leading to a plaza filled with groups of people beneath the trees and a bandstand in the centre. Some animals—a handful of wide-horned cattle, and sheep, some black and others white. Beyond them, the tower of a church rose above the shadowy peaks of distant hills beneath a windswept sky streaked with clouds.

I leaned across and pointed at a flat-roofed single-storey building facing the square. It appeared to be a school, with a number of young children playing in the courtyard.

'What's that?' I asked. 'It looks like a school.'

'It is. A Basque school, an *ikastola euskadi*. See the name over the archway? The authorities set them up in smaller towns like Guernica and Durango during the civil war and moved as many children as possible into them, well away from the big cities like Bilbao and Madrid. To keep them safe from the fighting and the bombing.'

'They look happy.'

'They do. It looks like some of them are playing hide and seek. And you can see those three girls skipping, just like you do.'

'It's very peaceful, Papá,' Andrés said, 'with a civil war going on.'

'It was a quiet market day, even though open markets were forbidden at the time. You see the time on the Santa María belltower?'

'Half-past two,' Andrés replied.

Papá removed his right hand to reveal the other photograph. He held both pages up to us. 'By eight o'clock, it looked like this.'

Gernika—después, Guernica—afterwards, the other title read.

I peered at the apocalyptic scene of shattered buildings smouldering beneath a pall of smoke, flames raging here and there. The charred and grisly remains of limbs and body parts barely recognisable as animal or human lay scattered across piles of burning rubble beside multiple black bomb craters. Trenches and cellars lay blasted open, those who may have taken shelter in them buried alive.

I gasped at the ruins of the school, struck with horror as my heartbeat faltered. *Those poor children!* I looked away for a full minute, nauseated, fighting to calm myself, before glancing back.

The shadows of three firemen from a brigade unit stood pumping water at the conflagration. Fractured tubes the size of relay batons glinted in the blackened wreckage.

Andrés pointed them out. 'What are they?'

'They're the aluminium shells of phosphorus grenades. The bigger ones are thermite bombs,' Papá replied, 'used to create a firestorm across the town. Imagine the damage, especially when the people or animals caught fire.'

Andrés stared at the two photographs, shaking his head. He pointed at the earlier photo on the left-hand page. 'Is this one of Abu Xavier's photos too?'

'They both are. He was working in Bilbao at the time so he could have visited Guernica any day before the bombing. He showed my mamá, Marina, and me the pictures when he developed them back in Barcelona.'

'So it may not have been taken on the day before the bombing?'

'Knowing him, he'd have done everything to find a shot he'd taken as close to that date as possible.' He glanced at Andrés, frowning. 'I do remember one thing that concerned him. Some other world-famous photojournalists working in Spain *staged* the photographs they sent out for publication. Breathtaking shots, full of drama. Prize winners, some of them. They looked authentic, but they weren't. They were posed many kilometres behind the front lines, using actors dressed for the part, complete with cartridge belts and rifles. They cheated, in other words.'

'Why?'

'Because they couldn't get close enough to the fighting. Or were afraid to. Or too lazy.'

'How could they get away with it?'

'Tricks of the trade, I once heard him tell Mamá. Blurring the background so the locations couldn't be verified. Your abuelo refused to do the same. All his shots were genuine. In the case of Guernica here, we know it was a market day, but they turned most of the farmers away. The town was already full of retreating Republican soldiers and refugees.' He circled the animals in the plaza with a forefinger. 'But it looks as if a few farmers got through the cordon anyway, as we Basques always will. We're a determined bunch, *cuando el empuje viene empujar.* When push comes to shove.'

Papá told Andrés the bombing had been carried out by German Luftwaffe pilots of the Condor Legion flying the latest Heinkel bombers, on loan from Hitler to General Franco's Nationalists.

'By eight o'clock the town was in ruins and up to a thousand people were dead,' he said. 'We don't know the exact number. Guernica didn't just change world opinion against the Nationalists, it also changed my life forever.'

'You came to Mexico?' Andrés asked.

'I did.'

'So we owe Guernica our lives, Alicia and me?'

Papá closed the album. He spread both hands across the

cover, smoothing it out. 'You could say so. When Abu Xavier saw the extent of the carnage and took these photographs, he made up his mind to send me here. On my own. It happened as quickly as that.' He snapped his fingers; the piercing click beside my ear made me jump. 'A month later, I boarded the steamship *Mexique* in France, in Bordeaux, with the other selected children. We arrived in Veracruz in early June.'

'How old were you?' Andrés asked.

'Twelve.'

'Did Abuela Marina or Abuelo Xavier see you off?'

'Papá was working in Asturias, but Mamá came to the França station the day I left.' He drummed his fingers on the photo album for several long moments before he broke the silence. 'I never saw her again.' He pursed his lips as the silence lengthened. 'You don't have to ask. She died at the battle of Ebro River a year later. In July. Papá told me in a letter.'

'How?' Andrés asked.

Papá stared at Andrés, holding himself in check, it seemed to me. 'All right. She was evacuating three wounded volunteers from Benifallet and the ambulance received a direct hit. She's buried with them in the Rasquera cemetery in Tarragona. At least she had the dignity of a proper burial. Not a mass grave like many others.'

He shook his head. 'Before she died, she wrote to me whenever she could. Many postcards. Almost one a week. I lost count. They arrived every few months aboard the ships bringing them, in little bundles held together with rubber bands, sometimes with a letter from Papá.

'At the school in Morelia, we used to listen out for the postman every afternoon. Señor Arturo, on his red bicycle, with his pea whistle. Such an unmistakable sound! So shrill we'd hear him coming down the street and watch the *portero*, the gatekeeper, open the gates for him. A big fat man with a loud voice, he was. Always laughing. So loud we could hear his conversation from the classrooms even with the windows closed. It was exciting when he distributed the letters, but for me, almost always disappointing because the ships from Spain weren't frequent.'

Papá replaced the photo album in the suitcase and took out one of the beige cigar boxes. He placed it on his lap. He ran his fingertips over the two rampant lions facing off against each other in the logo embossed on the lid, as though reading them and its *veni vidi vici* motto in braille. He did not open it. He leant forward instead, placed it on the floor between his feet, and sat with his shoulders hunched.

And then, vigorously shaking his head, his fearful growl shattered the silence. '*Guernica!* This takes me back, damn it!'

I jerked sideways and glanced up at him, alarmed. Andrés placed a restraining hand on his forearm. Papá looked at each of us in turn, then closed his eyes. He spread his arms across our shoulders and gradually tightened his grip, his fingers digging into my flesh until it hurt.

An icy foreboding rushed through me. I twisted around and loosened his fingers, then held his hand in both of mine on my lap. A rush of empathy overtook me. About to cry, I began stroking the back of his hand, desperate to comfort him, but unsure how. When I looked up at his tormented face it blurred through my welling tears and I looked away.

Thankfully, moments later, he relaxed. He opened his eyes and took a deep breath.

'Very well,' he said, 'since you want my story, why don't I begin on 29 April 1937? I am twelve years old. It's late in the afternoon during a thunderstorm in Barcelona. Imagine you're sitting beside me as you are now, in the little kitchen at the back of our house. Abuela Marina is opposite us, looking unusually serious. Abu Xavier has just developed the photos of Guernica I've shown you, as well as several others not in the album. We watch him put them down one at a time on the mustard-yellow plastic tablecloth. Face up. In silence. We have no idea what he's going to say, but his expression is so stern and the photos so shocking we know it's going to be terrible.'

He held Andrés and me rapt in a long moment of shared suspense before he told us what happened next.

His storytelling, as always, held us spellbound.

VICTOR: In Barcelona, Spain, 29 April 1937

MAMÁ MARINA AND I stared at the freshly developed black and white photographs as Papá Xavier spread them across the kitchen table. He rapped the tabletop with the knuckles of his right fist several times and growled, '*Sobran las palabras.*' His face was so flushed it shocked me. 'Words are superfluous. Each picture speaks for itself.'

He scooped them up and looked across at me.

'Victor, I've added your name to those going to Mexico next month,' he said.

It took me a moment to understand what he'd said, before I reared back in my chair. 'What? *Me?* Going to Mexico?'

'It's either that or a choice between Great Britain, Belgium, France or the Soviet Union. You speak little French and no English or Russian, so Mexico is the obvious destination. Especially since their President Lázaro Cárdenas sympathises with our Republican Popular Front.'

He spoke so rapidly and the rain was drumming so loudly against the window I could hardly hear him.

'If the quota of those embarking on the steamship *Mexique* from Bordeaux for Veracruz on 26 May is full,' he went on, 'there are places available aboard the *Habana*, leaving the Santurtzi docks in Bilbao for Southampton on the twenty-first. Mexico or England. Either way, you are going. Mamá and I are agreed on this. I'm sorry. We have no choice.'

His warning frown and quick shake of his head as our eyes met discouraged me from interrupting him. 'It's for your own good, Victor. You're twelve years old. We will not have you sent to the front when you turn thirteen in July or *Dios no lo quiera*, God forbid, joining the siege in Madrid.'

He sat back, placed the photos on the table and crossed his arms.

'On my own?' I stammered.

'Yes,' Papá said.

Tense and breathless, I felt the world fall away beneath my feet. 'For how long?'

Mamá reached out and held my right hand in both of hers. 'Until the situation here is sorted out and things return to normal,' she said quietly.

'How long will that take?'

'*Quién sabe*, who knows? A year? Two?'

'Can't you come with me?'

'No,' Papá said. 'Mamá is needed here to run the ambulances.'

'Two years?' My eyes filled with tears I couldn't stop. '*Two years!*'

'According to some, but I will not lie to you.' Papá picked up the top photograph. He tapped the ruins with a forefinger. 'I've told you before, General Franco has Hitler and Mussolini in his pocket. They're using the civil war as a testing ground for their latest weapons. It pains me to say so, but the Nationalists might win. We Republicans have the heart and the will for a fight, but without the firepower, we're on the back foot. The armaments Stalin and Cárdenas are sending us don't match theirs.' He shook his head. 'It's another case of might is right, in which case we could become the righteous losers.'

'How will I contact you?' I asked. My voice was shaking so much I could hardly speak, a feeling of helplessness overwhelming me.

'All in good time. Arrangements will be made.'

'Can't I stay here in Barcelona?'

'You risk being handed a rifle and drafted where the fighting is.'

'Others my age have done it. Even younger.'

'Yes, and come back dead or mutilated in the back of ambulances. Ask Mamá. She has seen them. I will not risk it.

In Mexico, you'll have a future. They are setting up a special school in a city called Morelia for all the children selected to go. President Cárdenas himself lives there and he'll be taking a personal interest in the school. You can finish your education there if you're fortunate enough to be accepted for the voyage. Perhaps start a profession. In geology, maybe? I know you're interested—look at your rock collection—and you have the talent and the persistence for the study.' He stared at me, adding forcefully, 'Remember what I've always drummed into you. *Serás exitoso siempre que aproveche al máximo sus oportunidades*, you will succeed provided you make the most of your opportunities and don't waste them. Set your goals and work hard to achieve them, one step at a time.'

I was shocked. 'Finish my schooling there, Papá? Now you're saying it could be *longer* than two years?'

'We don't know for certain. We have to face the possibility.'

'Can't you change your mind?' I couldn't hold back my sobs as a rush of fear tore through me. I felt vulnerable, unprepared and utterly helpless. 'Please?'

'Our minds are made up.' Mamá handed me a handkerchief. 'Your safety comes first. Besides, Papá and I will join you as soon as the war is over.'

'Or I can come home?'

'Or you can come home.'

There was a tense silence. Flooded with disbelief, I found myself standing on the edge of an abyss. I looked at Mamá. 'How long before I leave, then? If I have to.'

'Three weeks,' she said. 'Whichever ship you're on, I'll come with you on the train, if I can. If not, I'll be at the station to see you off.'

'What about you, Papá?'

'I have to return to Bilbao to give these photographs to my friend, George Steer. He's a British reporter for the London

Times… and the *New York Times*. I was negotiating with him in Guernica after the bombing. The quicker we communicate this atrocity to the world, the better.'

'So if I'm sent on the *Habana* you'll be there?'

'If I'm still in Bilbao. Otherwise, no. I'm sorry.'

He stood, walked round the table, took my hand and pulled me to my feet. He put his hands on my shoulders and looked intently at me. 'I know this comes as a shock. It is a big ask. You might believe you won't cope, Victor, but we know you better than that. You're young. You're adaptable. And even if you have no say in the changes in your life right now, you have control over your attitude towards them. You decide what actions you take. Only you. You understand?'

He gathered me in his arms. 'We're depending on you to put your best foot forward. How you handle every challenge in the future will tell you—and us—the person you are.'

When he released me, I sat back stunned, my mind in turmoil. *If I leave*, I thought, *my friends will consider me a coward for avoiding the military service most of them will be undergoing. If I stay, I will consider myself a coward for backing away from the challenges of a future lived alone in Mexico for who knows how long.*

Papá was right. The decision was not mine. I had to make the most of the situation.

A fortnight later, the Ibero-American Committee accepted my application to join roughly four hundred and fifty other Spanish and Basque children—'orphans' they called us—selected to travel to Mexico from Bordeaux aboard the SS *Mexique*. Of course we weren't all orphans, but the Cárdenas Government used the term to generate sympathy among the Mexican people when appealing for donations to assist in our rescue.

We caught the train for Bordeaux on 23 May.

I have never forgotten the final confusion when the train pulled out of the França station. The last-minute shouts and whistles, the slamming of doors as the train gained traction, steel screeching on steel, steam and smoke erupting across the platform enveloping the crowd blurred through tears I could not control.

I gazed at Mamá's tall figure in her grey ambulance driver's uniform and wide-brimmed black hat with its stiff white feather fading as the train glided away. It drifted into the right-hand bend, picking up speed, hauling the carriages out into a bleak and overcast day until Mamá was out of sight and the soot-blackened graffiti-covered brick walls beyond the station slid past, the carriages rocking from side to side to the clattering rattle of wheels on the rails.

I pulled the window halfway down and sat back, but the incoming hot windgust carried the sharp smell of smoke and soot into the compartment and I slammed it shut. I closed my eyes and surrendered to the train's vibrations, the distance between everything I was familiar with and the unimaginable future looming ahead widening relentlessly. The clacking of the wheels on the tracks echoed in the darkness of my mind as the train gathered speed. It seemed to be calling out to me, *There's no going back... there's no going back... there's no going back.*

It was awful. I'd never experienced such despair.

Papá calculated the journey to Bordeaux would take ten hours. Three to Portbou close to the border, where we changed trains because of the narrower French railway gauge. Another three to Nanterre, where we stayed overnight and changed trains again, before travelling on to the west coast and our ship.

We reached Bordeaux late in the afternoon the following day and reported to the National Evacuation Committee reception centre. I was wearing my name tag—a palm-sized white hexagonal cardboard label on which my name and number were printed: *Expedición a Mexico*, it read, *Víctor Serrano, No 412*.

Some Basque and Mexican officials checked us in, and then a short, broad-shouldered Mexican lady in a bright yellow jacket introduced herself as *Señora* Cortés. Her thick braided hair was piled up on top of her head and dyed bright red—so bright you couldn't miss her. She stood out like a warning beacon. She told us she was in charge and called out our names through a megaphone, her deep, no-nonsense voice deafening us, while another Mexican *dama* handed each of us one of these blue suitcases. It was packed with clothes and things for the voyage, even candy. I've kept it ever since. *Como un recuerdo*, as a reminder.

Once we had the suitcase, we had to kneel in front of a young *sacerdote*, a priest—each of us in turn—who blessed us for the journey. I didn't mind so much, but all the older teenage Basque boys refused point blank. Every single one. They were having none of it. They were true socialists—maybe even communists—who had already been fighting on the front lines and they hated the Catholic Church for siding with Franco's Nationalists. When I saw their reactions, I knew there'd be fireworks sometime in the future.

The next morning we marched two-by-two to the Richelieu Quay, where the *SS Mexique* was tied up. Children of all ages. Many were crying, with a number of adults trying their best to keep order. The Mexican teachers and their assistants stood out in their yellow jackets, Señora Cortés among them.

There were also large and rowdy crowds of local people on the quayside who'd gathered to see us off, Spanish and Basque people living in Bordeaux and French workers who must have been Unionists taking time off. A group among them surprised everyone by singing the Republican songs *'El Ejército del Ebro'* with its rousing *'Ay Carmela!'* chorus, and breaking into *'Viva La Quince Brigada'* now and then, applauding and throwing handfuls of sweets at us when we joined in.

I was awestruck by the ship. Its immense size and sleekness and the length of the black hull with red at the waterline. Its central white superstructure rising in two decks to a pair of tall funnels painted dark red with a black band around the top, barely visible convection currents of exhaust steam pulsing skywards from them. White masts and derricks fore and aft arching above canvas awnings spread across the open promenade decks, a large flock of squabbling snow white gulls swirling above them.

The ship was due to cast off at three that afternoon and we started boarding at ten, after the last group arrived. We climbed the ship's gangway in single file and number order, the angle steepening as the ship rose with the incoming tide.

I was confined to my cabin with three other boys until the ship had cast off and we were underway. We watched the action through the open porthole as the quayside slid away, the hum of engines we'd barely noticed before rising to a deep and regular booming, the vibration of the four propeller shafts bringing the ship to life, the brown water of the Garonne-Gironde River estuary beneath us churning.

We were allowed on deck after sundown. I joined others at the stern, where the French tricolour billowed in the navigation lights.The ship was gliding out through the rivermouth and the Atlantic lay ahead. I distinctly remember the surface was a fearful black expanse streaked with long diagonal crests of breaking waves, while the phosphorescent wake foamed across the sea behind us towards the the coast awash with the lights of villages and the glow of distant Bordeaux. The giant half-circle of an orange waning moon suspended in the haze above the shore turned pale and shrank as it rose.

A black and crushing feeling of hopelessness overtook me as it dawned on me it was my last glimpse of Europe for an unpredictable time.

Thirteen days later I experienced the same suffocating desperation when we approached Veracruz on the Mexican coast just after dawn, my throat painfully constricted as I forced back my tears.

In Morelia, central Mexico, 20 June 1939

One morning two years later, the Principal of the school in Morelia, Director López, called me from my class and showed me into his office. A stranger was in there and the principal left us together.

I thought at first he was Vladimir Lenin, the likeness was so striking. I knew that Lenin was a leader in the Russian Revolution in 1917, and we had a picture of him among other political leaders on a classroom wall. The stranger had the same lean and bony face. The high round forehead and sweep of eyebrows over hypnotic Asian eyes, their piercing gaze frowning at the light, or maybe it was short-sightedness. The same straight nose and goatee around his unsmiling mouth.

He removed a pair of rimless glasses from the top pocket of his black suit, polished the lenses on a scarlet handkerchief and placed them on his nose. He peered at me over them, pushed them up the bridge of his nose with his middle finger, and examined me through them.

'Víctor,' he said, 'you won't remember me. I met you when you were only four and now you've grown up, but you're exactly as Xavier described you. I could have picked you out in a crowd. I am pleased to meet you. I am Kurt Lessing, a friend of your father.'

His Spanish was poor, his accent guttural. *He must be German*, I thought, *or Scandinavian*.

'I've brought you some things Xavier wanted you to have.' He shook my hand and then patted the seat of a chair he'd arranged facing his. 'Sit. Make yourself comfortable. Don't be nervous.'

A worn but polished brown leather briefcase was propped against the leg of his chair. He picked it up, placed it on his lap and fiddled with the buckle. He didn't open it but sat there patting it and shaking his head without looking at me for almost a minute, mumbling something to himself I couldn't understand. I think he was talking in Yiddish or some German dialect. It sounded as if he was praying. Perhaps he was.

He turned to me. 'I tell you not to be nervous when I should be telling myself. You must prepare yourself, my boy. I bring you sad news,' he leaned forward and placed a hand on my shoulder. 'Perhaps we get that out of the way first.'

He handed me the scarlet handkerchief, and without further hesitation, told me Xavier was no longer of this world.

'He faced a firing squad against the wall of La Modelo prison in Barcelona and died six months ago, on 29 January,' he said.

What he'd just announced seemed to deafen me. I watched in horror as he kept talking, mouthing words I longer heard or understood. It was horrifying, as if a door had slammed shut in my face. I screamed at him to stop. The space between us turned black and the room spun as if I'd fallen from a precipice. How long it lasted I have no idea.

I clung to my chair until my vision gradually cleared, and as his blurred face reappeared we stared at one another for a full minute. It's as close to madness as I've ever come.

Kurt placed the briefcase on the floor and stood behind me, squeezing my shoulders with both hands, before pouring a glass of water for me from a jug on a sideboard to his left. 'Be brave,' he said, as he handed it to me and sat down again. 'This is hard for you, I know.'

I could see him thinking it was as hard for him to tell me about it as it was for me to listen, as he went on to describe how Xavier had been arrested on 26 January, while photographing refugees retreating through the streets of Barcelona.

It was a so-called citizen's arrest, he explained. 'We were together at the time, when a gang of fifth columnists sympathetic to Franco seized him outside the Vallcarca hospital. They must have been in hiding in the neighbourhood. They held me as well, until they saw my German papers. They handed Xavier over to a detachment of Nationalist *regulares* soldiers who were looting nearby shops and houses at the time, street by street.'

Kurt lifted the briefcase to his lap again and withdrew the photograph album. I recognised it as Abu Xavier's at once. He flicked through several pages before handing it to me open at a page with several photographs.

'Take a look at these six photos,' he said, pointing. 'There was a film in Xavier's camera and these shots were on it. They were the last ones he ever took. Before his arrest, he handed his camera to me for safekeeping while he went to assist one of the wounded patients from the hospital.' He leaned across and pointed with a forefinger. 'That old man there, the one with both legs missing. He must have crawled down the steps and Xavier was helping him sit more comfortably against the wall. He was about to arrange the blanket over him when he was arrested.'

The photos showed several corpse-like starving figures, mutilated and bandaged, wearing ragged striped pyjamas, staggering down the hospital steps. One of them was limping towards the line of refugees passing in the street, his mouth gaping as though pleading not to be left behind.

The nearest refugees escaping the city were hauling and pushing two overloaded carts up the slope, one hauled by a skinny mule, the other with two old men straining against the shaft. Two women and a young girl were stooping to place rocks behind the rear wheels to prevent the carts from rolling backwards as they made their way uphill.

The old double amputee, breath steaming, sat half-naked in the freezing cold against the wall, watching. The rumpled blanket lay beside him as if he hadn't the strength to spread it over himself.

'You can see why Xavier went to help the old man,' Kurt said.

They took Xavier to the La Modelo prison where he was held for three days. He gave Kurt the keys to his house, and Kurt was allowed to take food and the latest local newspapers to him.

'I have a copy of one of them in here,' Kurt said, dipping into the briefcase again. He withdrew a newspaper from it and unfolded it across his knees before pointing at the headline. 'It's the first issue of the *Hoja Oficial de la provincial de Barcelona*. See the date? It was printed on 27 January, the day after the city fell. What do you make of the headline? *"Ayer se libero Barcelona! A la dos de la tarde, sin disparar un tiro, nacionalista las fuerzas al mando del general Yagüe, entraron en Barcelona"*. "Yesterday Barcelona was liberated! At two in the afternoon, without firing a shot, nationalist forces under the command of General Yagüe, entered Barcelona."'

When Kurt visited the prison two days later, the guards told him Xavier had been executed the night before by firing squad. They'd lined him up with several others and shot him for his sympathies with the Republican cause and for the work of his wife, Marina Serrano, with the International Brigades.

'They told me Xavier's body had been delivered to the mass grave at the Fossar de la Pedrera, the Cemetery of the Quarry on Montjuïc.'

When he'd finished, Kurt emptied the briefcase. He handed me Abu's Leica camera and a batch of photographs, newspapers and magazines. He told me he'd arranged with Director López for me to take three days of leave from school. He and his wife Frida were staying at the Hotel de la Soledad before continuing on to Los Angeles, and I was welcome to stay with them if I wished.

They were stressful days. I don't know how I'd have survived if I hadn't gone with him. I was overcome with grief, especially when I met Señora Lessing. I will never forget her. She was a short, rather plump and motherly woman with blond hair and a pale round face. She was wearing a midnight blue dress that offset her light blue eyes. I saw them filled with concern when we met. Although she spoke no Spanish, her sympathetic voice was so warm and comforting, the moment she gently hugged me for the first time in the courtyard of the hotel, murmuring her condolences beside my ear, I broke down and couldn't stop weeping. It's strange. I can still feel the softness of her body and the warmth of her breath, as well as smell her perfume when I recall that afternoon. A fresh and delicate scent like Mamá's lilacs.

For the next two days, waves of grief washed through me when I least expected them, even waking me in my sleep, but by the third day, I felt I was getting stronger. I willed myself to be.

Kurt told me one evening after dinner as the waiter was clearing away the empty plates, that he was a camera technician. 'I am an expert with lenses,' he said. 'That's how I met Xavier. I worked for Leica, for Ernst Leitz and his daughter Elsie, in Wetzlar. During the civil war, I used to accompany Xavier and other photographers in the war zones for months at a time, checking how the cameras performed in action, looking for improvements.'

He was Jewish, he went on, and the Nazis were targeting Jews during the 1930s. After *Kristallnacht* in November 1938, Ernst Leitz began arranging travel permits to save the lives of hundreds of his Jewish employees to get them out of Germany.

'Frida and I were among the last to escape. We left France aboard the SS *Sinaia*, from the port of Sète,' he said. 'We arrived in Veracruz a fortnight ago, along with the first sixteen hundred exiled Republicans looking for asylum.'

He pushed back his chair and stood. 'Stay here,' he said. 'I'll be back in a minute. I have some papers a group of us refugees printed during the voyage in my room. I think they'll interest you. They might remind you of your trip aboard the *Mexique*.'

He returned a moment later and handed me a sheaf of twelve folded newssheets.

'These will give you something to read while you're here.'

That night I read the banner of the first edition, dated 25 May 1939, the day the ship left France: *SS Sinaia—the Diary of the First Expedition of Spanish Republicans to Mexico*. When I'd read the cover and turned the page, a surprising illustration on page two caught my eye. A hand-drawn aircraft, stalled and falling through the clouds, was spiralling down towards the desert sands of the Sahara. It said the French academy had just awarded the writer and pilot, Antoine de Saint-Exupéry, their highest literary award for his autobiographical novel, *Land of Men*. When I asked Señor Kurt about it, he told me Saint-Exupéry was a famous aviator and journalist. He'd been in Spain reporting on the civil war since 1936 for the Republicans. He told me his most famous book was *The Little Prince* and I should read it if I ever got the chance.

I have never forgotten that conversation, or those three memorable days.

So I had become a Cárdenas orphan after all. I can see the irony now. But at the time? No. I'd just turned fifteen and grieving was painful. I was confused, particularly when Kurt and Frida left for Los Angeles and I was back at school with the others. I'd lost Mamá and Papá and with them my sense of belonging, my sense of direction towards a future I could look forward to. My conception of a home with them had lost all meaning. No more postcards. No letters from Papá. Time had come to a mysterious and frightening standstill. I felt paralysed, as if the world whirling around me and unfurling into the future was leaving me frozen in its wake.

One hot summer afternoon not long after Kurt's departure, I deliberately tortured myself by swimming laps alone for what seemed pointless hours up and down President Cárdenas's swimming pool, when he took a group of us out to his house with wide and shady verandas overlooking Lake Cointzio. I didn't care whether I lived or drowned as I counted the tiles along the bottom, my eyes stinging in the warm chlorinated water. There were one hundred and twenty-seven in each of thirty-five rows. Pale blue with dark blue spirals on them, like labyrinths, as if they'd been imprinted there by Ammonite fossils. The sequence of numbers as I counted was eerily hypnotic. Each number following its predecessor measured out the flow of time, yet I felt dreamily outside the flow, out of touch with the normal world of change and consequence. It was both comforting and terrifying, until President Cárdenas's wife, Mamá Amalia Solórzano herself, dived into the pool to convince me to end the session and join the others on the bus ride back to school.

During the next few months I often used to wander off on my own and walk around Morelia, unsure where I was going and what I was doing there, or play my guitar in a quiet corner of the school yard, sometimes with my best friend Guillermo Reyes, dazed and confused, but knowing I had to rely on myself from then on. It took me the best part of the following year to regain my equilibrium and rebuild the confidence to map out my future.

In Chihuahua City, Mexico—Friday, 30 April 1943, El Dia Del Niño, *Children's Day*

By 1943, when I was turning eighteen and matriculating in my final year, the school in Morelia was running out of money and support, and the political situation was becoming complicated. Nationalist General Franco was the leader of Spain, and he had called on the Mexican Government to return the remaining children at the school to Spain. The new President, Ávila Camacho, elected in 1940, agreed to ship us out. He was keen to wash his hands of what he considered an inherited problem irking many long-term Spanish immigrants across Mexico, who were sympathetic to Franco's Nationalist cause.

Fortunately for me and the others, Republican refugees were still pouring into Mexico. They saved the situation, by organising several boarding houses for us in Mexico City. So we moved into them and the school in Morelia was closed down.

At the same time, ex-President Cárdenas arranged a place for me and for Guillermo Reyes in UNAM, the *Universidad Autónoma de México*, in the engineering faculty, studying to become geological engineers—but there was one condition: we had six months' wait before the academic year began, and both had to re-join the *Ejército Infantil de Cultura*, the Children's Cultural Army, and work for that time in the campaign across the country, stamping out illiteracy.

We'd been members of the Children's Army for the past two years at school. In our spare time, we'd worked in Morelia, looking for kids and adults who couldn't read or write and wanted to learn. We spread the message that to become a true mestizo Mexican, you had to be literate. We worked in teams of ten or so, with a maestra in charge, to teach them how. Even the primary school kids helped—the cleverer ones. It was good fun, especially when Director López handed out "Good Mexican" certificates at Friday assemblies to those who'd recorded five successful cases who were now basically literate. Some of us even got our names and photos into the Education Department SEP magazine.

Guillermo decided to work at his home in Durango, so I started working there with him at first. Then we got a call from the teacher in Chihuahua City urgently requesting volunteers, so I went.

I clearly remember the day I joined the team. It was Friday, 30 April 1943, and it was *El Dia Del Niño*, Children's Day.

After running down the Calle Guadeloupe from my boarding house, I reached the Cathedral where we'd agreed to meet. I checked my watch and found I was half an hour late. There were already six others sitting on the cathedral steps. Panting, and about to apologise for being late, I took off my sunglasses and glanced up at the cathedral clock. It was stuck on ten-nineteen, showing just under an hour and a quarter earlier.

'Hola, I'm Victor Serrano, from Morelia,' I said, then pointed up at the clock. 'I thought I was late, but it looks as if I'm early.'

One of the young women looked up at me and laughed. She stood and lifted the book she was reading, her forefinger holding open the page.

'I'm Suré,' she said. 'So you're early, not late, just because the cathedral clock tells the right time twice a day? If that's the case I have time to buy myself another *paleta* fruit icy pole.'

A shock ran through me like a bolt of lightning. *Had we met before? Somewhere, somehow?* It was an otherworldly moment—and it was the same for her, she admitted to me later.

She was beautiful. Her face beneath her fringe was exquisitely shaped, her lively brown eyes captivating. Her thick black hair was drawn back in a ponytail and it shone in the sunlight, displaying her profile as she looked down at the others, her bronze skin glowing.

'Would anyone else like one?' she asked.

When no one answered, she handed me her book. 'Can you keep my place for me, Víctor? What flavour do you like? Pineapple? Mango? Tamarind? Vanilla with almond flavouring, maybe?'

'Vanilla with almond flavouring sounds good,' I said.

'I guessed as much. I like a man with good taste.'

Before I could dip my free hand into my pocket for coins, she'd slipped off her sandals and darted away in her bright ruby-red blouse and long green skirt, weaving barefoot through the many colourful families milling around the balloon and piñata sellers on the Plaza de Armas.

I saw her sprinting past the roasting corncob braziers, almost upsetting the peanut vendor as he cascaded a shower of what looked like salted and chilli nuts from an aluminium scoop held above his right shoulder into newspaper cones twisted into shape with his other hand. She tore past the fresh papaya with sliced lemon stall and the mango, sugar cane and pineapple barrows, before disappearing behind two magicians surrounded by packs of rowdy children, among them a clown on stilts swaying on alternate legs high above their *ooooohs* and *aaaaahs*.

I caught another sudden glimpse of her beside the dazzling acrobat in a body-hugging silver costume juggling five large Golden Delicious apples, taking alternate bites out of them, his hands as quick as striking snakes.

Beyond them all, I caught sight of her again, a flash of red and green, her black ponytail and scarlet ribbon flying from side to side as she glided across the grass before disappearing from sight behind the bandstand.

What just happened? Was she real? Will she reappear? I wondered.

My focus shifted to seven mariachi musicians in black and white playing a catchy Cri-Cri song in the shaded bandstand, the baritone at the microphone dressed as a singing cricket in a lime and orange fancy dress, a row of empty Corona beer bottles glinting along the railing.

Then I looked down at her book, read the title and was stunned.

She was reading *The Little Prince*, by Antoine de Saint-Exupéry. It was the last thing I expected. I recalled the article in Kurt Lessing's newssheet and his advice—and there I was, four years later, holding that very book in my hands.'

When I read the title I knew my destiny was revealing itself to me.'

I opened it and silently read the first words on the page Suré had reached. *"Aqui esta mi secreto. Es muy simple: Soló con el corazón se puede ver correctamente; lo que es esenciel es invisible a los ojos"*, "And now here is my secret. It's simple: It's only with the heart that one can see rightly; what is essential is invisible to the eye."

By the time I caught sight of Suré winding her way back towards me waving the two paletas, one scarlet, one white, I knew the quotation by heart.

When we moved into the shade of the cathedral and sat with our backs to the cool granite wall to enjoy the paletas, I surprised her by reciting the passage word-perfect.

Six months later, when it was time for me to go back to Mexico City to enrol, I kissed her goodbye when her sister Ariché, our chaperone, wasn't looking. Suré told me that moment beside the cathedral wall, frozen like the paletas at ten-nineteen, won her over even though the cathedral bells had been striking twelve and she'd barely heard me. *Igual de bien levanté la voz y le di a mi destino una mano amiga*, just as well I raised my voice and gave my destiny a helping hand.

I'd only known her for half an hour, but the moment was so precious it lasted many lifetimes for both of us... the memory of it always accompanied by the rich taste of our paletas.

Back in Saucillo, Northern Mexico, April 1968

Papá gazed at each of us for several long moments as if wondering how we'd responded to his story.

I didn't tell him an unbearable burst of shock had slammed across my chest when he'd told us Abu Xavier had been shot, and I'd heard Andrés gasp. 'No! You've never told us that before.'

'So... that's how I met your mamá,' Papá said after a few moments, picking up the photo album again. 'Everything I've told you today is a lot for you two to take in, but you must never believe Abu Xavier lost his life for nothing. I want to show you something special Kurt Lessing brought with him.'

He opened the album to a plastic sachet at the back and withdrew a postcard-sized photo of a grey, black and white abstract painting I had never seen before.

He held it out in front of us.

'This is a copy of one of the most famous anti-war paintings in the world. It's a mural showing the bombing of Guernica.' He indicated several features in turn. 'See the screaming women, the gored horse and the flames? See the dismembered soldier and the bull's head?'

'And the dead baby,' I said, pointing.

'And the dead baby, of course. It was painted by a famous Spanish artist, Pablo Picasso, in 1937.' He hesitated. 'Have either of you heard of him?'

'I have,' Andrés said. 'We've got some posters of his work up in the art classroom at school.'

'Well, let me tell you, Abu Xavier's photos published in the newspapers inspired Picasso to paint his masterpiece. So you were right, Andrés. If not for the bombing of Guernica, I wouldn't be in Mexico and would never have met your mamá.'

'In which case me and Alicia wouldn't exist,' Andrés said.

'And those three girls at the school would still be skipping,' I said, as if participating in a strange game of Consequences whose rules I didn't yet understand. I sensed the powerful beating of my heart racing against my ribs and added breathlessly, 'I wish they were.'

'This will interest you both,' Papá turned to another page in the album. 'I have a photo here of Mamá with you, Alicia, a baby in her arms. Most of the photos in here are Abu Xavier's, but not this one. This is Tía Ariché's work, right down to the tinting.'

He held the page open, but Andrés had a better view of it than I did and I had to push him aside to see.

'Can you believe it? Tía took it in black and white on the Kodak Brownie camera she was so proud of, before adding in the colours. This is your mamá. I'm sure you recognise her, Andrés?'

'Of course I do.'

Suddenly tense, I looked down at my clenched fists as Andrés spoke.

'What do you remember most?' Papá asked.

'Oh, her voice. Especially when she sang... and when she made me laugh.'

I felt a sudden uncomfortable chill. I had no memory of her, so her absence became unbearably present once again. Her not being there was all I could recall, and I felt cheated. The emptiness was agonising, and without warning, a paralysing thought crossed my mind. *Does Andrés blame me for Mamá's death? I've never asked him and he has never said so, but there's every chance he does, especially since I arrived in the house the month Mamá disappeared.*

'She was good at both,' Papá commented. He gave me a sharp nudge with his elbow. 'And that is you in the photo.'

Neither of them noticed my discomfort as the piercing thought persisted, *Have I hurt Andrés just by being born?*

My mind raced as I leaned across for a better look. Andrés was ten years my senior. He'd been a hero to me since my infancy. I held him in awe and became his shadow, clearly often much to his annoyance. We both shared the tragedy of losing Mamá at an early age. It cemented our closeness more strongly than we understood, but he'd known her for a period of ten years and was able to bring her to life more realistically than I could in my imagination.

Even so, he had hurt my feelings on more than one occasion when we were squabbling and he insisted the grief he experienced at losing Mamá had to be deeper than mine. 'You never knew her,' he used to say. 'Not really. I did. So how can you say you miss her? You can't lose someone you never knew.'

'How do you know?' I'd shout back. 'Because I never knew her doesn't mean I miss her less than you. I was inside her for nine months, don't forget, and with her for a month after I was born. She was *never* there for me again. At least you knew her for ten years. Her death left a bigger hole in my life than you think.'

I gritted my jaw and did my best to shut down my racing thoughts as I looked down at myself half-hidden in the folds of her bright green dress, my back to the camera, nuzzling at her breast. Concerned I'd be looking at a complete stranger I couldn't remember, I was surprised to discover it wasn't the case, perhaps because she so closely resembled Tía Ariché. Her long black hair fell on each side of her face, framing it, and her eyes, which struck me as remarkably like Tía's, were dark and liquid yet bright with humour. Despite her dark skin, Tía had rouged her cheeks and tinted her lips, unnecessarily glamorising her, because to me, she was way beyond pretty, she was beautiful.

Gazing at her with me in her arms, imagining myself drawing warm milk from her breast as my heart beat rapidly against hers, I concealed as best I could the confusion swirling through my mind. *It's bad enough me blaming myself for Mamá's death, but it's far worse suspecting Andrés may blame me too, perhaps along with others in the family. Even Papá? Surely not.*

'No wonder you liked her,' I managed to whisper, desperately quietening my mind.

'No wonder,' Papá replied. 'She took me by surprise on the cathedral steps when I was unprepared.'

As I studied myself feeding at Mamá's breast, a wave of anguish overwhelmed me. *Mamá loved me then, as a mother does, with a mother's nurturing love that can never be replaced.*

Papá smiled. 'Don't forget, she took one look at me and felt the same. Wouldn't you?'

'*Tú deseas*,' Andrés broke out laughing. 'You wish.'

'After a facelift, maybe?'

'Perhaps. And that's a big perhaps.'

'Can I have the photo, Papá?' I whispered.

Papá did not hesitate. 'Of course you can, if it's okay with Tía, but we'll keep it safe for you in here until you have an album or a photo wallet of your own.'

He turned the page and showed us two more photographs of Guernica taken in a different quarter of the town. In the foreground of the first, several buildings were facing a young leafy oak tree standing intact. They had escaped the bombing from the incoming waves of aircraft. Beyond them lay the town in ruins. The second photo showed an ancient, blackened tree trunk standing protected in a pillared rotunda, also untouched. The smoking ruins were visible beyond it.

'It looks as if time has stopped in one part of the town and is continuing in the other, as if two separate photographs, randomly ripped apart, have been joined together for dramatic effect.' Papá ran his finger along the jagged border between the ruins and the intact buildings. 'On one side, the way things were, and on the other, the way things now are. Things we'll never forget.'

He took a deep breath and I saw a tremor run across his shoulders. 'The oak trees are special to us. The old tree trunk has a history stretching back to the fourteenth century. It's called the *Gernikako Arbola* and symbolises all the traditional freedoms of the Basque people. It represents our *eusko abertzaletasuna*, our sovereign nationhood. The younger tree was grown using an acorn from the latest in the line. Those buildings behind it are the Casa de Juntas, the Basque Government buildings.'

I had little idea what he meant, but I loved the sounds of the words he'd just pronounced, the complex music in the way he'd accentuated them. The way the sounds became words carrying meaning, weaving images into existence in my mind: the *Gernikako Arbola,* the oak tree, so special to the Basque people.

I asked him to repeat them so I could whisper them to myself. He did, and we spent several delightful minutes echoing one another until I'd learned them. I spoke Spanish and Tarahumaran as fluently as could be expected of a seven-year-old turning eight, and these new Basque words fascinated me, even though I had trouble getting my tongue around them at first.

'We call the Basque language 'Euskara',' Papa said as he corrected me. 'Now there's another Basque word for you.'

He then said the living tree was so important its acorns were used to grow special seedlings—one to replace the current tree in case it died, others to send to diaspora groups of Basques who'd emigrated across the world.

He doubted we would qualify for one when I pleaded with

him but, '*Nunca sabes*, you never know. If you and Andrés send a special letter worded just right to the soft-hearted nurseryman, he might convince the current *lehendakari*, President Jesús de Leizaola, to allow him to send you one... even though he's currently in exile.'

'We won't hold our breath.' Andrés said as I voiced the new word I'd just heard.

While Papá continued talking to Andrés about the bombing, I busied myself writing out my new Basque words with a red crayon onto a blank page torn from the back of one of his sketch pads, which he withdrew from the suitcase for me. I interrupted him now and then to spell them out.

'I'll go to Guernica one day and hug that tree,' I overheard Andrés say.

'It will, without doubt, hug you back.'

Looking up from my completed list, I said, 'I'll come with you.'

I held my list out to Papá. '*Lehend-a-kari*, not *lehend-i-kari*,' he corrected me after a moment. 'Otherwise, it's excellent, *cariño mio*.'

'*Lehendakari*,' I repeated after him, '*el presidente vasco*. The Basque president.'

'You're right.' Papá sounded surprised. 'It was José Aguirre at the time of the bombing.'

'Yes, him. He looks like Balthasar, the one kneeling in front of Melchor and Gaspar in the stable, in Tía's picture on the wall in her dining room. You know the one I mean. He's got a long grey beard and wavy hair. He's wearing a blue rebozo wrapped around his neck and a dark brown cloak reaching the ground. He's carrying a jar of acorns in his left hand.'

'So the word conjures up all those images in your mind? Isn't that a miracle?'

'Of course it does. *Lehendakari, es su palabra*, that's his word,' I said, looking down at my list. 'That's what words do. They tell you everything you need to know.'

'About the person?'

'About everything in the world... it doesn't matter what,' I said slowly and shyly, stumbling over my words as I struggled to explain the mysterious relationship between sounds, words and meanings, between an image and the language describing it, as I began carefully sketching a green oak tree beside the words *Gernikako Arbola*.

'*Es su palabra*,' Andrés teased, his voice sarcastic. 'That's conjuring for you, my little miracle worker.' He leaned across and threatened to flick the top of my crayon, but I jerked it away and jabbed the pointy end into his ribs.

'Serves you right,' Papá said when he complained. 'Lesson one in good relations with a señorita. Never disturb her when she's concentrating on her work.'

When I'd corrected the list and completed the picture, I handed it back to Papá for a final check. He nodded as he read the words and was about to return it when he stopped abruptly. 'What's this word?' He pointed at the last word on the list I'd added as an afterthought. 'Is it meant to be *septicaemia*?'

'Yes.'

'And it tells you everything you need to know?'

'Yes.'

'Do you want the Basque spelling for it?'

'Yes, please.'

He took the red crayon and corrected my spelling, before handing me the list and giving me a tight and silent hug lasting for way longer than I'd expected—so long it seemed as though Mamá herself was reaching out to me through him, thrilling me and bringing me close to tears as I returned the hug.

I ran my eye down my list, sounding each strange new word in my mind, learning them by heart—and then I suddenly recalled a word Papá had used when telling his story. 'Papá, what's *Kristallnacht*? Is it English?'

'It's German. The Night of Broken Glass. When the German Nationalists smashed the windows in Jewish shops and houses in many cities in Germany and set them on fire.'

I made a separate column with my crayon and wrote 'German' across the top. 'How do you spell it?'

'Enough is enough. German now? You're going overboard.'

'No. How do you spell it?'

Papá gazed at me, bemused, his eyebrows raised. 'Really?'

'Really.'

I gave him a winning smile as I sensed him thinking, 'Trust you to insist!' as he spelled it out and I wrote it down.

* * *

Papá leaned down and picked up the cigar case from between his feet. 'Now we come to another chain of coincidences leading me to becoming a geologist at the Naica mine... this collection of rocks.'

He opened the case and tipped out a handful of rocks, each wrapped in thick tissue. He spread them with his right hand as Andrés and I shifted our positions to get a better view.

He picked one up and unwrapped a cluster of light pink selenite crystals. He placed it to one side. 'You've seen this type of crystal before,' he said.

'Abu Cerrildo's got lots of them,' Andrés said. 'Mostly clear white.'

'For the chess pieces he carves,' I added.

'This one here is special.' Papá said.

It was the first of its kind he'd ever seen, he explained. It belonged to his friend Guillermo, who had several in his collection. 'His were pale green, white and pale pink to red, similar to this one. Like the colours in the Mexican flag. Guillermo told me they came from the Naica mine over the border from his home in Durango. It's beautiful, don't you think? The first time he showed it to me I knew I had to have it, so we swapped. Guillermo struck a tough bargain—three of my sandstone fossils in exchange. Three for one. He always was *nariz dura*, hard-nosed.' His grin became a chuckle. 'But at least he paid for my Lulú lemon sodas next time we went to the cinema. Twice. To thank me.'

As he unwrapped the other rocks, some embedded with fossils, he told us he used to go on long walks with Abu Xavier when he was photographing landscapes and sunsets before the civil war, in the Ordesa Valley and on the slopes of Mt Perdido in Basque country, in the western Pyrenees.

'I found these up there,' he said. 'Papá started taking me with him when I was four years old. I'd be riding on his shoulders most of the time or looking for salamanders and tadpoles in the rivers with Mamá when he was photographing the rock walls and waterfalls.'

He held each rock out in turn, describing the black coiled nummulite fossils, the fan-like alveolina and the barely visible patterns of orbitoid shells set in the flat shards of sandstone.

He saved what he called his pride and joy for last—a fist-sized ochre-coloured nodule embedded in grey limestone. It was a silex sponge crystallised into quartz over many millions of years, he explained. Holding it up to the window he turned it this way and that, the sunlight flaring in amber sparks from its microcrystals like a mini chandelier.

'Imagine it growing on the seabed long before the Pyrenees were formed.' He looked up and smiled. 'When I first took it home, I used to picture myself diving in the ocean long, long ago while it was still alive, taking underwater photographs of it growing among others. And here we are, sitting in Saucillo, admiring it and listening to its story, like I'm reading to you from a book. We each have our story, including this sponge. Isn't that a miracle?'

'So your rocks are books and your collection is a library?' Andrés asked.

'That's what Papá used to call it—my *Biblioteca de la Naturaleza Rocosa*. My own Nature's Rocky Library, *registrando la historia de la tierra misma*, recording the history of the earth itself.'

'That's why you became a geologist,' I said.

'It is. And if I hadn't, I wouldn't have joined the Children's Cultural Army and worked in Chihuahua City, where I met your mamá. Now *that* was a chain of coincidences.'

'And we wouldn't be here to prove you did.' Andrés burst out with a laugh. 'So I was right. You did have rocks in your head... and still do.'

'And you inherited my genes.'

'So did I,' I said.

'Ah, but your rocks are *words* and you must never stop collecting them.'

We sat in silence, rewrapping the rocks as Papá packed them carefully back into the cigar case. He closed the lid and tapped out two unexpected drumrolls with all his fingers on it, before replacing it in the suitcase and closing it.

Then he stood, hoisted it to the top of the wardrobe, and ushered us back out into the lounge.

ANDRÉS

In Saucillo, Northern Mexico, 1967–1968

DURING 1967, ANDRÉS AND I often used to sweat alongside our Tarahumaran Abu Cerrildo, helping him clean his 1956 Golden Hawk Studebaker parked in the driveway of our house in Saucillo.

The car was a sight to behold. It was Abu's pride and joy. I can still see the excitement in his unusual almond-shaped dark brown eyes, his wide smile with a single silver canine crown standing out, the creases in his leathery skin deepening as he pushed back the brim of his sweat-stained white Stetson and ran through the car's mechanical qualities for anyone prepared to listen.

'Four gears and overdrive on the steering column gearshift,' he loved to boast, 'and she's powered by a *trescientos cincuenta y dos pulgada cúbica*, a 352 cubic-inch, OHV Packard V8. Would you like to take a look?'

He'd have the bonnet open and up in a flash, the engine block cracking like a shotgun as it cooled. 'Here she is, *mi bestia gruñona*, my growling beast. Naught to sixty in eight seconds. What do you think?'

We hosed down and polished the two-tone orange and cream bodywork and steam-cleaned the engine and chassis, especially after Andrés's monthly marathon training runs in preparation for the 1968 Mexico City Olympic trials. They were now a year away and Andrés used to run alongside the car for three or four hours over forty-two dusty kilometres on the gravel road from the right-hand turnoff at the Conchos overpass, westwards to the Naica mine where Papá was the Chief Geologist and Abu Cerrildo worked as a security guard; or we'd drive south towards Camargo on Highway 45D, the bitumen cutting through shady pecan and alfalfa orchards, and past green fields of jalapeño, maize and groundnuts.

I distinctly remember one Saturday afternoon in October

that year, when Abu first pushed back his seat and made room for me to sit in front of him and learn to steer while he changed gears and worked the pedals. I was seven years old. I fought to suppress my giggling excitement as my arms struggled to manage the car's unaccustomed weight. Such responsibility. Such trust.

He had the windows down and rhythmic mariachi music blaring as he shouted instructions at Andrés right beside my ear, deafening me. 'Glide, boy! Glide! Keep your feet close to the ground, each stride fluent and economical. Save your energy. Elbows in, and hands in line with your hips until you're sprinting, and then you wait for my instructions!'

It took me several kilometres to get the knack of the steering wheel. Whenever a distant cloud of rising dust signalled oncoming traffic, I resumed my seat and became Andrés's helper again. I passed a water bottle or one of Tía Ariché's special chia energy bars out through the passenger window when he needed them as he slipped along, his hands held low, his feet barely leaving the ground as though he was skating on ice, his clipped stride quick but deceptive in length.

'Just under two metres, *nieto*,' Abu had told him earlier, after measuring both our strides as we'd loped around the circuit lined with pencil pines in our backyard in Saucillo. 'You'll have to build up your stride length when you're sprinting. It will come. You're only sixteen.'

'Almost seventeen,' Andrés corrected him.

'I beg your pardon, seventeen next month. You are filling out, I grant you. The weights and gymnastics are doing you good. And kayaking with Alicia on the Conchos River and Rosetilla dam, of course.'

'Not to mention his favourite food he scoffs down when we're running up at Cerocahui,' I added, recalling Tía Ariché's mouth-watering tortilla, beans and squash and her chilles rellenos with three eggs and tomato salsa.

'Yes, her recipes are to *die* for.' Abu closed his eyes and sucked in his lips to kiss the four fingertips of his right hand. 'Like her second-to-none goat meat tacos *de cabeza* I can't resist.'

'They're all so filling, but greedy guts here, he always goes back for seconds. Even for *chica* Camila's cooking here in Saucillo,' I added with a grin, referring to the basic but always tasty meals our housemaid was teaching me to cook after school.

'And thirds,' Andrés said proudly.

'*Comes lo suficiente para engordar una palanca*. You eat enough to fatten a crowbar,' Abu commented, patting him on the back.

* * *

Andrés often seemed lost in a meditative daydream as he ran those longer distances beside the car. I used to wonder what he was thinking about. Was his mind blank as he counted the kilometres slipping by? Was he noticing changes in the passing scenery? The clouds changing shape in the upper winds? The sun climbing through the big sky, rendering it a paler blue?

Or was he concentrating on enduring the pain he was experiencing until it became second nature? Or maybe imagining creative new floor plans and designs for the houses and buildings I'd watched him drafting in his bedroom at home now he'd enrolled in architecture as a compulsory arts option to his Physical Education degree at the National Polytechnic Institute in Mexico City next year?

From then on, when I wasn't busy steering, I'd look out for a change in his expression signalling he was about to accelerate to a light canter or an occasional sprint, before easing back after a minute or two. He'd give a sudden, determined frown as he rose to the challenge, fluently lengthening stride, his arms driving his legs to a higher knee-lift. He seemed to float across the ground, his upper body perfectly balanced, Geronimo looking up with an occasional approving bark as he raced along beside him like his shadow.

'What do you think about when you're running faster?' I asked him once. 'What goes through your mind?'

'I have to decide in a split second whether I'm a frightened hare caught in the headlights of anyone who's going to chase me down when I overtake them on the back straight—or an Olympic champion with the killer instinct, like Billy Mills in Tokyo in 1964, and nobody's going to catch me once I kick in and take the lead. I'm training myself to feel I'm so fit and strong I'll grind them into the dust after turning into the home straight.'

He gave the characteristic burst of laughter I loved to hear and always shared, even though I may not laugh out loud. 'The other thing I do once I've changed gears is recite a poem to myself. It has the perfect rhythm for running hard and its meaning speaks to me. The school coach found it for the athletics team. It's called *If*, by an English poet, Rudyard Kipling. He was a runner too, so he knew what he was writing about. You want to hear the last verse?'

'Of course.'

'*Si puedes llenar el minuto implacable*
Con sesenta segundos de distancia recorrida,
Tuya es la Tierra y todo lo que hay en ella,
Y—lo que es más—serás un Hombre, hijo mío!
If you can fill the unforgiving minute
With sixty seconds' worth of distance run,
Yours is the Earth and everything that's in it,
And—which is more—you'll be a Man, my son!'

He nodded. 'Once I'm up and running, with overdrive still in reserve, I keep repeating, *Serás un hombre, hijo mío, serás un*

Hombre! as I race towards a target at the side of the road—a tree, a light pole or a sign a hundred or a hundred and fifty metres away. Before I reach it, I switch on the turbochargers and sprint the last thirty or forty metres flat out until I dip through the tape.'

When I heard that, the first time he raised his pace I teased him by shouting the refrain through the window, using words of my own, '*Serás un hombre, mi hermano!* You'll be a man, my brother! *Serás un hombre, pero no por un tiempo todavía,* but not for some time yet.'

'*Dices tú, ardilla.* Says you, chipmunk,' he shouted back.

There were times when he slowed his pace to recharge his batteries, as he put it. He'd signal to me with his left hand and I'd open the door and join him, jogging for anything up to a kilometre, careful not to trip over Geronimo as he bounded up to give me a welcome lick before they both picked up the pace once more and left me struggling in their wake.

I loved it. So much so that running became my other passion, after words and language. I knew I had a talent for both, as both came naturally to me. I spoke both Tarahumaran and Spanish by the time I was five and I was learning English at school and extending my Basque vocabulary with Papá when he had time to respond to my pestering.

As well as running with Andrés, I also ran in teams with other Tarahumaran girls my age and older when I was up at at Cerocahui. We'd chase a wooden *ariweta* hoop rolled between us with our sticks beside the river at Urique, or through the scrubby pines and oaks along the crest of the Copper Canyon for as long as we enjoyed the game. We were never conscious of the time, but revelled in the sheer exhilaration of the sport.

We learnt to perfect our skills, moving as lightly and efficiently across the rocky ground as our developing bodies allowed. When we watched the older women also running, we were aware we'd be doing so for a lifetime—perfecting the art of running and living up to our preferred indigenous name of Rarámuri, the light-footed ones.

And uncannily, through it all, I was conscious of Mamá, wondering if she was watching me and appreciating everything I did, as though I was doing it all as much for her as for myself, which of course I was.

* * *

Another thing I loved doing with Andrés was paddling one of the two small marine ply kayaks Abu Cerrildo made for us that year. They were smaller versions of his sea-going kayak, which he used on the Rosetilla Dam whenever we went there for picnics.

We helped him build them in his work shed in the back garden, both frames upside down on what he called his Pegasus saw horses. I say helped, but what I mean is we did our best to curb our enthusiasm and not get in his way or test his patience—on a good day handing him his tools, or screws, nails and glue when he needed them as he worked, whistling between his teeth. Occasionally he'd shove his hat back to scratch his forehead when things were going wrong, before swearing under his breath, apologising and making us laugh.

'Don't tell me you heard that. If you did, don't let me hear you repeat it.'

Once he'd covered the frames with the plywood panels of the hulls, we spent several afternoons painting them. Then he left us to our own devices. I chose a brilliant orange and Andrés a navy blue. When they were sealed and dry, we launched them on the Conchos River in full flood at the bottom of the garden.

It was such an adventure I could barely hold my excitement in check!

'Using these will give your upper bodies the strength you need for your running,' Abu told us, as he waded out waist-deep and helped us into the wooden seat, strapping our legs in place, 'but I have strict rules. You'll use them as part of your training program and sometimes on a day off, but only if I say so. You must never use them when I am not around to watch you,' he patted the safety jacket he'd shown us how to wear, 'and you will always wear one of these. When you are used to them, I will take you to the Rosetilla Dam with my kayak, and we can all paddle around it.'

Abu was right. Within a year, Andrés was broader in the shoulders and much stronger, and I was wirier, fitter and running faster.

In Mexico City, 1967

On a hot Sunday afternoon in early December 1967, in the foothills of the Paso de Cortés, in Zoquiapan National Park, I clutched Papá's hand, my heart thumping, as the leading group of runners bounded past us for the second time. They'd reached the halfway point in the eight-kilometre cross-country course.

Andrés was among them, running third or fourth. I caught our pre-agreed signal—a forefinger lifted to his right eyebrow told us he was feeling good, with plenty in the tank, all high-octane fuel waiting for the spark, as he described it.

I checked the stopwatch—thirteen minutes, thirty-five seconds and counting. Just under the national record pace for Mexican junior boys aged eighteen and below.

From the slope overlooking the course, we could see the line of runners as they laboured up the next hill, some now falling back, several walking at the rear, a handful stretching away at the front. Andrés was in the mix, standing out in his brilliant blue and white Saucillo High School colours before he disappeared over the top and into the pine plantations.

Clouds spilled across the crests of the two nearby volcanoes, Iztaccíhuatl and Popocatépetl, the sky a blinding sunlit blue. Stratospheric winds wiped away the chalky trail of a barely visible silver aircraft streaking across from east to west. *Has it just taken off from Benito Juárez airport in Mexico City? Are others lined up on the runway about to follow? Will their white trails entertain me with a heavenly game of tres en raya, noughts and crosses, emblazoned across the sky?*

I began imagining where I'd place my marks.

'Here they come,' Papá yelled, peering through his binoculars. 'Just two of them.'

I craned my neck to see, then fought my way to the front as the seated spectators stood, their conversations rising to a crescendo of cheers, my screams among them. Andrés and a taller runner, dressed in black, powered down the long slope beyond the trees towards us, shoulder to shoulder. A third runner was struggling a distant thirty metres behind them.

A hundred and fifty metres from the finish, as though propelled by an invisible rubber cord stretched between my willing mind and his, Andrés took a step to his right, and within several arm-pumping, smoothly accelerating strides, he gained a five-metre lead and slowly extended it, before he ducked through the tape.

In the last thirty metres of the race, the number 11 on his chest flapped upwards in his slipstream, and I saw beneath it through my excitement and my tears the Saucillo High School badge on full display—*el correcamino*, the roadrunner. Andrés was a roadrunner, but he was no Mexican chicken. *Eso es tan irónico*, that was so ironic, I thought. Irony was a fascinating new abstract word in my vocabulary whose meaning Papá had taught me recently and I was struggling to understand it. Particularly tragic irony. Papá had suggested that Mamá surrendering her life in exchange for mine was a good example. It gave the impression that cosmic forces had shaped my destiny in an unexpected and tragic way.

When I checked the stopwatch in my sweaty hand, I realised I'd forgotten to press the button. I quickly did so, only to discover I'd added half a minute to Andrés's time when the official timekeeper later confirmed before the medal presentation he'd run the course in a new national junior record of twenty-seven minutes and five-point-four seconds.

'It was Billy Mills who helped me win,' Andrés confided to us on the journey home. 'He coached me all the way.'

'What? Was he speaking to you in Oglala Lakota with someone translating for you into Tarahumaran?' I asked.

Papá gave a burst of laughter. 'Trust you to know he was speaking Oglala Lakota.'

'It says so on Andrés's poster,' I replied defensively. 'And Jim Thorpe on the other poster is a Sac and Fox. He speaks Algonquin.'

Papá turned back to Andrés. 'So what advice did Billy give you?'

'When we came down the slope to the finishing line, it was like I was running with him on the last lap in Tokyo, when the Tunisian, Mohammed Gammoudi, shoved his way through the gap between him and the Australian Ron Clarke to take the lead, and he chased them both around the turn into the home straight. Then he stepped to the right, just like I did today, and blasted past to win the gold.'

'Just like you did,' I said admiringly.

'You recall all that from the film of the race?' Papá asked.

'Remember I told you about Señor Valentin, the German coach who's visiting us this week during the year of the Cultural Olympiad? He showed us the film at school. The last lap. Three times. He was pointing out how rough it can get on the track, how we have to avoid getting boxed in, and what to do if we are.'

'You did well today,' Papá said. 'We're proud of you. The Olympic trials are next. Will you compete if your win today qualifies you?'

'If I get an invitation, maybe yes.'

'No maybes,' I broke in. 'Just a yes.'

Two weeks later, we learned that his win, along with other times he'd recorded, had earned him an invitation to run in the ten thousand metres at the Mexican Olympic Trials.

In Saucillo, Northern Mexico, 1968

Late evening, Sunday, 21 April 1968, a week after the Easter celebrations in Saucillo, the Olympic trials were televised.

I carried the loose wiring and the aerial while Abu Cerrildo lifted his black and white television out to his worktable on the back veranda. I climbed up into the pistachio tree and hoisted the aerial into the upper branches above the roofline of the house. I lashed it in position and Abu, fiddling with the controls, shouted that reception was as clear as he could manage.

I climbed down as he adjusted the volume. The *Telesistema Mexicano* sports announcer's voice was commenting on a track event. I leapt to the ground and rushed to Abu's side to check—the one hundred and ten metres hurdles for men had just finished. I glanced at the program. We had an hour to wait before Andrés ran the most important race of his young life.

He had enrolled for the February intake of students at the IPN, the *Instituto Polytécnico Nacional* in Mexico City, and we hadn't seen him since his departure. Papá had taken a week's leave to support him, even though he was not allowed to enter the Olympic stadium to watch the race.

Abu, the housemaid Camila and I settled into our chairs when the ten thousand metre runners were called to their marks. It was impossible to distinguish them in the growing twilight and on the steady long shot taken, I guessed, through a camera stationed on the stadium roof. Earlier events had involved closer cameras strategically placed around the stadium. We'd watched the muscles twitch in a tangle of sprinting legs one minute, a high jumper's distorted features as he sailed over the bar the next, or tracked a discus spinning high through the air across the stadium.

I was tense, searching for Andrés but not recognising

him, as twenty or so small, shadowy figures shuffled into a curved line at the start. A short delay, before the crack of the pistol set them off, the bunched pack rocketing into the back straight, runners jostling for position before settling into pairs and single file down the back straight for the first time, the pace easing into a fluid stride as they came to the end of the first lap. The field official turned the arm of the lap counter down to a number it was impossible to read, but I knew it was twenty-three.

Who is who? Where is Andrés?

Multiple bulbs in the four floodlight towers overhead were glowing but refusing to fire up. For three laps the camera angle didn't change and the shell of the stadium darkened further... until the floodlights flared alight, each with a startling explosive crackle, the runners now standing out as brilliant as day.

Andrés—*there* he was—running freely in tenth position, looking comfortable, the floodlights on his body throwing four shadows across the lanes, tracking every footfall.

José Garcia, who I'd seen in one of Andrés's *World Sports* magazines, was six or seven metres in the lead.

I imagined Papá following the race on his colour television in his Mexico City hotel—the white lines clear against the reddish tan of the rubberised tartan track, the deep green of the infield grass, the state colours of the runners' vests and shorts: Sinaloa scarlet, Jalisco orange, Chiapas black and yellow, Yucatán green, and Andrés in his Chihuahua silken blue, running well, still in the middle of the field,.

With ten laps to go, Andrés was holding his midfield position. A leading group, including Garcia, Juan Martínez and Pablo Garrido, played a game of catch me if you can, threatening to draw away.

The camera angle switched to a bird's eye view, and the distant figures circling the track were too small and mesmerising for me to follow. My attention was drawn instead to the stairway leading up to the Olympic cauldron. I decided to count the steps and imagined running up them, carrying the Olympic torch—ten grey steps between iridescent pink banisters per lap, ten laps to go. Each time the leader passed the halfway point down the back straight, I'd sprint up another ten, like scaling an Aztec or Mayan pyramid, to see how close to the cauldron I'd be at the finish. Then I'd climb the rest and light the flame to celebrate Andrés winning.

After ninety-three steps I'd reached the summit, my stomach churning and gasping for breath in my imagination. I stood beside the angled cauldron, panting, the torch raised in my right hand.

I watched start of the final lap, the camera angle switching back to close-up. I had a trackside view as it followed Juan Martínez, leading, with four runners chasing him at the bell. Mario Saldivar was his closest challenger... and Andrés was still in eighth position, the length of the home straight behind him.

I was overwhelmed as Andrés passed the bell. *Does it sound to him as it does to me, like the Chihuahua cathedral bell striking twelve for Mamá and Papá when they were nineteen and met for the first time on the cathedral steps in 1943?*

He ran the bend into the last lap, digging deep, his stride long but not yet at full sprint. He was beautiful to watch, so smooth, so fluent as he cruised past another runner in the back straight and another as he turned for home, holding his form and gathering gazelle-like speed over the last thirty metres in a controlled sprint, dipping through the finish in sixth position.

I leaned across to light the cauldron for him, sobbing with delight and pride.

Was it Billy Mills whispering to him in Oglala Lakota who inspired him to run so well, or Jim Thorpe in Algonquin this time?

Either way, it was a North American Indian sharing his secrets with a Central American Rarámuri Indian.

'*Sexto!*' Abu shouted. 'Sixth!' He sat shaking his head, looking down at the stopwatch in his trembling hand, and after a deep breath, 'In thirty minutes and forty-eight point four seconds by this watch. And he was making ground on Martínez and the others in the last lap. He gained at least ten metres. Did you see him?'

'He was brilliant.'

'He may have missed out on a place in the team this time, but you wait till Munich.' He gave me a hug and choked the breath out of me, before releasing me with a lopsided grin, his eyebrows arched upwards, his silver tooth flashing, 'He couldn't have done it without our coaching could he, *nieta*? You and me both.'

'You and me and Geronimo, Abu,' I said, 'and the Studebaker, of course.'

'Ah, *mi bestia gruñona*. We must not forget her. Or the kayaks.'

'And Camila's special nutritious diet,' I added, placing my arm across her plump shoulders as she ducked away, a blush rising beneath her olive skin to the silver coronet of her hair, pinned back with a large tortoiseshell comb.

I did not tell them I'd climbed the steps to light the cauldron, striving upwards with one goal in mind—to reach the top, determined to succeed without a backward step.

To do it on my own and please Mamá.

And I'd known for certain I'd concentrate on a *two*-lap race from then on. Just the two. No further. One lap cruising to the bell, the next a sprint to the finish. *Another twenty-two laps, like Andrés? Out of the question. The eight hundred metres.*

Eso me viendría bien, muchísimas gracias, *that will suit me, thank you very much.*

* * *

Six months later, the hallway telephone shrilled while Camila was preparing breakfast, the rich warm smells of coffee, *pan dulce* sweetbread and eggs Mexicana spreading through the house, carrying with them the sharper whiff of salsa made with pickled jalapeños, onion and tomatoes.

The phone went quiet before it shrilled again.

Dressed for school but still barefoot, my mouth watering and stomach rumbling, I slammed my bedroom door behind me and rushed down the corridor towards the dining room to answer it. I collided with Papá, who'd left the table to do the same. We both apologised and laughed, but as I retreated, I heard him raise his voice. It was so rare for him I froze.

'Enough, Andrés. *Enough.*' I flinched when he roared, 'I've warned you. How many times have I warned you not to get involved?' He glanced angrily in my direction, sending me a hurtful dismissive wave as he growled, 'I don't care what your peers are doing.'

I slid shut the dining room door before joining Abu and Tío Guillermo at the table. Tío was visiting us from Mexico City, where he was UNAM's Professor of Mining Engineering. The three of us sat in surprised silence, Papá's voice hoarse with concern and anger reaching us during the next fifteen minutes. Bursting with curiosity and straining to hear, I couldn't decipher the conversation. It ended when he slammed down the phone.

'You and I were both mistaken, it seems,' he said when he joined us, dragging back his chair. He snatched up his serviette before facing me. 'Running is not his only passion, he tells me. Politics is a part of student life. A part of *his* student life, he insists, from now on. He was one of the three hundred thousand in the silent march to the Zócalo last Friday. The *gran manifestación del silencio*, he called it, as if it was some sort of holy pilgrimage. Who knows what he's risking if the authorities find out? They'd have had spies everywhere in the crowd, fraternising with the students. With cameras, no doubt.'

'Is this the first time he's taken part in the rallies?' Tío Guillermo asked, swivelling his broad shoulders towards Papá, the taut brown skin on his shaved head shining as if polished, the tendons bulging in his bull neck, silver hair curling among the black in the inverted triangle of the open collar on his denim shirt.

'Apparently not. He joined both marches to the Zócalo last month as well, he tells me. He was there when they took down the tricolour and raised the anarchist flag, for God's sake. How disrespectful and dangerous was that?'

'Students will be students,' Tío Guillermo said, wiping his mouth with his serviette.

I was horrified. We'd watched the TV on Tuesday, 27 August, when the leaders of the huge crowd of students, teachers and workers of various unions who'd filled the *Plaza de la Constitución* had defiantly raised the revolutionary flag on the flagstaff.

'Red below the diagonal, pitch-black above it,' Abu had whispered to me when I'd asked as it rose up the mast, the breeze displaying it in black and white on his television set.

I'd been shocked as several light armoured cars, mounted with machine guns, driving three and four abreast, had driven through the crowd to disperse them, the granaderos riot police and a battalion of armed soldiers in support. Live rounds had been fired, occasional bullets ricocheting from the surrounding buildings, showers of pulverised brick spraying across the crowd.

And Andrés had been there.

A fortnight later, we'd watched the news again as busloads of government bureaucrats and public servants were driven to the Zócalo to take part in a rival demonstration supporting the government. The granaderos offloaded them and forced them to raise the national tricolour back in its place. Reluctant to participate, they'd been satirically baaing like sheep as the enforced show of support for President Díaz Ordaz backfired.

'We won't lose our tickets to the Olympics, will we?' I blurted out across the table. It was the first anxious thought that crossed my mind. Andrés's sixth position in the trials had earned him a place on the reserve listing for the Mexican Olympic team and with it, four complimentary tickets for him and his family to attend the Games on any two days of our choosing. We'd examined the track and field program and selected Tuesday and Wednesday, 15 and 16 October. 'I'd hate not to go. I've been looking forward to it for so long.'

'Never mind the Olympics,' Papá snapped. 'It's the least of our worries. I don't want to see him arrested and imprisoned for God knows what offence.'

'Or disappeared,' Abu murmured, 'like in the past. The *desaparecidos* during the railway workers' strikes in 1958. Remember them? Arrested and never seen again. And the doctors on strike for better conditions three years ago and arrested. Same unforgivable story.'

'Remember them?' Tío Guillermo frowned. 'How could we forget? Demetrio Vallejo is still in prison, for God's sake. Eleven and a half years. For daring to speak up and organise the railway strikes. Sedition, they called it. Other union leaders like him were thrown into the gulf from helicopters, according to the rumours. Dead or alive. Who knows?'

'Most of it true,' Abu said. 'Where's the justice?'

They all looked across at me, and in the tense silence,

Papá put a reassuring hand on my arm. 'Relax, *mijita.* Take no notice. This is men's talk, that's all. People sometimes do things to harm each other, but we'll make sure you and Andrés are safe. Come, put your shoes on and get your backpack. I'll drive you to school. You're twenty minutes late.'

Take no notice? How can I take no notice? I was too stunned to reply.

I looked back at Papá, my mind racing as the silence lengthened and I stood to go back to my bedroom.

Everyone at school had been talking about the strikes and daily violence for months, some more hysterically than others. Every new demonstration perpetrated by school and university students in Mexico City and across the country, each more dramatic and revolutionary than the last, seemed to mark another crucial social and cultural watershed in our anxious young lives. Fights between vocational and private school students on 22 July, brutally broken up by the granaderos. Demonstrations on 26 July by university students of the IPN Polytechnic in support of the vocational schools— Andrés among them, I discovered later, to my dismay. Days of rioting and school strikes followed, with buses torched in the streets—the granaderos using a bazooka, of all things, to blast open the carved front door of the Idelfonso Preparatory School and drag out rioters who'd taken refuge inside. And the peaceful march of fifty thousand students and unionists on 1 August, led by the rector of the UNAM, Javier Barros Sierra, protesting the heavy-handed tactics of the granaderos.

It all culminated in the founding of the *Consejo Nacional de Huelga,* the National Strike Council, to coordinate the protests and present a list of six demands to the president.

And worst of all the silent march we'd talked about at breakfast—I will never forget the images on TV when it ended after sunset with thousands of students holding up burning rolled-up newspapers and pamphlets to illuminate their faces, their mouths sealed with black crosses of masking tape, only to be followed by brutal running battles during September between students and the granaderos, supported now by the full firepower of the army and air force helicopter gunships, as they occupied the various university campuses, determined to stamp out the unrest before the end of the month.

President Díaz Ordaz was resolved to save the Olympic Games at whatever cost. They were due to start on 12 October.

In Mexico City, 1 October 1968

'Things are on a knife edge,' Tío Guillermo said, when Papá and I joined him at the Chihuahua City airport to fly to Mexico City for the Games. 'They could go either way. Did you see the news? IOC President Brundage has given Díaz Ordaz an ultimatum. Bring the students to order or he may cancel the Games.'

'Or transfer them to Los Angeles, God forbid.' Papá slowly shook his head. 'Knowing Ordaz as we do, he may see Brundage's threat as a license to crack down even harder on the students. So much for the peaceful Olympics.'

'*Toqué madera nuestra viaje no será en vano*, touch wood our flight won't be wasted,' Tío Guillermo said.

Papá and Tío Guillermo were both contracted by the Mexican Mining Industry Council to put the finishing touches to their mining display within the Ciudad Universitaria as part of the Cultural Olympiad, the year-long international cultural and economic program organised in conjunction with the Games. It was designed to illustrate how technically advanced and progressive modern Mexico had become.

I was excited by the prospect of escaping school for a fortnight and helping them.

Tío Guillermo had arranged for us to stay with him and his wife, Tía Sofia, in their unit on the seventh floor of the Chihuahua building beside the *Plaza de las Tres Culturas*.

Just over two hours later, I was in the window seat beside Papá as we descended. I was thrilled by the hazy spread of the city as we banked sideways to the left, dipping with unnerving vibrations in the seats and along the wings. I found myself peering up at the pale blue cloudless sky across a sheet of quivering aluminium one moment, before angling to the right as we levelled off and skimmed closer to the buildings and streets. They stretched out of view in all directions.

As we slowed in preparation for landing, we flew across a huge oval building squatting beneath us like a giant armadillo, sunlight flashing from the scale-like cones in the copper sheathing of the roof. Beside it, I made out six tall, bright yellow pillars and a magenta-coloured seventh. Shaped like polyhedrons, they transformed magically into seven stars in an elongated formation as we glided directly overhead and looked down from above.

Tío Guillermo leaned across Papá and pointed. 'The constellation of Ursa Major, and next to it the new *Palacio de los Deportes*, the Sports Palace for the Basketball,' he said.

Papá had allowed me to bring Abu Xavier's old Leica camera with me on the trip, and I took my first colour photograph of the seven stars below and the roof of the Sports Palace.

Moments later, we skimmed across a rectangular lake, its surface a glassy silver-green. I prepared to photograph the plane's reflection as it flashed across it, but it was far too quick for me.

'The Nabor Carillo,' Tío said, nodding at the lake, before the runway rushed towards us, the wheels squealing on concrete and the engines roaring, their reverse thrust slowing us before we taxied towards the terminal buildings.

We disembarked and entered the airport concourse, the ceiling above us decorated with spectacular balloons of different sizes and rainbow colours, patterned with the psychedelic Mexico 1968 logo and other Olympic icons.

Andrés was standing at the exit. When I saw him, I took off at a run and sprinted through the crowd. I leapt into his arms and gave him an octopus hug he was clearly unprepared for. Tía Sofia was standing next to him, smiling, petite and trim. She seemed delighted to see me, although my energetic and unexpected appearance must have surprised her and my exuberance almost knocked her over.

Andrés put me down and we greeted each other, sizing one another up with shared affection and curiosity—him with his new sparse beard and longish black hair trained back into an ambitious ponytail, the scarlet and black welt of a healing bruise beneath his bloodshot left eye; me an inch or so taller than I had been the last time he saw me. For a disturbing split second as we smiled rather foolishly at one another, I sensed how much we'd grown and wondered how our relationship may have changed. His deepened voice and the intensity and confidence he'd gained in so short a time were so striking I wondered if they'd raise a barrier between us.

He was wearing a smart, wide-brimmed black hat of a style I'd never seen before. Two long red feathers with black tips slanted up from the band.

'Where did you get *that*?' I asked.

He took it off and placed it on my head. It was too large and settled over my ears.

'It suits you,' he said. 'Now you've turned into an Aussie.'

'I've turned into a what?'

'An Aussie. An Australian.'

'Why?'

'It was given to me by a friend of mine, Tony Pickett. He's an Aboriginal Australian art student. He came here with a sculptor I got to know, Clement Meadmore. We helped him with his sculpture for the Cultural Olympics. They went home the day before yesterday. When I went to see Tony off at the airport, he gave it to me because I'd been admiring it. I'd told him I was part Tarahumaran and he thought I'd appreciate it. Which I do.' He took back the hat and pointed. 'These are the tail feathers of a red-tailed black cockatoo. Tony called it a *Kaarak*, named for its call. It's common where he lives.'

'I like it. It looks good on you, but it's not a magic hat. It hasn't turned me into an Aussie. I'm still a Mexican Rarámuri, and so are you. We'll never change.'

He smiled as he put it back on. 'No, it's not a magic hat and I'm still me. But it is Australian. They call it an *Akubra*.'

'*Akubra*? Is that an Aboriginal word?'

He gave a burst of laughter and shook his finger under my nose. 'Trust you. Yes, it is. Tony told me it means "something covering your head" in the Gathang language of his Biripi people, if I remember correctly.'

'A-ku-bra,' I pronounced each syllable of the word aloud and followed it excitedly with, 'Ka-a-rak. My first two Australian Aboriginal words.'

Holding both their hands, I dragged them along the concourse at a trot towards Papá and Tío Guillermo, who were making their way towards us.

An hour later, Tía Sofia served us a selection of tasty *aperitivos y bebidas*, appetisers and drinks. Andrés and I were standing among the polished green and multicoloured leaves of a jungle of indoor plants and hanging baskets on the balcony of the unit, four stories up. Open sliding windows overlooked the historical plaza,

Leaning across the window ledge beside Andrés in the clear air so high up, I was fascinated by the excavated Aztec ruins spread out below us. A flight of steps led down from the plaza to several circular and pyramidal platforms Andrés told me were the foundations of ancient temples in the market city of Tlatelolco, destroyed by Hernán Cortés and his conquistadors in August, 1521.

'I know about him,' I burst out. 'We're doing a project on him at school.'

He pointed out the ancient Hispanic Church of Santiago to our left. It was the first built by Franciscan fathers to replace the Aztec temples destroyed by Cortés, he explained; and the monastic college and convent of Santa Cruz beside it was opened fifteen years later in 1536, a school to educate the Nahuatl-speaking Indian children. In the background, surrounding the plaza on three sides, were modern buildings many storeys high. The tallest beyond the church was a skyscraper housing the Foreign Affairs Office.

'The other buildings are all apartments similar to this one,' he pointed around the square, 'so we have Aztec and Spanish colonial architecture next to a modern housing complex. Hence the name—the Plaza of Three Cultures.' He gave out a whistling sigh. 'You should have seen this area before it was cleared. It was a slum as far as you could see, a shantytown for railway workers, campesinos peasants new to the city and the homeless unemployed. Many indigenous Indian people were among them. Smoke, dust and filth everywhere. Not to mention rats. A place everyone else avoided like the plague, which you may have risked catching if you'd visited.'

'Where are the people now?'

'Who knows?' he replied, as Papá called him into the lounge. He shrugged his shoulders. 'They've moved on, God knows where to. Swept aside and under the carpet, as usual.' He paused, then added with thoughtful irony, 'Thanks to the Olympics.'

He glanced back at me as he strode away, 'So much for the Mexican miracle and all the promises of the revolution fifty years ago. The poor are still the poor and the illiterate are still uneducated. By the tens of millions.'

I struggled to grasp what he was getting at, puzzled by his abstractions and references to recent history and I was shocked to hear the hard edge of anger in his voice. I hadn't heard him speak with such bitterness before. Especially his last words as he disappeared inside, 'We have an ethical responsibility to care, *mi pequeña cabra*. To voice our objections and change things for the better.'

It was so out of character it made me wonder how much

else he'd changed… and then a reassuring glow ran through me at his remembering to call me his little mountain goat.

Moments later, I heard Papá raise his voice, 'I warned you not to get tangled up with the National Strike Committee. You're inviting trouble for all of us.'

I picked up on his clipped and heated tone and stiffened. Tuning in without looking around, I watched a family of four or five picnicking on a patch of lawn below. One of the older children redirected a plump brown baby crawling half-naked and with robust determination towards plates of food laid out on a colourful Huichol blanket. The dreamlike scene was a sundrenched tapestry beside the ancient excavations as I listened to the argument.

'Only the extremist *acelerados* among us want to interrupt the Olympics.' Andrés's raised voice was replying to a question I hadn't heard. 'And I'm not one of them.'

'So what *are* you looking to achieve?'

'Simple. We want to negotiate. We want to have an open democratic dialogue with the government, preferably with the president himself, which he denies us.'

'An open democratic dialogue with the president? Get real. Don't you know who you're dealing with? He's an autocrat who's got two more years of his six-year presidency to do things for Mexico his way. He and his self-elected PRI party leaders are deaf to criticism. He's going to take your demonstrations as a personal insult.' Papá sighed a long impatient outbreath. 'Is there anything else you students want?'

'We want all political prisoners released, even though he says there aren't any. They're all common criminals in the eyes of the law, according to him. We want indemnity and compensation for those who've suffered police brutality and the families of those who've died. And an end to the violence of the granaderos. In fact, we want them punished and disbanded, and their militant leaders dismissed.'

'You don't want much.' Papá's voice was cutting. 'You've heard the rumours—Cuban and Maoist agitators have taken over the student movement. Not to mention the KGB.'

'That's ridiculous. Yes, we have some communists among us, but very few. We aren't a political party looking to overturn the government or depose Díaz Ordaz and his cronies. The only constitutional change we want is to repeal the laws allowing for any public demonstration or dissent to be crushed with a show of force, no matter how peaceful it is.'

'Article 145 in the Federal Penal code?' Tío Guillermo asked. 'The one concerning social dissolution?'

'Exactly.'

Tío Guillermo agreed. 'I see your point. It is open to wide interpretation.'

'I warned you. The president will never concede,' Papá shouted. 'Don't you realise? If it wasn't for the Olympics, he might—*just might*—consider your demands, but it's too late. So you *are* jeopardising the Games.'

'No, we're not. Not deliberately. But the president *is*, him and his ministers, Echevarría and Barragán, by responding to us with such brutality.'

'Don't shift the blame, Andrés. *Se necesitan dos para bailar un tango*, it takes two to tango. The end result is the still same. And as for the brutality you mention, if you provoke a cornered snake, what will it do? It will strike. And not only that. By threatening the Olympics you're giving Ordaz an open invitation to go to any extreme to shut you down. I dread to think what he'll resort to next.'

After a brief, tense silence, Andrés's voice was surprisingly firm. 'I told you. Now the Games are only ten days away, the majority of us want them to go ahead successfully as much as everyone else. Take a look around. None of the street signs or decorations have been defaced. There's no graffiti on any of the venues or the sculptures. Hundreds of students are already working as volunteer guides and hostesses for incoming tourists and visitors. We haven't held up the preparations—'

'Except to point out the money could have been better spent.'

'Well, it could. You can't deny it, can you? You only have to look around the country at the widening gap between the rich and poor.' He paused for several long moments, the lengthening silence tense as he appeared to be gathering his thoughts. 'And we haven't interfered with any of the cultural events and exhibitions. In fact, I've enjoyed attending some of them.'

'For example?'

'Well, the art exhibitions, for a start.'

He said it with such unexpected enthusiasm I turned around. I leaned back against the balcony with my arms outstretched along the window ledge and gazed at him. His expression, more self-composed than the exasperation I'd expected, caught me by surprise.

'I've seen Paul Gauguin's *Vairumati*, painted in Tahiti. What a palette. Such colours and naïve application of the paint. But so alive, and every brushstroke visible on rough sackcloth, because he had no canvases. And Salvador Dali's *Cosmic Athlete*. It's fantastic, a discus thrower about to tear the sun from the sky and hurl it across the universe. René Magritte, his painting *The Memory*. Unforgettable. A woman in profile with a bullet wound at her temple and half the canvas jet black. And the music concerts. Samuel Ashkenazi on his violin. Dave Brubeck and Herbie Mann, jazzing up the crowds, most of them students, like me and my friends.'

Papá, his face flushed, glanced over and surprised me

with a grin. 'It sounds as if Andrés here has been broadening his education at last, *mijita*. Mexico will make a *hidalgo* gentleman of him yet.' He turned back to Andrés, giving him a reconciling pat on the shoulder. 'What about your studies? How are they going?'

'Good. As well as you can expect. Physical Education is straightforward. I have time for training and an effective coaching routine. So the running's going well.'

'You're looking fit... apart from the black eye.' They both laughed. 'I won't ask.'

'Did you see Abel Quesada's cartoon in Excélsior the other day? The woman with the black eye?' Andrés asked. 'Let's see if it fades by the twelfth.'

'I did.'

'Well, Abel is a friend of mine,' he pointed at the eye, 'and here's his inspiration. A subtle comment on the brutality of the granaderos.'

'Indeed. And your secondary subjects?'

'All of us on the architecture course have been helping Señor Ramírez Vázquez and the sculptors working on the Ruta de la Amistad, the Friendship Route.'

'We saw one of the sculptures when we were landing,' I said. 'Ursa Major.'

'Yes. The one beside the Sports Palace. It's called *The Big Dipper*. I like it.'

'Which ones did you work on?' Papá asked.

'Just the one. I helped the Australian, Clement Meadmore, with his sculpture—*Janus*. We put the steel rods and mesh framework in place and helped with the concrete pour. It looks simple now, but it was complicated. It took us months.' He pointed at the Akubra he'd hung behind the door. 'One of his Australian students gave that to me when he flew out.'

'The sculpture, what does it look like?' I asked.

'Imagine a long cube twisted up into a ring like an open Möbius strip, six metres high and the same across, its square ends facing in opposite directions. Then try pouring blackened concrete into it.' He grinned. 'We did. With difficulty. Meadmore had a great sense of humour. Beers all around when we succeeded. VB was the brand, I remember, because he was from Melbourne, he told us. Specially imported for the occasion. I had to write the project up as an assignment. I scored an A. I'll show it to you later. You can see the sculpture itself tomorrow, if you like. It's simple but impressive.'

'I like,' I said. 'Show us the whole city. Especially the Olympic stadium.'

'Of course. I can miss tomorrow's marches. They're all going to end up right here, in any case, at a meeting on the plaza down below. The Strike Committee members want to talk to us. I've heard a rumour they may be calling for a temporary truce.'

Tía Sofía appeared in the hallway and beckoned me to the bedroom she'd allocated to Papá and me.

Without a word, she pointed at two new dresses she'd laid out side by side on my camp bed—the first was a smart white blouse and mini-skirt combination with the Mexico 1968 logo imprinted on it in dazzling black op art, a labyrinth of wavy lines based on Huichol Indian designs. It was identical to those I'd seen several Olympic hostesses wearing at the airport, though theirs had been in pastel orange. It had a cloak attached to the back of the collar.

The second was a white trapeze dress with aquamarine running figures emblazoned across it.

'That's the uniform of the hostesses at the athletics,' she said, pointing. 'I thought you'd like it. Aquamarine for track and field. Each sport has a unique colour.'

'I love them both,' I said as I hugged her. '*Muchas gracias,* Tía Sofía. *Muchísimas gracias.* Are they my size? Can I try them on?'

'Go ahead. There's a full-length mirror is in my room, through there.' She pointed at the door on her right. 'We'll wait for you in the lounge.'

They both fitted, with a little room to spare. When I reappeared in front of everyone in the lounge I stole the show, parading along an imaginary catwalk and back, spinning to show the swirl of the trapeze skirt and balancing next on tiptoe in the miniskirt as if I was wearing stiletto heels. With Tía Sofía announcing for me, I was a leading model for Courrèges at the Paris Fashion Week in one dress, and a model for Mary Quant in Carnaby Street in the other.

For several electrifying, unforgettable minutes, the applause and laughter were intoxicating. I acknowledged my admirers and accepted a bouquet from Andrés—a bunch of fresh carnations, reds, whites, yellows and pinks. He withdrew them from a large crystal vase shaped like an Olympic torch on the coffee table, their long stems dripping water in translucent pearls I caught in my palm and gleefully splashed over him kneeling in front of me, before returning them to the vase once the show was over.

The only person missing from the audience is Mamá. Or is she here? I asked myself.

* * *

After breakfast the next morning, Papá was the first to leave the table. He was going to work on the Mining Industry exhibit. 'I'll see you all tomorrow,' he said. 'I'll be working late, so I'll book in to UNAM tonight.' He ruffled my hair before I could stop him and blew me a kiss. 'You enjoy yourself, *mijita*, and don't give Tío Guillermo or Tía Sofía too much strife.'

He gave Andrés a bemused look, shaking a forefinger, his eyebrows raised. 'And you, *mi joven rebelde con una causa*, my young rebel with a cause, take good care of her… and don't even think of enrolling her in one of your female student brigades we see on the news all the time.'

'Why not?' I asked. 'I might enrol myself—'

'No, you won't. *Todo eso de tirar sosténes*, throwing away and burning their bras. They're scandalous.'

'Scandalous? They're brilliant,' Andrés said, reaching for another slice of pan dulce. 'Even someone as old and patriarchal as you must have heard of *liberación femenina*, women's liberation?'

'*De todos modos no uso sostén*, anyway I don't wear a bra yet,' I pointed out.

Papá clicked his tongue at me, bending to pick up his briefcase and striding to the door. 'That doesn't qualify you to join.' He turned and raised his open palm. 'Enjoy yourselves.'

He closed the door behind him and clattered down the steps to the lift.

Tío Guillermo remained with us. He had agreed to take the day off and drive me and Andrés around the city to see the Olympic decorations, the sculptures and the sporting venues.

'We'll start with the Sports' Palace and *The Big Dipper*,' he said, nodding at me in the mirror with a confidential wink as we took the crowded lift to the ground floor. I returned it with a shy and awkward grin. I was self-conscious and unsure around him, so small and insignificant beside his overpowering presence, especially in such a confined space, even though I'd known him all my life.

'You've seen it from the air, so you know what to expect. And it's the closest. Just a few kilometres southeast of here. Then we'll drive across the city and see the sights.'

As soon as we turned into the traffic streaming along

Paseo de la Reforma Avenue and headed south, I relaxed and was enchanted. The city came vibrantly alive, the way I remembered it when Papá and I had come down to watch Andrés run in the cross country. White-painted tree trunks glided across the fronts of shops freshly painted in brilliant pastel colours as we passed, gaudy rectangular billboards advertising the Olympics erected over their open doorways, and *there*, on the left, the brilliant mural portraits of a man and a woman stood side by side three storeys high, completely covering the facades of two neighbouring flat-roofed buildings.

Occasional autumn leaves cascading from the liquidambar trees skittered across the car's bonnet and fluttered away in the slipstream. One became trapped and rattled in the windscreen wiper, so Andrés leaned half his body dangerously out to clear it, whooping to the music on the radio Tío Guillermo had switched on and surprising passers-by who looked around to watch his double-jointed gymnastics.

A huge bronze monument loomed up on the left. It was dedicated to the Aztec leaders Cuitláhuac and Cuauhtemoc—a gigantic warrior in war regalia, his spear raised threateningly against the sky. I read the names embedded in the pyramidal plinth as we passed.

'Do either of you know anything about them?' Tío Guillermo asked, jerking a thumb at the statue as he turned eastwards around it.

'The battle of *Noche Triste*,' I called out from the back seat. 'The battle of the Night of Sorrow. We've just finished a project on Hernán Cortés at school. Cuitláhuac and his warriors killed so many of his conquistadors that Cortés had to retreat from Tenochtitlán.' I struggled to remember. 'From Tlatelolco as well, I think. On 30 June 1520, wasn't it?'

'You're right, and from Tlatelolco,' Tío Guillermo said.

'It took Cortés over a year to rally his troops and retake Tenochtitlán.'

'Helped by the Tlaxcalan tribes,' I said. 'They hated the Aztecs.'

'Yes, and his African slaves. He had hundreds of them with him. I knew you'd know.'

He knew I'd know? Is he complimenting me? Or is it an ironic observation and he's being sarcastic?

'Cuitláhuac's spirit is alive and well,' Andrés remarked drily. 'He lives on in Alicia's DNA.'

'Yours too,' I said.

'Not tonight, I hope,' Tío Guillermo replied. 'Tonight, he and his warriors can leave us in peace to enjoy Tía Sofía's cooking. Don't you agree?'

'As long as we can call on him if we need backup against the granaderos.' Andrés laughed. 'And whatever Tía Sofía cooks, it'll have to be good to beat the Polytechnic Zacatenco campus canteen. It's five-star, believe it or not.'

'I guarantee you'll score hers a six, if not seven. How do fish enchiladas for afternoon comida sound?'

'What type of fish?'

'Tilapia, homegrown. A friend of a friend runs an aquaculture farm just outside Buenavista. They jump straight from the ponds into the pan.'

'There it is,' I yelled, as the giant armadillo I'd seen from the air swept into view.

We spent the next half an hour walking around the Sports Palace among other groups, most of whom I took for recently arrived tourists or athletes familiarising themselves with the city. The basketball stadium was closed to visitors, but we admired its intricate design and shining roof from the outside, the concrete paving around it decorated in bright vermilion and orange concentric semi-circles.

Beside it, the seven concrete pillars of *The Big Dipper* stood dwarfing us. I lay on my back to take a second photograph of them to complement the one taken from the plane. From that angle, the serrated parabola of the gleaming copper dome beyond the pillars was sharply etched against the bluest sky across which sunlit cirrus clouds swept in dizzying brushstrokes.

As I was kneeling to put the camera back in the case, Andrés nudged me with his foot. He nodded at two men strolling past. One of them glanced fleetingly at me in my hostess's uniform as I fiddled with the latch.

'Plainclothes security police,' Andrés hissed as they walked on, sending a quiver of fear up and down my back. 'Officers of the *Batallón Olimpia*, the Olympic Battalion. They're everywhere you look.' When they were out of earshot he spoke aloud, his voice sarcastic, 'Keeping us all safe and sound.'

I glanced around and picked out several other nondescript groups of men similarly dressed in casual clothes, strolling among the crowd in twos and threes. I'd earlier taken them for visitors.

'Don't let them worry you,' he said, walking on.

'I'm not worried.' I tried to sound convincing as I slung the camera over my shoulder and caught up with him.

'Sure. You don't look it. Ignore them. Relax.'

Back in the car, we crossed the city. I was fascinated by the elegance and graphic beauty of the Olympic signs and the venue icons, the transparent plastic banners imprinted with white doves and multi-coloured half-moons and the decorations strung across the buildings. There were balloons in eye-catching colours and various sizes; colourful two-metre-high hexagonal information pillboxes, regularly spaced along the pavements, carrying sporting venue icons on all sides. There were spectacular rooftop billboards telegraphing the message "*Todo es posible en paz*", "Everything is possible in peace", written in Spanish, English, French, Arabic and Chinese. There were smartly painted buses adorned with the psychedelic Mexico 1968 logo and sporting icons in pastel shades, vivid posters advertising the cultural Olympiad in shopfront windows and showy bumper stickers on passing cars. Even the lamp posts, I noticed, were painted in unique colours for each street—pink on Churubusco Avenue leading away from the Sports Palace, green along the Río de la Piedad we followed across the city, and orange on the Periférico Sur Ring Road we were then driving down.

'And they're blue all the way to Xochimilco,' Tío Guillermo said over his shoulder when I commented on them. 'You can follow them to the different venues. Each has a distinct colour. The committee even wanted to paint the pavements, but never got round to it.'

I was so enthralled I wanted to explain how the overall effect of the decorations and signs so joyfully communicated Mexico's vibrancy in 1968 it took my breath away, but I felt sheepish and the words I was looking for escaped me. 'It's wonderful, Tío. Truly wonderful. I'll never forget it,' was the best I could come up with.

Andrés turned and nodded at me. 'You're impressed, hey? Just wait. We have more surprises up ahead. The sculptures on the Friendship Route. Eighteen concrete ones, to be exact, and another four in bronze and steel. Are you ready?'

'We won't have time to stop at all of them,' Tío Guillermo said.

He lifted his thick-boned left wrist and displayed the dial of his gold watch embedded on a mat of wiry black hair. It showed eleven-thirty.

'We can stop for one or two you might want to

photograph—and slow down for the rest. You choose the ones you really like.'

I hesitated. 'How can I decide until I've seen them all, Tío? I need to compare them first, before I choose.'

Andrés gave a burst of laughter.

'Still pedantic as ever, *mi pequeña quisquillosa*, my little nitpicker. Will you ever change?' He leaned across the seat and stared back at me. 'You're going to make a brilliant lawyer.'

'Linguist, you mean.'

'*Oooh* yes. How could I forget? Our up-and-coming translator, our walking dictionary. Our own *La Malinche*, speaking in tongues—just like she did for Hernán Cortés.' He looked across to the right. 'Okay. Here comes the first sculpture. What do you think?'

I stared at the two towering sculptures, mystified. 'They look like a pair of bull's horns,' I said. 'One black, one white... or hockey sticks for giants.'

'We'd better not let the sculptor know.' Andrés laughed again. 'She might take you seriously and use you for a hockey ball. She's called it *Signals*. What about the next one? See it over there through the trees?'

'Ah, that one I don't mind.' I liked the way the vivid blue-green circular pieces slotted together like a jigsaw. Andrés said it was called *The Anchor*, constructed by a Swiss sculptor he'd met.

'It's nice,' I said, looking back.

I took the camera out and asked Tío Guillermo to slow down for the next one. I focussed and snapped the three monumental columns as we passed. They reminded me of those making up *The Big Dipper*, but their brilliant colour was a beautiful shade of purple I had never seen before.

'What colour's that?' I asked.

'Red violet, I'd say,' Tío Guillermo replied. 'Almost magenta. I don't know if there's a special name for it... plum, perhaps?'

'That was *The Three Graces*,' Andrés said. 'By Miloslav someone or other, from Czechoslovakia, as far as I remember.'

'Easily the best so far.'

And so it went, as we drove past another nine.

Then we drew into the parking lot of the Athletes' Village, where we stopped to buy a grilled corn *elote* each, covered in tasty melted *cotija* cheese and sprinkled with ground chilli and lime juice. Andrés took a photo of me eating mine sitting side-saddle on a three-metre-high maroon metal sculpture of the Mexico 1968 logo in the plaza. I climbed it using the Olympic rings for footholds.

Back in the car, we turned up Insurgentes Sur Avenue and followed the aqua lamp posts to the Olympic stadium.

I was speechless at the imperious sweep of its dimensions. We joined a tour group and were shown into an upper tier in the stadium with a view of the immaculate red tartan track, the immense expanse of lawn marked up for the field events, the water jump for the steeplechase, and halfway along the back straight, the ninety-three steps leading up the pyramid to the cauldron.

'I can't believe we watched you run right here,' I said to Andrés. 'You must have been jumping out of your skin.'

'I was impressed,' he admitted. 'At first. But once the pistol fired...'

'I can't *wait* for the opening ceremony. And for the fifteenth and sixteenth, when we'll be sitting here watching.'

'Me too. They can't come soon enough,' Andrés replied. 'I'm glad the black Americans from the United States have decided to come. They were talking about going on strike to protest for their civil rights under the Black Power movement.

The Games would have been a disappointment without them. Especially the sprinters.'

'What are civil rights?' I asked.

'Making certain everyone enjoys the same opportunities in society, no matter what your race or religion is.'

'Isn't that the case in the United States?'

'No, it's complicated. In some states, the blacks are separated from the whites. By law. It's called segregation— now there's another interesting word for you. In the buses. In the cafés. Even in the schools and universities.' He looked down at me with sudden seriousness. 'Don't worry about it. It's a long story, and anyway, they're coming to compete, so we will see them.'

'Good.' I held up the camera. 'I'll make sure I bring this.'

'You'd better. I'm looking forward to watching the Africans in the distance events. A few of them have been training in the IPN grounds and I've joined them doing speed work once or twice. They're brilliant runners, from Kenya. They're so... I don't know, so relaxed. So natural. So *streamlined*.'

'As if they've been running all their lives, like us?'

'Exactly. And they're friendly. Always laughing.'

'What languages do they speak?'

'They're from East Africa, so they must speak Swahili among themselves, I guess. Or tribal dialects.'

I looked up at him. 'Can you find out for me?'

His gaze met mine and he nodded, his eyes carrying the hint of a sardonic smile.

'Did you talk to any of them?'

'One, to start with—Kimaru Songok. He's a four-hundred-metre hurdler. He spoke to me in English, so we understood each other, more or less. He introduced me to some of the distance runners. Kip was one I remember. Wilson. And Amos. I forget the others. Oh yes, and Naftali, how could

I forget him? We ran some laps together and I enjoyed it.'
He smiled. 'They don't just have four on the floor. They
have overdrive and rocket power in reserve. It's going to be
interesting. They asked me about Juan Martínez, and when
I warned them he was a front runner with stamina to burn,
Kimaru told me that's exactly what they were looking for.'

When we returned to the Periférico Sur Ring Road,
'We've saved the best two sculptures for last,' Andrés said.
'And there they are, over on the left.'

We stopped at both.

The first was Australian Clement Meadmore's *Janus*, just
as Andrés had described it—a solid black cube twisted into
an upright ring six metres tall, its ends facing in opposite
directions parallel to the ground. We climbed the steps
carved into the volcanic rock on which it was placed so that
I could shoot it close-up.

I liked the simplicity and flow 'Why is it called *Janus*?'
I asked.

'Janus was a Roman God with two faces, front and back.
He could look both ways at once. See the ends up there, facing
east and west?' Andrés replied. 'He was the God of doorways.
The God of beginnings and endings. He could see into the
future and the past simultaneously. *Es pore so que Enero se lleva
su nombre*, that's why January's named after him.'

'But why is it black?'

'I asked Tony the same question. He told me Meadmore
had dedicated the sculpture to an Aboriginal hero of his.' He
bent and pointed out a name and the date 1894 carved into
the concrete at the base.

'*Jandamarra*,' I read aloud as I focussed the camera.

'Tony told me he fought a war against the invading British
colonists, just like Cuitláhuac when he defeated Hernán
Cortés.' He waited for a moment as I took in what he'd

said, before going on, 'Jandamarra saw the disastrous future unfolding for his people when the colonists arrived. He fought to save his tribe from the annihilation he saw coming.'

Then we drove on to the last sculpture a short distance away.

'Now *this* one takes the prize,' I said as we parked.

'It's called *Articulated Wall*,' Andrés said as we left the car. I focussed the Leica. 'It's also Señor Ramírez Vázquez's favourite, but I'd say it comes a close second to *Janus*. What do you say, Tío Guillermo?'

'Oh no. No, no. You two can fight it out. I never get involved in family matters when blood's about to be spilled.' He gave me a shrewd look and placed his hand on my shoulder. 'I know what this little cat's like when she's got her claws out.'

I walked around the sculpture, taking several photos, before stepping back to admire it. Standing seventeen metres tall and a brilliant yellow, I counted thirty-three identically sized rectangular slabs of reinforced concrete, one above the other. I read their dimensions on the information placard. Each was twelve metres long, one and a half metres wide and half a metre thick. They were mounted on an invisible central steel axis with a tiny but visible gap between them, each block placed slightly askew from those above and below it. In three sets of eight, their edges curved out and back to create a wave-like effect up the column, with five at the base and four at the top, complementing the spiral.

It was brilliantly designed, the play of light and shadow across it captivating.

'Ten!' I yelled, sprinting around it. 'Ten out of ten, without a doubt.'

'That settles the matter, and no blood spilled.' Tío Guillermo laughed as Andrés caught up with me and attacked my ticklish ribs, as always, with the bony fingers of his left hand. 'Time to head for home and enjoy the tilapia.'

We turned off Insurgentes Sur Avenue, intending to take a shortcut through the back streets, but we were held up behind a long column of army trucks filled with soldiers.

'Probably the paratroopers,' Andrés informed me. 'They're in the city all the time these days.'

'But they're all armed.'

'They always are. They've been attending our demonstrations lately to give the granaderos backup and make sure we keep the peace. We're used to it.'

When Tío Guillermo turned onto a parallel street to overtake them, I was astonished at the time it took, truck after truck still visible on the adjoining side street as we passed.

When we passed the front of the column, there were five rubber-tyred armoured vehicles leading them, similar to those I'd seen on TV in the last few months driving through the scattering demonstrators to disperse them. My stomach churned at the memory and I fought to prevent myself from throwing up.

'I'm feeling car sick,' I shouted, desperately swallowing the saliva pouring into my mouth. Tío Guillermo pulled up, allowing me to open the door and sit with my head between my knees in the fresh air until the nausea passed.

When we pulled into the Chihuahua building car park at last, I raced to the lift lobby, sheepish with relief and embarrassed by my nausea. I took the steps at a light jog to regain my composure.

They'd arrived in the lift just before me and the front door to the flat was open when I reached the corridor. I hugged Tía Sofia when she offered me her motherly concern, before moving to the balcony, sliding open the windows and leaning out to look down.

There were small groups already gathering on the plaza beside the church to attend the political meeting Andrés had mentioned. Others were arriving through the entrances to the laneway on the left and right. Many were carrying red carnations in bunches and single flowers. Others had them in a buttonhole or visible in a shirt pocket. Andrés had told us earlier it was an emblem the students had adopted.

A *pajarero*, a seller of songbirds, stood out among them. He was so unexpected I changed the film and snapped him making his way across the paving. The tower of bamboo cages strapped to his back swayed with every stride. Each cage was decorated with red and yellow crepe paper hibiscus flowers and filled with shadowy, fluttering pairs of dark blue songbirds and orange-chested green parakeets.

The church bell sounded three o'clock when Tía Sofia served the tilapia enchiladas for a late *comida*. Aromatic smells pouring from the kitchen the moment she opened the oven door enriched the lighter hints of spice and garlic lingering before then.

'Can we go down and join the students on the plaza now?' I asked when we'd finished.

Tío Guillermo looked at me, carefully refolding his serviette. 'It's not a good idea. Not after the way you were feeling just an hour ago.'

'I'm fine.' I widened my eyes, giving him my special pleading look. It always worked with Papá. 'There's nothing wrong with me now.'

'You're too young, Alicia. It could get rough down there.'

'There are other kids my age in the crowd, even younger. There is even a pregnant lady pushing a pram, with two little ones following her.'

'Even so, you've had a long day.'

'Please?'

'You heard me.'

His patience is running out. Perhaps just one more. 'Please?'

He pursed his lips. 'Are you going down, Andrés?' he asked, his tone irritated.

Elated, but not showing it, I knew I was winning him around.

'No, I'm not planning to. It's my day off training and I'm looking forward to an early night.' Andrés turned and bowed to Tía Sofia. 'Especially after the best enchilada I've ever tasted. Seven stars, Tío? Ten, in my book.'

'Please, please, please. Just for a little while. I want to feel what it's like to mix with students and school kids, even school kids my age, getting together to speak up for a just cause.'

Tío Guillermo leaned back and looked at Andrés again, drumming his fingers on the table.

It wasn't much, but it was enough. I gazed directly at him, mustering my most beguiling smile. 'Pleeeease?'

'Alright,' he said at last, glancing at his watch. 'You rest up here until five-thirty, and we'll go down for an hour. No longer. When I say so, we come straight back upstairs. No ifs, no buts.'

'Gracias! Gracias, Tío!' I squealed, surprising myself by running around the table to hug him. 'I can take the Leica with me and get some more shots.'

Now all I had to do was convince Andrés to join us. I knew he was enjoying a rest day between training sessions. I didn't say a word, just looked at him with as pleading an expression as I could muster.

'No, it's my day off—and *nothing* comes between me and my running,' Andrés said when he saw my look. 'Nothing. You above all people know that.'

'*Please,* please, please, please… I want to finish the film in the camera,' I begged him.

'Alright, I'll come,' he surprised me by reluctantly agreeing.

'I wouldn't do it for anyone else. Only for you, to take your photos.' He gave me a quick dry laugh, his voice touched with sarcasm. 'You never know, they might go down in history, *pequeña cabra*.'

'Like Abu Xavier's Guernica,' I agreed excitedly, ignoring his tone and triumphant at convincing him to change his mind.

* * *

We took the lift down to the plaza and it was packed, people streaming in through both entrances. Tío Guillermo showed his displeasure with an exasperated shake of his head as we exchanged looks and joined the flow. 'We're not going to enjoy this.' He gave me a thin smile. 'There must be ten or fifteen thousand people here already.'

I held up the camera and snapped his expression just as I was jostled sideways. 'At least let me use up this film, Tío. I've just changed it. I've already taken two—one of you and one of the *pajarero* over there. There are twenty-two exposures left.'

'*Only* twenty-two? As long as you make it quick.'

He frowned down at the red carnation he was carrying. Andrés had removed one for each of us from the vase. I saw Tío notice some people around him were not carrying one, so he threaded it through a buckle on the camera case slung around my shoulder.

Tía Sofia had snipped the stem off mine and pinned it to my top pocket.

Beside me, Andrés acknowledged two smiling dark-haired girls his age in the passing crowd. He threw the nearest one his carnation. She caught it, giving him an approving look before they both turned jauntily away. I snapped them too late, capturing the girl with the carnation waving Andrés goodbye with it over her shoulder as they disappeared towards the church, where someone was talking through loudspeakers.

'That's Gloria,' he said, 'and the other one's Ana María. They're in my architecture class. Gloria worked with us on *Janus.*'

'She likes you.'

'Who doesn't?' he responded at once, with a teasing self-effacing expression, leaving me unsure whether he was joking or serious.

So I took him at his word and dug my elbow into his ribs. 'Me, for one, when you're boasting.'

We worked our way to the back edge of the crowd close to the church, the voice on the speakers clearer now. A group of schoolboys in maroon and khaki uniforms in front of me restricted my view, even though one of them, whose features I recognised as Tepehuán Indian, flashed me a brief smile and stepped to one side when he saw my dilemma.

When I raised both arms above my head to take a hopeful random shot, Tío Guillermo took me by the armpits and effortlessly lifted me to his broad shoulders without so much as asking. I almost dropped the camera, but the position was perfect. I had a bird's eye view across the plaza and was able to balance my elbows on his bald head. He was rock solid each time I said I was about to take another shot.

I ranged the camera across the crowd and took several shots in quick succession. The first was the pregnant lady with the black pram, standing stock-still and listening intently, with her two little kids—*are they twin girls?*—squatting on the paving beside her, playing what looked like cat's cradle with a web of black string. I was delighted when the nearest of them stuck out her tongue when she saw the camera.

Another was a broad view of the Chihuahua building. A central balcony window on the third floor was wide open, a border of white sheets drawing attention to it, a pair of black loudspeakers at each end of the window ledge. I took it to be the hallway beside the lift shaft. There were several figures in the window, one of them speaking into a microphone.

'The Strike Committee,' Andrés said as I took the shots. 'Just as I thought. They want to call the demonstrations off. They're concerned about the number of granaderos and riot police already here. They must be able to see something from up there we can't.'

'Clearly, they know something we don't,' Tío Guillermo agreed.

The reaction from some rowdy groups in the crowd to their announcement shocked me. They began shouting in unison, others joining them, '*No queremos Olimpiadas, queremos revolución*. We don't want the Olympics, we want a revolution.'

The chant became deafening, drowning out whatever warning the student was shouting down at us.

'*Malditos extremistos*, bloody extremists,' Andrés yelled at us. 'I should have known they'd be here.'

I was surprised to see a single line of helmeted soldiers placed an arm's length apart at the base of the building, facing the crowd. They were standing at ease beneath the concrete overhang, bayonets fixed, as though guarding the entrances to the stairwells and the line of shopfront windows. An officer stood at the centre, his uniform immaculate and his polished epaulettes shining, a large orange megaphone in his right hand.

'It's the presidential guard, by the look of the uniforms,' Andrés said.

I photographed the officer, before raising the camera to focus on two helicopters that appeared out of the growing dusk high above us, one painted in dark blue police colours, the other in army grey camouflage.

The crowd quietened as they circled for several minutes, seemingly observing us, until two brilliant red flares were fired from the top floor of the Foreign Affairs skyscraper to our right. I took a dramatic shot of the flares falling against the darkening sky, trailing what looked like flames. They exploded on the paving between the church and the Chihuahua building, people beneath the line of their descent screaming as they fought to escape the shower of sparks.

The church bell unexpectedly rang out, tolling six and silencing the crowd. People close to me looked up at the bell tower, some laughing, others clearly counting out the chimes. I held my breath, the eeriness of the moment leading me to suspect it was a warning signal.

For several minutes the student's voice crackling over the loudspeakers urged the crowd to disperse, before falling silent as the police helicopter swooped directly at us. Tension rippled through the crowd as it also fired two flares aimed at the plaza, this time one red, one green, with the same incendiary descent and explosive result. The crowd scattered as they struck the ground. The helicopter skimmed low across the buildings, before soaring up and hovering over us, alongside the army helicopter once again.

The stunned silence lengthened, underscored by the consistent *whup whup whup* of helicopter blades.

Then a group of helmeted soldiers carrying rifles with bayonets fixed burst from behind the church wall to our right. They charged forward and took up positions in front of the church, facing the crowd. In a strange, dreamlike sequence, a side door of the church opened and I photographed a large number of men in plain clothes pouring down the steps, the door slamming shut behind them. The first of them showed a sheet of paper to the surrounding soldiers, who let them through. Wearing white gloves on one hand and carrying black pistols in the other, they melted purposefully into the crowd.

One of them passed so close to Andrés he could have reached out and touched him.

Andrés looked up at me. 'The Olympic Battalion. And they're armed. It means trouble.'

As he spoke, I heard the sharp crack of a gunshot, followed by several others. I ducked when I heard their terrifying echoes. I raised the camera again, fighting to control my shaking hands, to capture a soldier in the line beneath the eaves of the Chihuahua building, who had slumped to his knees and toppled forward at the feet of the others.

The officer raised his megaphone and spoke into it, his voice screeching until he adjusted the instrument and yelled at the crowd to leave at once. When he repeated the order, there was another sharp sequence of gunshots coming either from the roof of the church above us or from an upper floor of the Foreign Affairs skyscraper beyond it.

The officer was flung backwards against a shopfront window, hurling aside the megaphone. He slid down the glass, a smear of red marking his descent. He sat on the paving rocking himself, his legs outstretched, clutching at his chest, his mouth wide open coughing gouts of blood across his uniform.

In a shocking otherworldly moment, I read the name of the shop above his head in bold black print—*Fotos Exprés*.

I rushed to take the shot as Tío Guillermo lifted me down. He took hold of my hand, and we turned to run for the lift well at the far end of the building. The panicked crowd surrounding us rushed with one mind towards the same exit, their screams and shouts incoherent, trampling over those who'd fallen, papers flying as they threw aside the pamphlets and leaflets distributed among them earlier. An older man tore off his white shirt and waved it overhead in surrender. He staggered across our path before Tío brushed him aside. Others were scrambling for cover behind the vehicles in the carpark and crawling beneath them.

When I looked around for Andrés, he wasn't with us. I screamed a warning at Tío Guillermo. We slowed and he leaned down to shout in my ear, 'He must be ahead of us. Did you see him go?'

Seized with a terrifying degree of dread I screamed at the top of my lungs, 'No. He must be back there.'

We fought our way back through the chaos of running and falling bodies, kicking aside an overturned black pram, slipping on abandoned shoes and sandals, a handbag, paper cups, a scattering of empty food cartons.

We found Andrés lying face down beside the outstretched body of the blond-haired teenage schoolboy who'd been standing in front of me moments before beside the Tepehuán Indian. A bullet had smashed through the base of the schoolboy's skull and blood was seeping from beneath his body, spreading across the slate tiles on each side of him like a pair of wings with red and black-tipped feathers.

Andrés was groaning, his left calf bleeding into his jeans, shredded where a bullet had torn through them. Tío Guillermo turned him over, a grazed contusion evident beneath his hairline and across his nose where he'd struck the tiles. His eyes were glazed and unfocused.

As I looked down at him the world swirled around me, leaving me frozen with shock. For a moment I had no idea where I was. I doubled over and heard myself scream as though I was someone else, before I heard Tío's voice calling for the camera case. Barely comprehending, I handed it to him. He unclipped the strap, tore off the carnation and bound Andrés's leg above the knee.

Below the wound, his left foot protruded at a grotesque angle.

Tío stood, took me by my upper arms and shook me, before taking my face in both his hands. He leaned down to look into my eyes with unforgettable intensity. 'Listen, cariño. We have no time. You have to get away from here. Run. Run as fast as you can. I will take Andrés to the Green Cross Hospital. *To the Green Cross Hospital.* Remember that. Now Go. *Go!*'

He turned me around and pushed me away so violently that I almost fell. I regained my footing and stooped to pick up the camera. I stood unmoving in another moment of indecision, watching Tío use his teeth to tighten the knot on a white handkerchief he wrapped around his left hand before lifting Andrés across his back and right shoulder. He manoeuvred Andrés's arms around his neck and gripped both his hands in his right.

'Go,' he shouted again, leaning forward and balancing Andrés on his hip, his trailing legs off the ground. He took his first lunging step towards the exit, his left hand a cloth-bound white fist raised for balance. 'Go. Run like you've never run before.'

Helpless, I could not budge. The world spun around me, my terror-stricken mind a void as I lost all sense of time and watched a formation of soldiers advancing like black spectres across the plaza towards the pandemonium of screaming people, trapped by armoured vehicles and soldiers at the exit to my left. Some were firing from the shoulder, some kneeling before advancing again and others sliding into prone positions, one or two with their rifles balanced on the bodies of the fallen.

Closer, in stark black outline, the pregnant woman was crawling away from her pram. She was pinned as if paralysed in the blazing beam of a spotlight directed at the plaza from the police helicopter.

Is she searching for her children among the wounded? Did they try to run? Were they trampled in the stampede? And the horrifying question struck me, *Will the spotlight focus next on me?*

I tore my gaze away and my mind cleared as though I'd received an electric shock.

I had seven exposures left. I levered rapidly through them on automatic focus to the end of the film, before packing the camera back in the case and snapping it shut. I sprinted along the parapet beside the Aztec excavations, reached a flight of steps leading down into them and leapt down it, three steps at a time.

When I ran along the pathway between the pyramids, the lights in the Chihuahua building were switched off as if someone had cut the power supply. I looked back up to see rapid flashes of gunfire from several open windows on the second and third floors to the right flaring against the pitch-black backdrop, as though someone in there was striking matches.

Less than a hundred metres ahead of me another line of soldiers was advancing in formation, bayonets glinting. They were detaining some people, herding them at bayonet point to the corner where the steel paling fences met. They corralled them there. They were allowing others through. Women and girls, I noticed.

As I passed one of the pyramidal platforms, I climbed partway up and concealed the camera in a crevice between the rocks in its foundations.

I joined two women rushing in silence towards the exit gate, dragging a small girl between them and, I could not believe it, a brown silky terrier straining ahead on a leash, as if they were a family out for a brisk afternoon walk.

When we reached the advancing soldiers they scrutinised us, parted and directed us through. Others on guard at the exit gate inspected us, grinning at my hostess's uniform and confiscating a woven decorated Huichol basket one of the women was carrying before ushering us on.

We did not speak as we walked down Central Lázaro Cárdenas Avenue beneath the trees, a long line of empty army trucks parked beside the pavement.

A short way along we passed several soldiers eating tortillas handed out by someone in the back of a truck, their rifles stacked against the side of the vehicle. They took no notice of us as we passed, seemingly oblivious to the uproar and the sharp crackle of intermittent gunfire on the plaza.

A light rain began to fall when we passed the last truck.

I separated from my rescuers, took shelter beneath the awning of an empty takeaway restaurant and sat at one of the tables. I struggled to assure myself I had escaped. The cordon of soldiers had allowed me through. I had not been detained at the gate.

Shaking uncontrollably as I realised I was safe, I gasped for breath and sobbed when the rain strengthened in a series of wind gusts, drumming on the canvas overhead. It ran down in a blinding sheet before swirling across the pavement towards the gutter. *Just as it was across the plaza*, I imagined, *turning a deeper red as it washed away the blood, including Andrés's.*

The full horror of his shooting flooded through me, and my stomach churned as I acknowledged it had been at my insistence we go down to join the demonstration. *I've ruined Andrés's life. And the metallic smell in the air before I turned to run—what was that? The smell of gunfire or his blood?*

One of the women I'd been walking with burst through a curtain of water. She shook it from her hair, sat beside me and put her arm around my shoulder. When she asked where I was going and she didn't represent a threat, I told her everything. Who I was. That Papá was at work. That I was living in the Chihuahua building and couldn't return. That the last time I'd seen them, my tío had been on the plaza carrying my brother Andrés to safety—he had been shot in the leg. That I had to make my way to the Green Cross Hospital to meet them.

'You mean the Dr Rubén Leñero Hospital,' she said, as I wept in her arms. 'I am Ava. The other lady is my sister, Carmen. *Ven con nosotras*, come with us. We live just around the corner next to the Francisco Medina Ascencio Primary School. We are teachers there. *Te llevaré al hospital mañana*, I will take you to the hospital tomorrow.'

* * *

Señora Ava arranged a straw-filled mattress and bedding on the floor of a storeroom for me. The shelves were crammed with books and files. I thrashed from side to side in the musty darkness for what seemed hours, panting, before I fell into a fitful sleep.

When I woke it was still dark. I lay half-conscious, uncertain where I was. I stared uncomprehendingly at a wedge of electric light streaming across the unfamiliar ceiling through the partly open door. It threw shadows from the peeling paint in barbed and jagged patterns so terrifying I screamed in sudden panic for Tía Ariché.

When Señora Ava appeared at the door, I rushed sobbing into her open arms. She led me to her bedroom, where I curled up beside her in the warm bed, trembling. I tried to calm myself, staring across her shoulder at the green flower-patterned curtains lightening with the dawn. When she fell asleep and began to rhythmically snore, I shut my eyes against nightmarish images arising from the night before, dreading what waited for me in the morning.

After breakfast, Señora Ava drove me to the hospital. The traffic and pedestrians were so chaotic we had to park a street away.

At the hospital, a line of ambulances emblazoned with green crosses and others with red, as well as private cars, were banked up in the emergency driveway. Nurses and paramedics unloaded wounded patients onto grey-blanketed gurneys scattered in a triage area on the lawns, or lifted others from wheelchairs and stretchers back into their vehicles before they accelerated away to relocate them elsewhere. A group of white-and-blue-coated doctors worked purposefully among them.

When we reached the front of the queue, two armed soldiers barred our way.

'If you're bringing in someone wounded,' one of them instructed Señora Ava, 'or you need attention yourselves, report at the triage area over there. Otherwise, you have to leave. No visitors are allowed in this morning. The hospital is out of bounds.'

'We're looking for Alicia's brother,' Señora Ava placed an open palm behind my shoulders and gently pushed me forward. 'He was shot last night.'

'His name is Andrés Serrano,' I murmured. 'He's eighteen. We're from Chihuahua.'

'I wouldn't know,' he said. 'I'm not the registrar. You'll have to leave.'

'Can we talk to the registrar? Or is there a list of patients we can check?' Señora Ava asked.

'No, and no. As I said, I can't help you and you can't go in.'

As we walked away, he shouted after us, 'You can check at the Servicio Médico Forense mortuary on Chapultepec Avenue if he's dead. If he's not there, try Campo Militar Numero Uno. They're taking the bodies there to identify them… or you could even try the Panteón Civil de Dolores cemetery as a last resort.'

I heard his barked instructions even though I jammed my hands over my ears. His words sparked a fearful burst of foreboding deep within me, coupled with overpowering rage that rocked me to the core. I stopped, spun around and stared at him, speechless and shaking.

'*Cállate! Eres un bastardo cruel e insensible.* Shut up! You cruel and callous bastard,' Señora Ava shouted. '*Tu desperdicio de espacio sin cerebro!* You brainless waste of space!'

She placed a protective arm around my shoulder. 'Take no notice, *cariño.* He doesn't know what he's saying.'

Her violent reaction calmed me, though my heart still raced unbearably as we drove back across the suburb to the Chihuahua building.

We found it cordoned off. Soldiers and granaderos surrounding it waved us on. They refused to allow us to park.

As we drove past, I glimpsed civilians crammed into the backs of three army trucks in the carpark behind the building. Most were young students clearly in shock, some shirtless, some with bloodied faces, others being herded by granaderos towards the vehicles at bayonet point. I assumed they'd been arrested hiding in the apartments.

We had to wait at one point to allow a garbage truck to drive slowly off the plaza. Several stiff-fibred street brooms were clipped to its sides. The fogged-up windows of the driver's cabin were closed as powerful jets of water showered over it from tankers parked on each side of the laneway, washing away the blood and gore splattered along the chassis. Beyond it on the plaza, I caught sight of a gang of street cleaners working frantically. Partly obscured by sunlight flashing from the wet flagstones, they were hosing down and scrubbing the paving clean of blood and debris.

Back at the house, Señora Carmen had spread a batch of the latest newspapers across the table. She was cutting out articles related to the massacre as Ava searched through the telephone directory for Tío Guillermo's number.

'Take a look at these, Ava,' she said, adding without looking up, 'and you Alicia.' Then she puzzled me when she asserted that every headline reflected the influence and control the president and his PRI party had over the press. Although she was addressing Ava, I was pleased she'd included me in her remarks, treating me as if I was an adult. 'Not to mention the radio and television stations,' she added bitterly. 'They're censoring everything. All the information reaching us. Especially with the Olympics so close and the eyes of the world on us.'

She slid the cuttings she'd completed across to me. 'Just take a look.' She turned back to concentrate on the newspaper she was working on.

I glanced through the cuttings. The headline for *El Sol* read, '*Barrío el ejército con un foco de subverción en Tlatelolco*', 'The army has averted subversive activities in Tlatelolco'. The *Novedades* was headlined, '*El ejército mantiene tranquilidad y se informa oficial mente de 29 muertos*', 'The army maintains calm and reports an official count of 29 dead'. The *Excélsior* reported the Presidential Press Secretary had declared, '*20 muertos, 75 heridos y 400 presos*' '20 dead, 75 wounded and 400 arrested'.

'You see what I mean?' Señora Carmen said when I'd read through them. 'It's false news. They're lying about how many died. They cleaned up the plaza during the night and removed the bodies. We may never know how many were killed.'

'They still are cleaning up. We saw them when we drove past,' I said.

'The editorials suggest the massacre was the result of Cuban communists and Maoist agents infiltrating the student movement. Look at this example.' She cut out the next paragraph with her scissors and slid it across. It was taken from *La Prensa*. I read: *'Terroristas Extranjeros!'* 'Foreign Terrorists!' And above it, in smaller print, *'Armas de alto poder se utilizaron contra las tropas'*, 'High-powered weapons used against the troops'.

She took the cutting back, raised her pencilled eyebrows and gave me a bird-like glance as she explained that according to the government's so-called official reports, the communist agents among the students had started the shooting by posting snipers in the Chihuahua building and on the church roof and firing at the soldiers.

'The army retaliated and the president is taking credit for a job well done,' she said. 'He thinks he's confirmed Mexico's reputation as a stable modern nation by crushing the demonstrators. He believes might is right and the means justify the end.'

'Communist agents?' I asked. 'Is it true? My brother Andrés says it's not.'

'Of course it's not.'

'But why would the students use snipers to shoot the soldiers?'

'It wasn't the students. I suspect a conspiracy, most likely planned at the highest level and carried out by the Olympic Battalion. They used the army as a pawn.'

I frowned across at her. 'What do you mean as a pawn? Like in a game of chess?'

'Gunfire came from the top floor of the Foreign Affairs Office tower at the start. Ava and I saw the first flashes. So did the first two red flares. Students don't have access up there, let alone the roof of the church.'

'But why shoot their own soldiers?' I asked again.

'To get the army to respond in the worst possible way. Which they did.'

'I took a lot of photographs when it started,' I said breathlessly. 'And I saw gunfire too. It came from windows in the Chihuahua building when the lights went out.'

Her eyes lit up. 'You took photos? You did? Where's your camera?'

'I hid it. On one of the pyramids.'

'In the rain? It will have ruined the film.'

'No, it's in a case. Under a rock.'

'You have to retrieve it. You must. Your pictures, they'll be important under the circumstances.' She gripped my hand, squeezing it as she spoke. 'Listen to me. Whatever you do, don't give the film to anyone you don't know for developing. Use someone you trust or do it yourself. I'm sure your papá and tío will understand.'

Then Señora Ava called me over to the phone. 'It's your Tía Sofia. She has your Papá's number at the university.'

* * *

When Papá arrived, he told us Tío Guillermo had rescued Andrés. In the confusion, the soldiers at the exit had seen his left hand wrapped in the white handkerchief and waved him through to the carpark. They mistook him for a white-gloved member of the Olympic Battalion dealing with a student he'd arrested. He'd driven to the hospital, where Andrés was now receiving treatment in intensive care, with countless others.

'Andrés was conscious and under sedation when I saw him but he has suffered. He came round in agony on the back seat of Tío Guillermo's car.'

'In agony?'

'In agony. He must have been so sick with shock he could barely endure the pain. He says it was excruciating. He told me one thought had run through his mind—he had to survive. He had to stay alive, even though there were moments when the pain was so unbearable he hoped to pass out again.'

The searing agony he experienced with every bump and vibration struck through him with such ferocity he couldn't control his screams, Papá told me. 'He said it was without doubt the worst twenty minutes of his life. But you know our Andrés. When he described how bad the pain was, he joked that at least Tío Guillermo didn't need a siren. Everyone heard them coming. He's in reasonable spirits now, even though the damage to his leg is extensive. The chances of saving it could go either way. He may need an amputation.'

'Oh, no. *No. No. No!*'

'He may. We aren't sure yet.'

'If he does, will he ever run again?' I couldn't bear the idea of him on crutches or confined to a wheelchair.

'Run? Who knows? But walk? Yes, I'm sure.'

'How soon?'

'Within a fortnight, with crutches, they told me, and later with a prosthetic if he has an amputation. We can only wait and see.'

We returned to Tío Guillermo's unit in the late afternoon when Tía Sofia let us know the granaderos and police had released the Chihuahua building from lockdown after they'd entered and ransacked all the units. The power and water supplies had resumed.

Just after sundown, Papá and I recovered the camera from the pyramid. I was relieved to find it where I'd left it, undamaged, though the case was stained with what I feared at first might be blood, since Tío Guillermo had handled it and placed it on the ground between Andrés and the dead schoolboy—but it proved to be water.

Papá wound the film to the end and extracted it, and by

mid-morning the next day, we were examining the twenty-four enlarged colour photographs he had personally overseen being developed in the UNAM graphics laboratory darkroom.

He had arranged for all of them to be printed, even though two negatives were out of focus—the shot of the seller of songbirds I'd taken from high up in the unit and the portrait recording Tío's disapproving expression when we'd first joined the crowd.

Tío Guillermo gave a snort of laughter as he tore it up and threw the negative in the waste bin. 'We don't need that. We can do without the photo of a handsome man like me being mistaken for *el Coco*, the Bogeyman.'

Papá spread them out across the table and examined each in turn, before sorting them in the order of what he considered their dramatic impact.

'This one is without doubt the most sensational.' He placed it face up on the table. It showed the sharply focused pregnant woman crawling helplessly centre-stage frozen in the beam of the helicopter spotlight. She was staring directly at the camera, the upturned black pram behind her, her mouth gaping and her eyes filled with horror, the body of the schoolboy with wings of blood in the foreground and the ominous shadows of soldiers advancing across the plaza in the background.

Then he picked it up again and examined it more closely. 'What on earth are they?' he asked. He pointed at five metallic-blue shadows flying high across the cone of light. 'Swallow-tailed butterflies? Moths? Surely not. Not during the night.'

'Are they bats?' I asked.

'No, they're songbirds,' Tío Guillermo replied, peering over his shoulder. 'Slate-coloured solitaire thrushes, by the look of them. See the long tails?'

'Oh no,' I groaned. 'They killed the pajarero.'

Papá looked at me, before peering back at the photograph. 'I don't see any broken cages.'

'They must have been smashed in the stampede and cleaned up this morning,' Tío Guillermo suggested.

Papá next selected an earlier shot of the same woman standing attentively beside the pram before the shooting. Her two little girls squatted next to her with their hands entangled in the cat's cradle, one with her pink tongue sticking out at the camera. They were framed on the left by the Tepehuán Indian shuffling aside for me, and his fellow schoolboy with the blond hair standing in profile on the right, glancing sideways with his mouth open as though protesting that the Indian had shoved him aside to make room for me.

My heart sank as a rush of painful guilt tore me apart. *Such a change in fortune for him with the slight shift in his position because I wanted to take a photograph.*

Papá peered down at the two photos for a long time. He leaned across the table on his outstretched arms before he stood upright, crossed his arms and expired a whistling breath. 'My God, I'm back in Barcelona thirty years ago.'

'Why so?' Tío Guillermo asked.

'It's like I'm with Papá Xavier when he showed Mamá and me his photographs of Guernica taken with the same camera.' He tapped each photo in turn. '*Antes y después*, before and after. The only difference? His were black and white.' He picked each photo up in turn. 'Tlatelolco before and Tlatelolco after.'

Tío Guillermo nodded. 'You wouldn't read about it.'

Papá glanced sharply across at him, frowning. 'No, no. You would, if someone wrote about it. We're looking at our history here. This is a decisive moment, a watershed in the story of Mexico. *Una segunda Noche Triste*, a second Night of Sorrow.'

Tío Guillermo stared knowingly at him. 'And I'm looking at the author, who's just thought of the perfect title for his book and has selected the ideal pictures for the front cover.'

Papá gathered the photographs together and replaced them in the manila folder, before asking drily, 'Where do you suggest we start? With Porfirio Díaz and his overthrow in the revolution in 1910? Or with Lázaro Cárdenas and his reforms in the late 1930s? We both knew him personally when we were kids, after all.'

'We swam in his swimming pool.'

'Enjoyed his wife's food.'

'And rode his horses. What more do you need?'

'You're right,' Papá cupped my face in his hands. 'Young *mijita* here, with her abu's camera—and poor Andrés, with his new-found activism—are sending me on an important quest to record the outrage and grief we all feel at last night's murderous attack.'

'Never to be forgotten.' Tío Guillermo's said bluntly. 'Those photos record not only the facts, Víctor, they represent our collective revulsion at the shameful bloodshed. They symbolise the outpouring of our deepest emotions. You have to publish them. You must. We're all witnesses.'

Another tense silence followed before Papá nodded and held up the manila folder. 'One thing's for certain, Díaz Ordaz and the PRI have given up the moral high ground and any political legitimacy with this obscene act of violence.'

'And they'll lose the support of the middle classes and the intelligentsia. It'll be interesting to see how our writers like Octavio Paz and Carlos Fuentes react, let alone Elena Poniatowska and all the others.'

'Not to mention the rest of the world.' Papá frowned, placed the folder on the table and struck it repeatedly with a forefinger as he spoke. 'The massacre could be just the start.'

'Of what?'

'Of a movement leading to full democratisation.'

Tío Guillermo gave a burst of cynical laughter. 'Good luck with that. The phoenix of democracy rising from the Tlatelolco ashes? You'll need several lifetimes.'

'However long it takes.'

'Don't hold your breath. Mind you, you could be right. Your experience in extracting precious metals equips you well for digging out the truth.'

'If there's any to be found.'

'I'm sure you'll find it, even though it may be rare these days.'

* * *

The doctors did not allow me to visit Andrés for four days, but I accompanied Papá and sat in the hospital café while I waited for him. I did the schoolwork I'd been assigned, read books I'd selected from Papá's collection, or, when I got bored, practised the latest chess moves Papá had taught me on the miniature travelling chess set Abu Cerrildo had carved for me from crystals taken from the Cave of Swords—dark brown Aztec warriors on one side, facing white Spanish conquistadors on the other.

I sat at the same table each day with a view over the courtyard. A bar of sunlight widened across a line of potted *Anemia mexicana* ferns, keeping me abreast of the time, the satin greens of their prolific leaves steadily brightening. After midday, when the sun slanted across the chessboard or the open pages of my book, I'd order another Lulú soda and lunch, before moving to the next table in the shade. Papá joined me there before we headed home.

I had time to read Mamá's precious battered copy of *The Little Prince* twice and worked my way through a primary school version of *Yolanda Learns to Speak Nahuatl*, which Señora Ava lent me.

On the fourth day, I struggled through the first part of Carlos Castaneda's *The Teachings of Don Juan: A Yaqui Way of Knowledge*, which Papá was reading at the time. Attracted by the thought I'd gain an insight into the Sonoran Yaqui Indian language and culture, I'd snuck it into my satchel without his knowing.

I was learning about the mysterious effects of the playful spirit Mescalito in the peyote leaf on anyone who chewed it or drank the juice, imagining myself communing with lizards foreseeing the future and flying after smoking the Devil's weed, when Papá appeared and sat down. He had a fit when he saw the book, before roaring with laughter. He snatched it from me. Faces at other tables turned in our direction and smiled when he showed them the cover.

'It's all a fiction,' he assured me. 'The shaman Don Juan Matus does not exist.'

Late that afternoon, we joined Andrés in the ambulance as the paramedics transferred him to the Dr Eduardo Liceaga Hospital, the General Hospital of Mexico City, for his amputation.

'Why can't they save his foot?' I'd asked Papá, when he first gave me the news.

'He's too badly injured,' he'd explained, 'He has open fractures of the tibia and fibula.'

A crushing burst of shock and deep despair overcame me as he explained that fragments of the high-velocity bullet were still lodged in the torn ligaments, bone and tendons. The risk of infection was very high. Blood clots were developing in the lower femoral artery and he was losing sensation in the limb.

'The surgeons have told me repair is out of the question. Even if they are able to fix it, the chances are his foot will never function as it should. And the pain is severe at times, but Andrés has been remarkable. He understands and accepts the situation. He says it will be a relief to no longer experience such pain each time the sedatives wear off.'

I will never forget the drive. It was a Sunday, and the church bells rang for evening vespers as we drove across the city. It felt as if we were riding with Andrés to his doom. Holding his hand in the back of the ambulance, I couldn't speak. I could barely see him at first, his face blurred as tears slid down my cheeks.

'Relax, *mi pequeña cabra blanca*,' were his first words to me, his face pale and his eyes large and glassy, their pupils dilated. 'Anyone would think it was you having your foot cut off.'

Me having my foot cut off? I leaned forward, my body shuddering, and grasped his hand in both of mine. I held it to my forehead as if begging his forgiveness for indirectly causing such an unimaginable change in his life.

'I wish it was me instead of you,' I managed to whisper.

He stroked my hair as we pulled into the hospital driveway. 'No, no. Don't pity me. Look at it this way—I dodged the other bullet. I'm the luckiest man alive.'

My eyes brimmed as I fought to hold my composure. His innocent comment reminded me of the prostrate blond schoolboy lying next to him, the memory so vivid I felt sick.

'Come on, I need you to be strong,' he went on quietly. 'As strong as you've always been for me. You have to help me through this.'

Sobbing, I lifted my face close to his. He put his cheek to mine, and when the rear doors opened, my tears gleamed on his skin and in his sparse beard, before I realised he was crying too.

A jolt of shock tore through me. *When is the last time I witnessed that? Can I ever make it up to him? And if so, how?*

'Give me a smile to remember,' he said, as the hospital

orderlies lifted him out and onto the gurney, 'like you usually do. One with my name on it.' He glanced at me for a tense moment, his eyes wide and glistening. 'Ah, that's more like it. *That* is the Alicia I need around me.'

He lay back as they wheeled him away.

He needs me? My adored brother Andrés, who's been dealt a hand of winning cards until now, when my insistence on him joining me at the demonstration brought him such misfortune, now he needs me?

He had no idea how confused I was, how close to impossible it had been to keep my fear and guilt in check and respond with a self-conscious half-smile to his coaxing.

Or does he? I wondered. *And it's his way of calming me down.*

I turned and clung to Papá as Andrés disappeared through the double doors of the emergency entrance. Papá hugged me for several minutes in the dusk before I choked back my sobs and broke away. I watched him push open the hospital doors and when I followed him in, I stifled the dread flooding through me.

* * *

Early the next afternoon, Papá and I were allowed to visit Andrés in the intensive care unit.

It was a blazing hot Monday, the start of a week that seemed .never-ending. The opening ceremony for the Olympics was due on Saturday, 12 October. It was so close and yet so far, like an end-of-year school vacation that couldn't come soon enough. Or a longed-for birthday circled on a calendar, preceded by countless dates that never diminish, even though you cross them out.

I sat in the car squinting against the glare as we crossed the city, focussing the camera and feigning taking candid shots of the colourful streets and passers-by, wishing time would pass more quickly, and working out how I'd fill the intervening days, conscious that impatience made it drag more slowly.

It was a relief to come in out of the stifling heat and skip ahead of Papá down the long, whitewashed corridor on the third floor, beneath a row of spinning fans. I followed the six-inch green line painted on the floor leading to the swing doors of the ICU, making sure my sandalled feet landed squarely on it and didn't encroach on the forbidding minefield of the ochre tiles on either side.

I waited for Papá at the door, edgy with excitement, peering on tiptoe at the outstretched patients distorted through a frosted glass window, swirling figures in white and green weaving among them as though they were underwater.

'Settle down, *muñequita*,' he said when he reached me, placing a restraining hand on my shoulder. 'I've warned you. We don't know how he'll be feeling. We have to be prepared.'

'I know, but it's Andrés. Won't he be alright?'

'I hope so, but it's a lot for him to take in. And he'll be sedated against the pain.' He looked down at me before pushing open the door. 'We'll let him do the talking, shall we? If he's able.'

We took our bearings as we entered and saw Andrés lying opposite us across the ward. His eyes were closed, his face grey and sallow, a clear drip feeding into the back of his right wrist. I thought he was asleep. He was leaning back against pillows arranged around him as though he was in an extended armchair, an intricately crocheted white cotton blanket thrown across his torso. His left leg was encased in what looked like elasticised bandages from his thigh to his foreshortened calf. It was raised in a bedside sling, splints on each side of his knee holding it rigid.

I stared at him, appalled to see him so helpless, so wounded. When his eyes flashed open his enormous pupils were black and glazed. It took him a moment to focus. He tried to smile, a momentary flicker at the corner of his lips when he recognised me, before lurching away and holding his right hand out to Papá.

For several minutes no words passed between them. He did not look back at me.

When he closed his eyes again, tears slid down beside his nose into his beard, triggering a series of racking sobs rising from deep within me and doubling me over.

I turned and ran gasping for the door, burst into the corridor and slid down against the wall, where I sat with my head between my raised knees, my body shuddering. I gave out several agonised howls before taking deep convulsive breaths for self-control, my outpouring prompted as much by fury burning deep within me as despair.

Moments later, a laboratory technician appeared, pushing a two-tiered trolley loaded with rattling phials and instruments. She stopped beside me at the door. I ducked my head and gazed at her sandals encased in blue plastic overshoes.

'*Estás bien?* Are you alright?' she asked.

When she saw I was unable to reply, she squatted in front of me, tore several sheets from a roll of paper towels on the lower shelf of her trolley and handed them to me.

'*Déjame traerte un trago de agua*, let me get you a drink of water.'

I shook my head and managed to stammer, '*Gracias, pero no, te seguiré*, thank you, but no, I'll follow you in.'

She steadied me as I staggered to my feet. '*No te apresures. Entra cuando estés lista*, don't rush. Come in when you're ready.'

I stood uncertainly at the door for several minutes after she'd disappeared, but when I was about to enter, Papá appeared and held out his arm to stop me. With a hand on the small of my back, he guided me down the corridor away from the ICU. He strengthened his grip when I struggled to break free and run back to Andrés.

'Let me go, Papá. I haven't said goodbye.'

'You can't.'

'Why not?'

'I was asked to leave. They're preparing to transfer him to the orthopaedic ward.'

'So soon?'

'His surgery went well enough for them to move him. They need his bed for another urgent case.'

'That's good, isn't it?'

'I'm sure it is.'

When we stopped beside the lifts, he led me to a wooden bench beneath the window, patting the slats to his right.

'Listen to me, *mijita*, we believe you should stay away until he's well on the way to recovery.'

I sat beside him, stunned. '*We?* Doesn't Andrés want to see me?'

'You know he does, but not right now. By *we* I mean the doctors and me. It doesn't do him any good to see you so upset.'

'I couldn't help it.'

'I know.'

'It just happened.' Helpless, and for a moment feeling unwanted, I stiffened in a burst of fury at the unfairness of it.

'I know, and so does he.'

'I won't do it again,' I snapped.

'I'm sure you'll try not to.'

'I won't. I just *won't*.'

'Look, he has a lot to deal with. You're aware of that. His life has been turned upside down. He has to start again. With everything. He has to learn to make adjustments. Simple things to start with.' He held out a fist and extended a finger in turn, 'Like getting out of bed and dressing, eating and drinking, sleeping… even breathing, I suspect. He's exhausted after the surgery and full of different drugs. You saw the way he looked.'

'He looked terrible. And when I saw him crying…'

'He's in shock and he's confused.'

'So am I.'

'I know, I know.' He put an arm around my shoulder and pulled me to his side. 'I'm going to arrange counselling for you when we're home. There's one thing you must be clear about—it was not your fault. None of us knew what was going to happen.'

'But if it hadn't been for me—'

'No, no. You're not to blame, not in any way. You were interested in the crowds and curious about the demonstration. Besides, you wanted to use the camera. It's natural for someone your age. I'd have done the same when I was young.' He leaned forward and looked into my eyes. 'It was a coincidence, a chance accident, you understand?'

'An accident?'

'Yes.'

Despite his words, dreadful feelings of self-blame flooded my mind, as they had when Tía Ariché had told me about Mamá. I shook my head to dismiss the overpowering sensation.

'I can't bear to think of Andrés never running again. Never *ever*,' I said. 'Not the way he does now.'

But I will, the sudden determined thought arose. *I'll keep running for him. For both of us. And for Mamá, as we did in Urique Cemetery.* At precisely the same moment, it seemed, stunning doubts flashed across my mind. *But only for as long as I enjoy it. I have neither the desire nor the talent to succeed at world-class level that Andrés does. They are his dreams, not mine.*

131

'Look, we don't know what the future holds,' I heard Papá continue. 'Right now, he's about to experience a hurricane of different emotions as he comes to terms with what's happened.'

'We can help him, can't we?'

'Yes, we can. We can encourage him. And support him. But it's up to him. He has to realise what's happened and acknowledge the extent of it. There's no going back. His life will be different. He has to learn what he can do and not get depressed by what he can't. Too much grieving won't be good for him.' He took a deep breath. 'Or anger. Or depression. It's going to take him some considerable time before he accepts the situation.' He tapped his temple with a forefinger. 'In here.' He placed his hand over his heart and bent to clutch his ankle. 'As well as in here… and down here.'

'How long will that take?'

'It all depends.

'What about you? You'll visit him, won't you?'

'I will, as often as visitors are allowed.' He took my left hand in his and lifted it to his lips, briefly kissing my fingers. 'As for you, *mijita*, you can go to the Games with Tía Sofia on the days we have the tickets for, and watch the rest of the events on her colour television. Tío Guillermo and I will come with you when we can, at least for part of the time. You can take the camera.'

'I'll take the best photographs I can to show Andrés when he's ready to see me.'

'I know you will. He's sure to appreciate them.'

He withdrew his arm from around my shoulder and leaned forward with both hands on the bench as he prepared to stand. I put my hand on his chest. 'Just one thing, Papá. If Andrés can't go to the Games, why should I? Won't it upset him? It seems so unfair.'

He sat back and patted my knee. 'Don't overthink the

situation, *mijita*. He's just as likely to be upset if you don't go. It's what you both came here to do, so do it for him.' He raised his eyebrows and gave me an appreciative glance. 'I'm pleased you care so much you're putting yourself in Andrés's shoes to understand how he'd feel about you going without him, but I'm sure he'd feel far worse if it prevented you from doing so. So go. Enjoy it. Without a second thought.' He stood and pulled me upright. 'And let's hear no more about it.'

We were the only two descending in the lift when he turned to face me. He gave me a long, searching look, and with both hands on my shoulders, applied some downward pressure. 'Don't let Andrés's troubles weigh you down, cariño. When you take your photographs, take them for him.' He released his hands, cupped my face, and then surprised me when his next words echoed my recent thoughts. 'And when you run in future, why don't you run for both of you? Until the day comes when he can run for himself.'

'He will?'

'I wouldn't say it if I didn't believe it.' I looked up at him as he nodded, as if he was certain about something I now so strongly doubted. '*Siento en mis huesos*, I feel in in my bones.'

About to contradict him, I stiffened and did not reply as unexpected thoughts raced through my mind. Andrés was ten years older than me and had been a hero to me since I was young. I held him in awe and had became his running shadow, often much to his annoyance. We both shared the tragedy of losing Mamá at an early age and running cemented our closeness more strongly than we acknowledged, especially since he was able to bring her to life for me as we ran more realistically than I could in my imagination—as he had in the cemetery three years ago.

When we stepped into the foyer, Papá withdrew a small brown envelope from his back pocket and handed it to me.

'You're responsible enough to look after these.'

I lifted the flap and emptied eight tickets to the *Estadio Olímpico Universitario*, the Olympic Stadium, into the palm of my right hand. I stared down at them, speechless, before fanning them out with a scream of delight. They were blue with a yellow band through the centre, four dated 'Tuesday 15 Oct' and four for the next day. They all showed the icon of a running shoe for athletics, an archway with the number three, indicating our entrance gate, seated figures and the numbers 31135–31138 and two symbolic clocks indicating our entry and departure times—eleven and five o'clock. On the back was a graphic oval showing the seating in the stadium, a red arrow indicating our seats were on the second tier next to the rail, partway down the home straight.

I raised my arms above my head, tickets in one hand, envelope in the other, spun around Papá several times and tore out into the glaring afternoon sunlight when he opened the door for me. Breathless and jubilant, I gave him an energetic long-lasting hug.

'Better not lose them. Guard them with your life.'

'Trust me, Papá, I will. With my life. They are perfect.'

* * *

I woke while it was still dark on Saturday morning, immediately alert and bursting with anticipation.

Without waking Papá, I put on my trapeze dress and tiptoed into the lounge. I switched on Tía Sofía's colour TV and, with the sound muted, watched the build-up to the opening ceremony.

They were showing a repeat of the arrival of the Olympic torch at Veracruz six days ago. Seventeen swimmers in a relay were side-stroking from the cruiser *Durango*, each holding a torch in the air and lighting the next torch in sequence until the flame reached the shore.

The swim was interrupted by a brief flashback I hadn't seen before. It showed the moment the torch had arrived a week earlier in the Bahamas, at the place where Cristobal Colon—Christopher Columbus—had landed, coincidentally on 12 October 1492, on the island of Guanahaní. He had renamed the island San Salvador. The flame was used to light a cauldron modelled on an Aztec brazier dedicated to the fertility goddess of corn Xilonen, set on a pedestal in the town's plaza. I was amazed when the commentator mentioned the original brazier on which the replica was modelled had been unearthed from a pyramid in Tlatelolco years before.

A rush of excitement raced through me. *From the same pyramid where I hid my camera? From the same crevice? It has to be. It just has to be!*

I followed the journey of the flame from Veracruz through towns and cities in the south-east. It ended up in the late evening on an upper tier of the Pyramid of the Moon in Teotihuacan, where a spectacular Aztec ceremony of the New Fire was performed. It was the first, the commentator said, since it was last performed by Montezuma in 1507.

The ceremony was underway when Tía Sofia appeared. She opened the curtains, allowing shafts of blinding sunlight to pour across the room. She switched up the sound and settled cross-legged beside me on the carpet.

She put an arm around my shoulders. 'I should have known you'd be up. Did you get any sleep?'

'Enough, thank you. I can't wait for the Games to start.'

'No! I'd never have guessed.' She gave me a teasing smile. 'Are you hungry?'

'A little. What are we having?'

'Quick and easy *molletes*. Something you can eat in front of the TV without being distracted.'

'Oh, yum.'

'Would you like bacon topping with yours? Or tomato and jalopeños? Or all three?'

'All three, please. Can I help?'

'You stay where you are and give me a running commentary. I'll start with coffees for the two snoring señores.'

By mid-morning, the Olympic stadium was packed to overflowing when President Díaz Ordaz and a group of dignitaries arrived. They took their seats to a twenty-one-gun salute, a fanfare of trumpets and the singing of the national anthem. Five colourful gigantic balloons representing the Olympic rings floated skywards, and the athletes appeared in their multicoloured uniforms, marching in time and in disciplined rows and columns into the stadium to the regular drumbeat of a military band. They circled the stadium and took their places on the grass in the centre.

The formality of the athletes surprised me. I gave a burst of laughter each time I saw someone skip to get back into step, and when Tía Sofia asked what had amused me, I explained I often did the same at school, but for the opposite reason—to be the only one deliberately *out* of step.

When the president's voice rang out, declaring the Games open, and the Olympic flag was raised, a rush of anger rose like bile in my throat. I switched off the sound and glanced away. I couldn't bear hearing his voice or looking at him as he spoke. The thought of Andrés lying helpless on the plaza below and now in the hospital bed was unbearable.

I switched the sound back on when the mayors of Tokyo and Mexico City exchanged another smaller Olympic flag on a pole, which Tía Sofia explained was the Antwerp flag, first handed across in the 1920 ceremony in the city of that name.

'I've been reading about it,' she said. 'I thought I'd show some interest, even though I'm not a sporty person, especially now the Games are going ahead here. Guillermo was concerned they'd be transferred to Los Angeles.'

The wind was up, and the flag wrapped itself around the head of the guardsman carrying it, blinding him. He had to feel his way up the six steps onto the pink dais, applause ringing out when he didn't trip over. He untangled himself and handed the flag across, the band playing *'La Zandunga'*, an Andalusian waltz. I recognized it after a few bars—Andrés had recently been mastering it on his guitar following Papá's instructions, and I'd been unsuccessfully following him in the background.

At the same time, an astonishing cloud of multicoloured balloons was released.

'Do you know how many there are?' Tía Sofia asked.

'Ten thousand?'

'More.'

'Twenty?'

'Twice that. Forty thousand of them.'

'Wow! I'm glad I didn't have to blow them up.'

I held my breath as the torchbearer appeared to a fanfare of drums, conch shells and reed flutes—and then I recognized her.

'Tía Sofia, it's Queta Basilio,' I squealed. 'They've chosen a woman to light the cauldron! She's our hurdles champion. I saw her on TV at the Olympic trials.'

Dressed in white, her black hair tied back with a white sash and holding the torch high in her right hand, she circled the track in an anticlockwise direction, before mounting the steps to the cauldron in the back straight. She looked fit and strong as she bounded effortlessly up the stairway that I'd imagined climbing during Andrés's race. At the top, she turned, held the torch high and out towards the athletes, before lighting the cauldron. The flame erupted and the crowd roared.

The athletes' oaths were read, the national anthem played again, an enormous flock of pigeons was released, and the Games were underway.

* * *

Ten days later, with the Games still in progress, I upended the envelope and tipped all the photographs I'd taken across an open space on Andrés's bed. He watched me with a patient, bemused look, hands behind his head, his latest plaster cast raised on a pillow.

His calmness surprised and pleased me, but I wondered how he was feeling deep down after his second operation. Papá had told me the surgeons had removed a further section of bone from below the knee when unexpected complications had set in after the first amputation.

Looking back on it now, I believe the painkillers had numbed him and the extent to which the trajectory of his life had altered had not yet sunk in.

I busied myself by concentrating instead on sorting the photographs into as close to their calendar sequence as I could recall.

The first was the shot Andrés had taken of me in the parking lot of the athletes' village, sitting on the metal sculpture of the Mexico 1968 logo, about to bite into the grilled corn *elote*. I pointed at three African athletes walking past in their army-green tracksuits, "Ethiopia" imprinted on the back, and tapped my forefinger on the one looking across at me. I hadn't noticed him at the time the photo was taken.

'Can you guess who this is?' I said.

He picked up the photo and peered at it, without looking up. 'It's got to be Mamo Wolde, second in my race, the ten thousand metres. My God, what a runner. I've seen the replays over and over. Him and the Kenyan I trained with, Naftali Temu, battling around the last lap and down the final straight, Wolde leading until the last fifty metres when Temu sprinted past. I told you the Kenyans had an extra gear and overdrive.'

'They were followed by Gammoudi, weren't they?' I asked, relieved I'd remembered the name, especially since Andrés had mentioned him to me before.

'Yes, and then our Juan Martinez, who led for most of the last five laps, as I warned the Kenyans.' He gave a sympathetic pursing of his lips, 'The Australian, Ron Clarke, followed them home in sixth.'

'At least he finished. I remember you said he may not, may even have *died* because of the altitude.' I hesitated, unsure whether I should have referred to the dangers associated with the Games because of the altitude, before changing the subject with a question. 'What was Naftali's time again?'

'Twenty-nine minutes, twenty-seven seconds or so.'

'And yours at the trial?' I asked, before looking up at him and flinching when I realised how insensitive the question was. I held my breath before he replied.

'Don't remind me. Thirty minutes forty-eight point four seconds, according to Abu Cerrildo. A second slower by the official timekeeper.'

'I prefer Abu's stopwatch.'

'So do I, even if it puts me a lap behind at the end.' He looked down at the photo and shook his head. 'It's hard to realise I'll never have my time recorded as an able-bodied athlete again.'

I felt as if he'd slapped me hard across the cheek. I had no reply, so I reached for the next photo. 'I managed to get this one for you,' I said breathlessly. 'Tía Sofia took me to the athletes' village. We spoke to Kimaru Songok. He remembers you. So do some of the other Kenyans. He arranged for us to meet Naftali and I took this shot of him. I took the print back to him the other day to get him to sign it for you.'

I handed him the photograph. Naftali was standing in the plaza wearing his red tracksuit and barefoot, the gold medal around his neck. He'd printed a message across it—'*Kwa* Andres, *bahati nzuri na maisha yako ya baadaye*' and signed it '*Rafiki yako*, Naftali Temu.'

I saw Andrés wince and frown before he flicked the photo back on the bed, face-up. I pointed at the inscription. 'It's Swahili. It says, "For Andrés, good luck with your future, your friend, Naftali Temu." Kimaru translated it for me.' I gave him a shy half-smile, hoping to lighten the mood. 'He forgot the accent on the *e* in your name.'

'Thank you, but I don't know whether to laugh or cry.' He held my hand for a moment. His palm was dry and hot. 'You know how it is when you've just been given something brand new? A bike or a new pair of shoes? And you spend the next six months looking for every bike or pair of shoes of the same make you never noticed before? Well, that's me right now. Every time someone comes in here, I notice they have a whole left leg and mine is missing.' He tapped the photo. 'It happened when you walked in and when I looked at Naftali just now. He can still run. So can you. I can't.'

Stunned, I had no idea how to respond.

'It's hard. It might be different when I get my prosthetic. They've already measured me for one.'

'Will it arrive soon?'

'They have no idea. Until then, it's a wheelchair.' He let go of my hand, stretched and put both of his behind his head again. 'I hate to think of myself as disabled. Hate it,' he growled, before taking a deep breath. 'But guess who's going to be pushing me around?'

The vivid image of me pushing him in his wheelchair along the Conchos River footpath at a fast trot flashed through my mind. 'Geronimo?' I suggested to distract him. 'Pulling you from the front using his lead as a harness?'

'Geronimo. Now, there's a thought.'

'Do you want to see the rest?' I asked, to change the subject.

'Sure. Show me what you've got.'

We ran through them, beginning with Tuesday's events. The discus and javelin finals. The pole vault. Tall and slender Wyomia Tyus of the USA winning the women's one hundred metres, and the Kenyans, Amos Biwott and Ben Kogo, first and second in the steeplechase, both clearing away down the home straight.

'What about the men's two hundred metres?' he asked. 'Did you photograph the finish?'

'I did. The end of the race and the medal presentation.' I was excited he'd asked. Papá thought they were the pick of the photographs and had been full of praise for them.

'The medal presentation? Show me.'

I selected the three photos I'd taken, one of the race, two of the presentation.

The first showed black American Tommy Smith bursting smoothly through the tape ahead of the Australian Peter Norman, with another black American, John Carlos, close behind in third. It was slightly blurred, suggesting the effect of speed.

'You should have heard the spectators at the end of the race,' I said. 'They were going mad because it was so close, but that was nothing compared to what happened at the medal presentation afterwards. It was late in the afternoon. I had to concentrate on the light and focus the Leica, so it took me a while looking through the viewfinder as they took their places on the dais. Before taking the shot, I looked up to check the settings. When I looked over at them, I couldn't believe it, Andrés. Tommy Smith and John Carlos weren't wearing shoes. They had their tracksuits rolled up and were both wearing black socks. Here, look for yourself.'

'So they are. But look at what else they're doing. You caught it beautifully.'

I didn't reply at once as I recalled I'd had to refocus to ensure I captured all the details. As the Stars and Stripes flag was raised and the Star-Spangled Banner sounded, they lowered their heads. At the same time, they raised a fist wearing a black glove—in the Black Power salute, Papá told me later—Smith's on his right hand and Carlos's on his left. I'd snapped two shots, catching them as they stood with their heads bowed and arms upraised, with Peter Norman gazing at the flagstaff. I remember the spectators around me were shocked into a sudden prolonged silence before bursting into deafening jeers and shouts of outrage at the defiant show of obvious disrespect. While I wasn't aware of the deep political meaning behind their protest, the courage and daring they showed in facing the hostility of the spectators thrilled me, and I blocked out the noise.

'When Papá and I looked at the photos yesterday,' I said, 'we noticed all three of them, including Peter Norman, are wearing those round yellow badges over their hearts. See them? I borrowed Tía Sofía's magnifying glass and read what's printed on them.'

'What?' Andrés held up the photo to squint at it. 'I can't make it out.'

'The "Olympic Project for Human Rights", whatever that is, and look at Tommy Smith. He's holding an open brown cardboard box against his left hip. See the green leaves in it? Papá says it must be an olive branch.'

Andrés frowned at me and said one of the TV commentators had confirmed they had both broken other forbidden Olympic protocols—in Smith's case by wearing a black scarf around his neck and in Carlos's a beaded necklace visible in the open collar of his tracksuit top.

'He said they were protesting on behalf of the American Black Power organisation. The scarf and black socks represent the poverty many black Americans experience.' He looked more closely down at the photo. 'And Carlos's beads; see them there round his neck? The black ones? They symbolise the estimated two million slaves who died in the ships carrying them to the Americas, following the Middle Passage across the Atlantic. How brilliant!'

'And the *gloves*,' I said excitedly. 'Papá says they must have shared the same pair—one each. He says it took a lot of courage for them to do what they did. All three of them, even the Australian. He says they'll be remembered for a long time, but it's going to cause them heaps of trouble. The Olympic Committee won't stand for it.'

Andrés thrilled me when he tapped the photo with his forefinger and said, 'You don't know what you've done here, *pequeña cabra*. You've captured another moment in history with Abu's camera. Papá can use it in the book he's planning.' He raised his right fist, clenched in a salute. 'Black Power! I told you about it before the Games when the black athletes were considering going on strike, remember? Here it is in action.' He raised it to his lips and gave it a kiss. 'I love it... love it... *love* it.'

In Saucillo, Northern Mexico, 1969 – ongoing

THE YEAR 1968 WAS pivotal in my relationship with Andrés.

Three weeks after his surgery, he returned home to Saucillo to recuperate, taking leave from his studies. The evening before his arrival Papá forewarned us we we'd have to be patient and understanding with him. He called Camila and me into the lounge just on sunset. I'd been jogging round the circuit in the back yard, where Abu was carving his latest selenite crystal chess miniatures.

'We're going to have to be very careful with Andrés tomorrow,' he said. 'It's not just the physical pain he has to put up with, it's learning to do the simple things we take for granted—'

'Like what?' I asked, panting.

'Like moving from the bed to the wheelchair. Using the toilet. Washing and dressing.'

'He was already doing all that when we saw him in hospital, wasn't he?'

'He was, and he is becoming self-sufficient; but now he has to learn to be kind to himself. He has to give himself time to adjust to the changes. Get used to having no left foot. He has to recover emotionally and come to terms with not being able to run the way he used to.'

'That's going to be hard for him.'

'Yes, it will. Very difficult.'

'What can we do, then?'

'Be patient. Help him, whenever he asks you to. Be aware he'll be grieving as he reorients himself. It won't be easy.'

Why not? I wondered. *He is Andrés, after all. He's a fighter.*

'He's strong, isn't he?'

'Of course he is, but think about it. Put yourself in his place. His life's been turned upside down. He'll be angry and depressed. He'll find it hard to accept what's happened to him, let alone come to terms with it and start rebuilding his life. He'll be asking "Why me?" and we'll need to encourage him to keep going, to believe in himself, to find the strength to overcome the hardships he'll have to face. Step by step.'

'Will it be as difficult as you say?'

'It will. For him—and for you. He's on another journey now, just as he was for the Olympics. A journey to find a new vision for himself. To develop a new mindset as he learns his limitations. And that will affect your relationship with him.'

'Él podría sorprenderos a todos, He might surprise us all, Señor Victor,' Camila said. '*Si el es el Andrés lo conozco.* If he's the Andrés I know,'

'He might.'

'No! He *will*,' I said fiercely.

Within days I discovered how much Andrés had changed.

The first time I pushed him in his wheelchair for a short walk along the paved section of the Conchos River embankment, I floundered helplessly in a gravelled section where the concrete had broken up. We were a kilometre from home.

'Look out!' he screamed, as the left wheel dug into the sand. The wheelchair lurched sideways before swerving so violently the handgrip was torn from my grasp and he toppled clumsily out, despite my desperate efforts to prevent it. He saved himself from falling to the ground by clutching an armrest and hopping crazily round the wheelchair on his right leg.

Geronimo rushed around us, barking excitedly, as if we were engaged in some new game.

I was so relieved he hadn't crashed to the ground and he looked so comical dancing round the upturned chair, I gave out a nervous laugh, but guiltily stifled it when I looked at his red face. I was shocked to see his expression contorted with pain and rage.

'Are you blind?' he screamed. 'Look where you're going, you little idiot. You could have torn open the sutures.'

On the verge of tears, I helped him right the wheelchair and he levered himself back into it, adjusting the right footrest. He reached forward and gingerly felt the stump through the compression sock.

'I'm in enough pain as it is, without you making things worse,' he said, his voice a growl.

'I'm so sorry, Andrés,' I said in a strained whisper. 'I didn't mean to.'

I saw him set his jaw and he did not speak to me again on the way home. I could barely breathe as I pushed him back to the house.

When we kayaked together on the Conchos River later that week, I took his irritable outbursts of frustration at the pain and discomfort he experienced with the seat and positioning of his legs personally, even though he was not directing them at me.

'My God, it's worse than being stabbed in the leg with a knife, Alicia. Multiple times… and the pain at night! I can't sleep. My medications are useless.' Then he added in a wild outburst, 'This is no way to live! I can understand why some people in my circumstance would rather die.'

I suffered unduly as I towed him back to the landing, unable to please or calm him. My feelings swerved between empathy and distaste. *At least you're alive*, the thought kept running across my mind. *You should be grateful for that—and for everything we're doing for you. Stop feeling sorry for yourself.*

In spite of Papa's advice I soon ran out of patience. I found it impossible to tolerate his moodiness. I had never known him to be so negative and quick to anger, so mean, moody and emotional. So self-absorbed. I knew he was suffering but had no idea how to deal with the changes in his personality as he grappled with the evaporation of his Olympic dream and the effects of post-traumatic shock.

My emotions were so mixed I came close to hating him, though I never dared to say so. I was relieved when he returned to Mexico City a month later, to fit his prosthetic limb and continue with his architectural studies.

He did not return for over a year.

During that time Papá and Abu Cerrildo updated me on his progress.

'He enjoys his studies,' Papá told me once when I asked, 'and he's doing well at them, but he can't stand his prosthetic foot. He considers the design primitive, and it's only a temporary "stop-gap", as he puts it. It's too stiff. Yes, he can walk on it, but he can't run, and if there's one thing you and I both know about him, running was his life.'

'*Is* his life,' I corrected him. 'I don't think that's changed. It's just frustrating him that he can't'

'*Is* his life. So guess what?'

'I don't know.'

'Take a guess.'

'Is he going to ask whoever made it to design a better one, maybe? With more flexibility?'

Papá laughed. 'Close, but you know Andrés. He's impatient, and so determined to run again he's working on it himself. He asked Abu the other day to dismantle the old wooden rocking horse you kids never play with anymore. You know, the one he made for you with the single leaf of a car spring bouncing it. He wants to use the spring leaf as a foot, somehow.'

'How?'

'Who knows? *Está obsesionado...* he's obsessed with the idea.'

'Wouldn't it be too heavy? And even stiffer than the foot he's got?'

'You would think so, but let's wait and see what he has in mind. He won't be using the whole leaf, after all. I guess he'll be using part of it and thinning it down.'

I had to smile. 'If he succeeds, he'll make a great long jumper. Bouncing like a kangaroo.'

Papá was right. When Andrés came home for a week during his long vacation the following July, he'd regained his previous enthusiasm for the idea of running—this time as a Paralympian, assuming the Games would eventually include athletes wearing prosthetics —and his zest for living.

He had changed, and I found it a joyful relief to share his company again. He spent hours with Abu in the work shed cutting a segment from the curved leaf of the spring, grinding it back and shaping it to the template he had in mind.

'Like the rear leg of a galloping horse, *mi pequeña cabra,*' he explained one afternoon as I watched him working with the grinder, short-lived showers of sparks shooting across the workshop. 'If you examine it at full gallop closely it curves back and forward like a Spanish inverted question mark.'

'Like Abu's scythe he uses on the lawns?'

'Exactly, but flattened, to give traction.'

When he took it back to Mexico City with him, he was still puzzling over how to attach it to his amputated leg.

I enjoyed spending time at the dining table with him each evening, watching him work on a project he was due to present for his architectural studies. I was especially interested when he introduced me to the house designs of the Australian architect Glen Murcutt. He had photocopied a number of Murcutt houses from articles in architectural magazines held in the Polytechnic Institute library. One in particular had caught his eye—a small, neat wood and corrugated iron farmhouse he thought ideal for the Sierra Madre environment. He was redesigning the floor plan and simplifying its structure as part of his project.

'You remember *Janus*, the sculpture I worked on and you photographed?' he asked one evening. 'I've been trying to contact the sculptor, Clement Meadmore. I don't know if he'll remember me, but I want to ask him if he knows Glen Murcutt. I want to find out if he's published any books with his work in them. If he has, I'll ask him to get one for me. There's no harm in trying.' He tapped the picture. 'Can you imagine how practical little houses like this would suit the slopes of the barrancas?'

I look back on that week with some amazement. It was as if the next twenty years of Andrés's life were being foretold and about to unroll before us.

After qualifying in 1974, he established an architectural business in Chihuahua City, designing farmhouses throughout the state, and in particular, in the Sierra Madre. Then he received an invitation in 1980 from his old coach, Señor Valentin, to join a select worldwide team of amputee athletes testing prosthetic equipment being produced by the German Ottobock firm, acting as their representative in Mexico.

By the mid-eighties, he was running again with a refined prosthetic and he never looked back. He became one of several freelance amputee athletes testing the latest developments at Ottobock. Their aim was to convince the Olympic Committee to allow their ongoing use in the Paralympics after the 1988 Seoul Games.

He often hinted that if he was fortunate enough to represent Mexico in a future Paralympic Games, he'd like to use me as a training partner.

'I'm sure the prosthetics will get the green light,' he said.

'So make sure you keep fit for me, Alicia. You'll be doing us both a favour.'

I told him I would, and I've kept my word.

* * *

As for me, those years flew past.

I did well and primary school and excelled at secondary school as I matured, when I strove to come top of the class and win as many academic prizes as I could. I did so both to win Papá's ongoing approval and to impress on the women in my extended family and the neighbourhood that I was never going to meekly fill the expected role of housewife and mother as they had done.

I'd live my life on my own terms. I chose to ignore their frequent warnings I was heading for a fall, and their suggestions that if Mamá had lived she would have been horrified.

'I can't imagine what Suré would have to say about your attitude, Alicia,' was a frequent critical refrain I heard from the mothers of girls with whom I shared sleepovers when I was old enough. 'You'd be thinking and behaving differently if she'd lived.'

Without Mamá's guidance, femininity was the last thing on my mind. I developed a steely and, I like to think, resilient independence as I adapted to the physical and social changes I faced as I grew up. What mattered to me was Papá's pride in my progress and the fact that he encouraged and financed me to undertake tertiary studies, allowing me to enjoy the same opportunities as Andrés.

I turned to our maid Camila as a surrogate mother when I needed to. I sought her guidance and comfort when I experienced my first period and needed information in matters of sex; or when I was beset by anxiety in my relationships with girls who hated my attitude and resented my success—and my occasional, always short-lived, crushes on boys.

I'll always thank her for designing and sewing the lime green blouse and flare pants decorated with sequins I wore for my fifteenth birthday, my celebratory coming-of-age *quinceañera*.

'No, I am *not* going to wear one of those,' I said to Camila, pointing at the customary lacy and glamorous white and pink gowns other fifteen-year-olds selected from, during my fitting at the dressmakers. 'Never! If anyone insists, then I won't be attending.'

'So what will you wear?' she asked.

I rifled through the pantsuits hanging in a display wardrobe and selected a smart green safari suit. 'Something like this.'

Camila raised her eyebrows and gave out a quiet chuckle. 'Only my Alicia,' she said quietly. 'You won't be the belle of the ball wearing trousers.'

'Exactly,' I said, 'but at least I'll be true to myself.'

I scandalised the many guests at the gathering and to this day, haven't heard the end of it. The fact that I reflected my 'personality' in a blouse and flare pants rather than a frilly gown, and did away with the religious ceremony, was seen by many as an unforgivable insult to tradition.

I enjoyed the party though, and appreciated the symbolism behind the rites of my initiation into Mexican womanhood. When the music began, Papá led me to a chair and removed my leather sandals when I extended each leg in turn, replacing them with a pair of smart black high heels. I'd practised dancing round the tiled kitchen in them for weeks. Then he pulled me up into his arms with an exaggerated flourish and we took to the open floor in the coming-out waltz, before many of the guests joined us.

Later, I exchanged my bunch of flowers for a sceptre at the banquet table and walked away with it at the end of the night—a woman at last, but strictly on my terms. I was simply asserting myself and following tradition as I chose.

I completed my Masters in Linguistics and Applied Linguistics at Guadalajara University in 1983, before spending the next four years at the West Virginia University in Morgantown, completing my PhD studies. I selected the West Virginia University because Papá had often been invited to speak at geological conferences there, the state being the coal mining capital of the United States.

In 1987, I defended my thesis. I had prepared a comparative study of structural aspects of the languages of the Five Civilised Tribes—the Cherokees, Chickasaw, Choctaws, Creeks and Seminoles. It included a lengthy appendix on the Cherokee language, in particular, how it was affected by the forced removal of the tribe in the winter of 1838 from their homes established in the Appalachians when gold was discovered on their land. They were evicted and forced to march to Oklahoma in the shameful historical episode known as the Trail of Tears. Many died of starvation and hypothermia during the trek, forcibly undertaken during fearful winter storms.

Once qualified, I took my first posting as a tutor at the University of the Basque Country in Bilbao, Spain, in the School of Linguistics and Philology in 1988.

Late in 1989, when I was twenty-nine, I came to a fork in the road and my life took a sudden, unexpected turn.

ALAIN

In San Sebastian, North Western Spain, November 1989

I FIRST SAW ALAIN Leroy in mid-November 1989, in northwestern Spain. I'd spent two years tutoring at the San Sebastián campus of the University of the Basque Country. I was in the last month of my tenure. One early morning, I was running on my favourite steep, cross-country trail leading up to the Itxina cliffs in Gorbeia Park. When I came out of the beech tree woods and ran across the flat open field beside the Aldabide River, I saw a blond kayaker in the pool below the roaring waterfall. There was another dark-haired man on the riverbank filming him as I ran past. The cascade was in full flood, the water more turbulent than I'd seen it before.

I stopped to watch the kayaker and catch my breath for a couple of minutes. He was freestyling in a green whitewater kayak in the surging backwash and in the return current swirling by the bank—spinning, looping and bow-stalling his kayak almost to the vertical. Then he performed the quickest double Eskimo roll I'd ever seen, followed by a single roll, even quicker. He was obviously enjoying himself, showing off to the camera. He knew what he was doing. His technical skills were brilliant. The kayak was like an extension of himself—as it becomes when it's handled by an expert.

Another kayaker appeared at the top of the rushing falls. He did an aerial dive, shooting the white water and hurtling down the last three rocky steps in a vertical drop of twenty metres, before joining the blond kayaker in the pool, where he began practising the same manoeuvres with a similar level of skill.

* * *

On the following Saturday afternoon, I was working on my usual shift as a casual waitress in the crowded beachfront Café de la Concha on the waterfront in San Sebastián, when the blond kayaker walked back into my life with one of his friends. With an excited shock of recognition, I watched him select an empty table out on the patio, close to the railing above the sand.

Then he approached the counter. 'Hola, good day. I'll have three flat whites, thanks.'

His broad accent and the cadence in his voice were both surprising and catching. Uncertain whether he'd recognised me or not, I didn't respond at once. He repeated the order in carefully emphatic Spanish, his accent this time comically mispronounced, '*Puedo pedir tres cafés blancos planos, por favor?*'

'Of course you can,' I replied. I saw his surprise at my use of English, and couldn't resist teasing him by adding rapidly, '*Si no te importa repetir el pedido en tu español, está muy bien.*'

'Come again? And slower this time, *per favor.*'

'Of course you can, as long as you repeat your order in Spanish. It's a rule of the house for new customers. The manager insists, or I get the sack and you don't get served.'

His dark brown eyes lit up. 'Well blow me down. A sheila with the smarts.' He held up three fingers on his left hand and waved his right hand palm down to indicate flatness. 'Can she brew *tres cafés blancos planos* as quickly as she can crack a joke, do you reckon?'

'She can do her best.'

'That'll do me. I'll start the timer.'

'Are you sure it's three? There are only two of you.'

'Yes, make it three. Ben's gone to make a phone call.'

'Do you mind me asking where you're from?' I asked, reaching for the glasses. 'I hate to tell you, but your accent doesn't suit your Spanish.'

'We're from God's own lucky country.' He grinned. 'Have a guess.'

'Australia? Or New Zealand, maybe?'

'Oz,' he replied, 'and never mind the maybe, I'm definitely not a Kiwi. We're all from Perth, over in the west.'

'Ah, the land of the Akubra.'

'You got that right,' he said, clearly taken aback.

The delight in his expression captivated me as I turned away to prepare the coffees—his eyes alight in his wind-burned face, his unruly sun-bleached hair, his stocky, square-shouldered body in his sleeveless dark blue t-shirt and denim jeans, but especially the lively energy in his charismatic presence. He must have been swimming or kayaking earlier, judging by the faint fresh smell of salt and sunshine he brought in with him.

I prepared his order. 'There you go, three flat whites as ordered. Do you want anything to eat with them?'

'Thanks, but no. These'll do the trick. You made them, so I reckon they'll go down a treat.'

You've used that line before. The thought flashed through my mind. *You'll have to be more original with me.* 'If they're so good, sir, we'll see if you come back for seconds.'

'Bound to, but what's with the 'sir'? I appreciate the formality, but let's do away with it. I'm Alain... that's Alain with an 'i''

'Hi, I'm Alicia... Alicia with two.'

'Alain Leroy.' He lifted a forefinger and touched his temple in an elegant salute before picking up the tray, 'I'll catch you later.'

An adventurer, so devil-may-care! I thought, as I watched him thread his way back between the tables, balancing the tray above his head, avoiding collisions with other customers with a practised, athletic swaying quickstep. When he reached his table, I saw his absent friend—Ben he'd called him—join them.

He didn't come back to repeat the order, and when I saw

him and the others stand to leave, I walked across to clear away the empty glasses and wipe the table clean. We passed one another as they headed for the stairway to the exit.

'Thanks for the coffees, Alicia,' Alain said. 'We've been called away, but we'll see you next time.'

'Only if you come in at the weekend. I work the afternoon shifts.'

When I spoke, the tallest of the three, the lanky, dark-haired man who'd been filming the kayakers beneath the Aldabide waterfall, leaned forward with his head cocked to one side, his green eyes bemused. '*Alicia*, already? You two know each other and we're left in the dark?' He peered at me, gave a dry, knowing laugh and clapped Alain on the shoulder. 'You sly old dog, Alain! I *have* seen her before. She's the runner we saw up in Gorbeia Park.'

He turned to the third man in the group—I took him for Alain's younger brother, though a taller, more solid and muscular version of him and wearing John Lennon glasses. 'What do you know, Ben? The boss here has been working his charm on the *señorita* here behind our backs, by jeez.'

'That's a lookup for the books.'

'Yes, it was me.' I threw them both a smile. 'But Alain and I have only just met. I'm the one who prepared your coffees. I stopped to watch you kayaking the other day because I'm a kayaker myself. It's part of my fitness training. I love it. The double Eskimo rolls you two were practising up there were amazing. I have enough trouble with one.'

Alain took a step forward. 'It's a case of use it or lose it, I reckon. They're part of our training routines. Thanks for putting these two reprobates back in their box. They've been trying to get me paired off for most of this year.' He pointed at the others in turn. 'This lookalike is my young cousin Ben—another Leroy—and this skinny streak having a go at us is my so-called good mate, Tony Drummond. Take no notice of them. Alicia. Look, the coffees were excellent and we'd have ordered seconds, but we've received an urgent call and have to go. If you're interested, we'll be testing our sea kayaks in the bay off Zurriola Beach first thing tomorrow morning. Why don't you join us?'

'Off Zurriola Beach? It can get wild out there at times. Aren't they predicting storms later tonight?'

'Exactly the point. The wilder the better, to test ourselves and our equipment to the limit.'

'What time?'

'Sparrow fart. Just after sunup.'

I laughed. 'I'll listen out for it and see how I feel.'

'In which case, we'll see you later if we see you.'

'Not if I see you first.'

He looked back as he climbed the steps. He peered back at me for a moment, and I believe he shaped the words, 'Here's hoping,' at me before he disappeared, but I couldn't be sure, as he turned away to join the others.

Come on, girl, I chastised myself as I walked to his table, jostled by other customers. *Get real. You're not sweet sixteen. He's someone you've crossed paths with twice by accident. It doesn't mean you turn your brief encounters into a narrative with a romantic outcome, no matter how good he makes you feel.* I smiled inwardly at the ironic thought. *Just get on with your woman's work—clean up after him; the one principle you've fought against all your life!*

* * *

I woke to the rumble of thunder and the rain drumming across the rooftops, followed by the alarm I'd set for five o'clock. I didn't baulk at the idea of going to Zurriola Beach in the rain and kayaking in a stormy sea. I liked to live in the moment, vibrant and alive, drawing strength from the vulnerability I faced in taking reasonable risks... and besides, I didn't want to believe the image of Alain saying something I didn't catch before he left the café would be my last memory of him.

I arrived at the beach two hours later and sat soaked but exhilarated on the curving windswept wall at the end of the promenade beside the southern groyne, just as the sun was breaking through.

I watched two kayakers plunging wildly down the thumping right-hand breakers before gliding out again down the glassy dark green channel of the central rip. Six or seven surfers in colourful wetsuits rode the waves beside them or sat waiting on their boards on the swells behind the breakers. The sunlit golden rain was washing down the gleaming line of multi-storied buildings on the waterfront, their windows glinting.

A white Toyota LandCruiser was parked beside me on the promenade. A third sea kayak lay on the trailer linked to it. A magnetic vinyl label showing a map of West Africa was pasted on the driver's side door. The Niger River snaked in an elongated dark blue crescent from the Guinea Highlands, through Mali, Niger and along the northern border of Benin to the delta on Nigeria's Atlantic coast. The title 'Kayaking Expedition down the Niger River' was printed across the top, underscored by the graphic depiction of a sea kayak.

I watched Alain—his blond hair clearly visible now—ride another breaking wave curling towards the beach, avoiding a collision with a surfer attacking the same wave. He paddled with tenacious skill, blades flashing, to stay ahead of the crashing crest until it swept him into the shallows and onto the sand. He stepped out, dragged the kayak beyond the backwash and without a pause in his momentum, sprinted towards me in his red bathers, his lithe, wet body lightly tanned and gleaming. He leapt at the seawall, his extended leg springing from the brickwork and with both hands on the parapet, spun in one gymnastic movement and landed beside me, facing the sea.

'Hola,' he said, his lively brown eyes smiling, white lines in the tan at their corners spreading towards his temples, his blond hair spiked every which way. 'Did that impress you?'

'Not bad.'

'You ain't seen nothing yet.'

'Oh, haven't I? How do you know what I have and haven't seen?'

He laughed. 'There's plenty more where that came from, trust me.' He glanced out to sea as Tony turned his kayak into the rip and paddled out for another run. 'You've got the best seat in the house up here, but that's no excuse.'

'No excuse for what?'

He nodded at the kayak on the trailer beside us. 'For sitting here on your bum watching us two Aussies put in the hard yards out there. In our case, it takes three to tango, so why don't you show us what you've got?' He gave me a wide, inviting grin and a gentle nudge. 'Or was it all talk yesterday afternoon and very little action?'

'Try me,' I said, and for one vivid moment I was back with Andrés when we were younger, racing our kayaks headlong across the splashy Rosetilla dam, the Sierra Madre mountain winds roaring across its surface.

'You're on! I like a woman gutsy enough to accept a challenge when she's offered one, but before you do, it is dangerous out there. I wouldn't want to see you drown. I'd be sorry to lose you this early in our relationship.'

'Oh, we have a relationship, do we?'

He threw back his head and laughed aloud, a characteristic I'd noticed in the café and liked. I felt a rush of pleasure at how easily I'd prompted his reaction. He looked at me with mock seriousness. 'Well, you never know. I've always been an optimist and I've already counted my chickens. Now I'm getting my ducks in a row.'

'*Así me estoy involucrando con un avicultor?*'

'Come again?'

'So I'm getting involved with a poultry farmer, am I?'

He gave me a comical shrug, 'That's me. I've got all my eggs in one basket and you're among them because you're here and it's now and I'm glad you've come. But seriously, how much white-water experience have you had?'

'None in the open sea, but plenty on the Chattooga River in South Carolina and the Kanawha in West Virginia when I was at university there.'

He looked thoughtfully down at the sand and nodded. 'Didn't they film *Deliverance* on the Chattooga?'

'Yes, on parts of it, and trust me, there's some wild whitewater in there. Woodall Falls, Jawbone, the Corkscrew, Crack-in-the-rock...'

He laughed. 'Okay, okay. You've convinced me. If you're sure you can handle it, come in and join us. It'll test you and the kayak to the limit, but it's seriously good fun. The kayaks don't have fins, so steering them can be tricky. They have three full-length protective keelsons though, and they help, and the paddle blades are feathered to suit the open ocean. As long as you come in straight and don't ride diagonally down the breaking wave you won't capsize.'

He jumped onto the paving and I joined him as he began offloading the kayak from the trailer. He patted the white hull, 'This is a "Kittiwake Sea Adventure", built in Norway, but designed in Sweden. It's the best I've come across for the open sea. The sturdiest and most stable by far. I met the maker, Ingvar Hansen, when he was out in Australia and he agreed to sponsor us.'

'Sponsor you?'

He pointed at the door of the Toyota. 'We're aiming to kayak down the Niger from the source to the sea.'

'Looks like quite a challenge, I'd say.'

'Exactly… and it hasn't been done before.'

I admired the kayak's elegant lines, its length along the waterline with the widest point behind the cockpit. 'It is a beautiful design. I can't wait to try it out.' I looked across at him as we undid the straps. 'By the way, there's something I've been meaning to ask you, Alain. What was it you said when you were leaving the café yesterday? I didn't catch it.'

'When, exactly? I can be talkative at times."

'Just before you got to the top of the steps.'

'Oh, right. It was "Glad we met". I wanted you to know if I never saw you again, I was pleased we'd met.'

Oh, that means a lot to me. I stopped what I was doing as a warm thrill ran right through me. 'I feel the same.'

He glanced back, his eyes sparkling, and in a broad American accent said, 'It's our destiny, sweetheart, so here's looking at you, kid. I think this is the beginning of a beautiful friendship.'

'Oh, play it, Sam,' I reflected his drawl back at him with my own, 'the tune you played in Casablanca when we were there, please play it again.'

'Again? Did you say again?' He gave me a smile so catching it had me begging for more. 'We'll *always* have Zurriola Beach. Someday you'll understand.'

'I do already.'

Minutes later, as the rain eased, barefoot and in my soaked white jeans and blouse, I adjusted to the length and breadth of the kayak and the unfamiliar size of the double paddle as I skimmed seawards along the rip.

It was invigorating. My body responded to the hull,

balancing it, evening out its movements in the current. The glassy blue-green water flooding beneath me had an irresistible muscular feel to it, no different from the swirling eddies and whirlpools in the rivers on which I'd spent so many wild, exciting days when I was younger.

Out in the calmer water of the bay, I circled behind the breakers for a while, reading the frequency and angles of the swelling surges before the breaks, recalling the body surfing techniques Andrés and I had learned on holiday in Mazatlán.

On his next run out, Alain ranged alongside. 'You alright? Not getting cold feet?'

'No, I'm getting used to it. It's impressive. A lot to take in.'

'Join me on my next run. I'll talk you through it. You'll be fine.'

He manoeuvred his kayak to my right and I followed him, slightly behind, as we accelerated up the swell he'd selected. I tracked him to the crest and the next moment was on my own as the breaker picked me up and hurled me shoreward, the kayak responding to my instinctive steering, using alternate blades, thrusting backwards and sideways on either flank to straighten the kayak, just as I used to on the most turbulent sections of the Chattooga River.

The kayak surged through the breaking water, flying spume momentarily blinding me, before the wave dumped me and I found myself gliding up towards the sand and sliding back. I turned the kayak with a twist of my body and poled across to the beginning of the rip, following Alain, with Tony ahead of him, to begin a second run. Exhilarated, I gave two irrepressible screams of joy, both Australians looking back at me, laughing, Alain giving me a thumbs up.

For the next hour, Alain and I rode the waves separately and together, while Tony paddled ashore and set up his camera and tripod on the beach, filming both the action on the water and the cityscape behind us.

By mid-morning, the rain had cleared and we stowed the kayaks back on the trailer.

I sat on the seawall once more, pleasantly exhausted, the sun drying my clothes, a faint grainy powder of salt evaporating on my forearms and my face. When Alain and Tony were dressed, they joined me and we shared a thermos of steaming black coffee, drinking it from the one cup, and eating bread roll sandwiches Tony had prepared.

'Here you go, get your laughing gear around one of these,' he said, handing me one. 'They're my gourmet sanga specialty, genuine West Aussie fritz and sauce.'

I sized him up now he was at close quarters. Just under six feet tall and lean, he was fit and wiry, his physique the carbon copy of a long-distance runner. His black hair was crew cut and his face was thin, his nose long, with a prominent bridge. The turn of his lips to my mind displayed a hint of cynicism, if not a touch of cruelty. His green eyes were sharply intelligent, and two parallel vertical lines etched between his thick, dark eyebrows confirmed his intellect and powers of concentration. His Adam's apple was distinct and his voice deep, its tone dry and sarcastic. He put me on alert, striking me as someone with a quick native wit, someone not easily fooled.

I liked what I saw, especially the way his personality seemed to complement Alain's in the short time I'd seen and heard them together—Alain's Caesar to Tony's Cassius, without the betrayal. He'd make a good friend, I thought intuitively, one I could trust and turn to when needed. I was aware he sensed my approval.

'Impressive.' I held the roll in both hands and peered at it, thick slices of polony drenched in tomato sauce visible between the halves.

'You mean the roll?'

'What else?' I took a bite, holding the greaseproof paper

to avoid spilling the crumbs, before wiping a dribble of sauce from my chin. 'Actually, it's not bad, but it could do with some chili and a squeeze of lime.'

'Chili and lime? Sacrilege! It's not a burrito.'

'She's got a point, Tone,' Alain said. 'Wait till she's eaten as many as I have and they've destroyed her taste buds altogether.'

'We need the calories, Al. You're always begging me for more.'

'Keep them coming, mate. They do the trick.' Alain turned to me. 'You impressed us out there, especially when you tried your Eskimo roll for the second time in the open water and couldn't get back up. We both watched your recovery after bailing out. You were back in the kayak right side up in what, forty seconds? Complete with your paddle. How did you manage it? We thought for a moment there you'd have to body surf the kayak back to the beach.'

'You ain't seen nothing yet,' I said, and he gave me an appreciative sideways nod.

'There was a hippo after you, maybe?' Tony asked. 'Or a croc aiming for you like a torpedo with your name on it?' He tapped the camera balanced on the parapet beside him—I noticed the trademark Eclair NPR 16mm stamped across the bodywork. 'I filmed the whole episode. It'll be interesting to see how you turn out. The camera never lies.'

'No, it won't.' I laughed. 'Not if I have any say. You'll cut the scene or I'll sue you for a fortune. Surely you've heard of copyright and the invasion of privacy?'

'No chance, Aleesh. It was a top take. The last for the day, in fact. My martini shot. You're in the can and there you stay.' He gave me a wide grin, his expression to my mind somewhat cynical. 'So sue me, because it's not all I've taken. I also know what you look like from behind when you're running. I shot you the other day up by the waterfall when you took off.' He laughed. 'A long shot, zooming down to a close-up. A very cheeky close-up.'

I suppressed a flash of embarrassed annoyance. 'So how did I look?'

'In one word, eye-catching.'

'That's two.'

'Not if it's hyphenated.' His voice was filled with sudden passion. 'Perhaps I should explain. I'm always on the lookout for surprises when I'm shooting. I want to capture the unexpected, like you just now, caught in a difficult situation. I like to hold my viewers' attention—give their imagination and curiosity a serious nudge. Give them something to remember.'

'And your retrieval technique surprised us,' Alain said. 'You must be right-handed.'

'Yes, I am. It's taken a lot of practice, just like you two, I guess. At home in Saucillo, the Conchos River flows along the bottom of the garden and my brother Andrés and I used to have competitions rolling in our kayaks on it. My abuelo, my grandad Cerrildo, he used to time us.' *I can't remember ever winning, but I got close once or twice.*

Alain gave me a long, speculative look. I wondered what he was about to say. 'That explains it, then. Talking of hippos and crocs, Tone and I have got some good news and bad news for you. Which would you like first?'

'Oh, the bad, of course. Get it out of the way.'

'Right. You remember meeting Ben at the café?'

'Your cousin with the glasses? The other Leroy. Yes.'

'Yes, him. Well, he's been called back to Australia. His father has been killed in a car crash back in Albany.'

A burst of empathy rushed through my chest. 'Oh, *no.* How is he?'

'You can imagine. Not good. In shock, with his mother critical as well.'

I frowned across at him. *What are you two doing here, then? Shouldn't you be supporting him?* 'How's he coping?'

'Reasonably under the circumstances, so far from home. He insisted we leave him to sort things out and come here as planned. He had to make some calls home and was going to start packing up his gear. We're catching up with him at twelve.'

'We offered to help, but he gave us the flick,' Tony added. 'That's Ben being Ben. He prefers flying solo. Law students, they're all the same—too smart for their own good.'

He offered me the last of his bread rolls, and when I shook my head, he took out his red-handled Swiss army pocket knife, cut it in half on the brickwork, and shared it with Alain.

As I watched him, I thought, *Ben must have a lot of arrangements to make. Transport and airline bookings, for example. I can help him.* I turned to Alain. 'Does Ben speak Spanish? Or know his way around San Sebastián or Bilbao?'

'His Spanish is worse than mine, and no, we've only been here for three weeks. We've been training in Catalonia up till now.'

'When does he have to be home?'

'Yesterday,' Tony said. 'Or better still, the day before.'

'As soon as possible. A week at the latest.'

'Why don't I help him? I can organise his travel through the university. I know the logistics officers who fix up travel and accommodation every day of the week. They work miracles. Let me talk to them.'

'Excellent,' Alain said. 'Every little helps.'

'Let him know I'm here to assist… in any way he needs.' *Including providing someone neutral for him to talk to if he needs it,* I thought. *Sometimes the ear of a sympathetic third party helps in his circumstances.*

'Thanks. It's good of you. I know he'll appreciate the offer,' Alain said, meeting my eyes. 'Now then, are you ready for the good news?'

'*Soy todo oídos.*'

'Come again?'

'I'm all ears.'

'It's simple. With Ben pulling out, Tony and I want to invite you to join us on our expedition down the Niger River in the third kayak... What do you say?'

I peered around and jerked a thumb at the vinyl insignia on the door of the Toyota. It was the second time he'd mentioned the expedition. 'You're inviting me to kayak down the Niger River with you? And you're asking me what do I say?'

I was taken aback, afraid I sounded obvious and stupid in twice repeating his question. I needed time to absorb what he'd suggested. My instant response to a proposition so outlandish was to refuse. *And yet...*

'From the source to the sea. Like I said, it's never been done by canoe or kayak,' he went on. 'It's been tried a few times during the last three centuries, without success. By Mungo Park in 1796, for example. Twice. He died nine years later on his second attempt. The French explorer René Caillié tried, from Timbuktu in the 1820s, and the Lander brothers, among others, who explored the lower reaches. We intend to be the first.'

I looked away across the sand at the incoming breakers, collecting my thoughts, as a surfer in a yellow wetsuit ducked beneath the curling crest of the next incoming wave before reappearing from the tubular spray and racing diagonally down the slanting face. He or she flicked up and over its peak at the end of the run and glided back out into the bay.

'Everything's organised,' I heard Alain say. 'We leave for Algeciras in a month. And now we're short one member,' I heard. 'You.'

I looked back at him, the angled sunlight rendering his brown irises in flecks of gold and hazel. As I had in the café, I found him strikingly attractive. His sculpted cheekbones, the smiling curve of his lips. His dimpled chin. He raised his eyebrows. 'So what *do* you say?'

'I say thank you for considering me, and I say thanks for the lack of forewarning, Alain.' I shook my forefinger at him, then placed my right hand on his shoulder. 'And I say tell me more because right now my answer's a definite no. It's outside my comfort zone, too far from anything I've ever planned on doing.'

'Way to go, girl, now you're talking,' Tony gave a single barking laugh. 'I like your style. Don't dive in until you know the water's deep enough.'

'Okay, here are the stats. We're looking conservatively at five and a half months for the trip, allowing for weather, wind, current and breaks along the way. Especially the wind, the Harmattan, the dust storms it raises, but reports suggest it's very mild this year. The river's just over four thousand kilometres long. We should easily manage three kilometres an hour for eight to nine hours a day, kayaking with the current. We've been training for it on the rivers in Catalonia since late August.'

'You want me to give up five and a half months of my life kayaking down a river full of crocodiles and hippos, as you put it, in the middle of nowhere in West Africa? With two men I've only just met?'

'Chance of a lifetime,' Tony said. 'You'll be in darkest Africa with two Aussie blokes who are second to none in most respects. Think of the memories you'll pass on to your grandkids. How can you refuse?'

'Too easily, especially if you expect me to survive on nothing but your fritz and sauce *sangas*, as you call them. Now I've tasted one, the answer's a definite no. No, no and no.'

No to the sandwiches, the thought crossed my mind, *but a definite yes to you, Alain, even if that takes a four thousand kilometre paddle down the Niger.*

'How about we throw in some chili and lime as a sweetener?' Alain said.

'*Eso me gusta más*, that's more to my taste. Keep talking.'

'There'll be no cost to you. We're fully funded and we each have a daily allowance when we need it. Tony's filming a documentary of our progress, so there'll be your share in whatever publicity and income results—'

'Money's not driving the doco,' Tony interrupted him, 'as long as we recover costs. Nor is fame. I don't want to produce what *National Geographic* might classify as a travelogue "work of art".' He raised his hands and flicked the first and second fingers on both to indicate inverted commas. 'No. I want to let my imagination run riot. I want to give my viewers a raw, lived experience with a storyline highlighted by surprises. To give them something memorable. To make them curious. Think about it. We're calling it *River of Dreams*, but who'd want to watch three kayakers paddling down a muddy river for five long months compressed into an hour? You know what I mean?'

I know exactly what you mean, I thought, as the image flared in my mind of an upturned pram and a fallen pregnant lady dressed in black, trapped on all fours in the helicopter spotlight on the Tlatelolco Plaza at the mercy of advancing soldiers firing their rifles...

'We call them moments of *pura vida* in Mexico,' I said, 'when you face life at its most dangerous and you must survive it.'

'Or not,' Tony said.

'Or not.'

'We'll arrange all the vaccinations and medical insurance for you so you *do* survive it,' Alain broke in, 'as well as the visas. And we'll repatriate you to anywhere you choose at the end of the trip. But we'll need to get a wriggle on. Our deadlines are catching up. And as for Tony's sangas, we'll be buying fresh supplies from the towns and villages along the way.'

'*Dondé está la guinda del pastel?*' I asked.

'Say again?'

'Where's the icing on the cake? There has to be icing to get me over the line. The cherry on top. Right now I'm negotiating for an extension to my contract at the university.'

'What do you do there?'

'I'm a lecturer in linguistics.'

Alain stared at me for several moments before snapping his fingers with a flick of his right hand. 'You're a linguist? My God, you're just what we need—a translator. Think of all the West African languages you'll come into contact with. The Malinké dialect spoken in the Fouta Djallon Mountains at the source of the river, just for starters.'

'I bet that cherry makes your mouth water,' Tony said.

I tried not to show my surprise. 'You're right. It does,' I said.

What a coincidence! Of all the languages he could have chosen, how on earth did he pick Malinké? It was spoken by some Mandingo slaves in the early years on the estates in Georgia and the Carolinas. I'd studied the syntax and semantics when I was a postgrad student at the West Virginia University, preparing the appendix for my PhD thesis on the Cherokee language and the Trail of Tears. I was investigating whether one language had influenced the other over time.

I took a deep breath. 'Alright, tell you what, give me time to think it over. I have some loose ends to tie up. My tenure at the university ends in a fortnight. My father's in his seventies back at home, so I'll have to clear it with him and the family. My brother Andrés is hoping to become a Paralympian and he may ask for help with his preparation—he's in Germany at the moment, developing prosthetic running blades. The next Olympics aren't until Barcelona in three years' time, so that should be okay. Meanwhile, I'll see what I can find on Malinké in the university library. How does that sound?'

'No boyfriends?' Tony asked. 'Or similar complications?'

'None. Nothing permanent.' I gave him as meaningful a look as I could muster. 'Not right now, thankfully. Not again.' *If I'm going to be cooped up at close quarters with you two for five and a half months a romantic relationship has to be the last thing on my mind, never mind Alain having all his eggs in one basket and me already feeling the way I do about him. I'll deal with it as things develop.*

'How long will you need?' Alain asked. 'We'll have to organise a replacement from Australia quick smart if you knock us back.'

'Why don't I help Ben get home to Australia first?' I said.

'Sounds fair.' He stood and turned towards me, extending both hands to help me down from the parapet. 'Let's catch up with Ben and get him sorted.'

'I'll give you my answer once he's gone.' I took his hands. *'Pero es probable que sea sí.'*

'Now that I can translate and it sounds like a probable yes.'

'It is.'

When I hopped down to the paving, he took me in his arms and gave me a reassuring hug I sensed we both wanted to last.

I heard him whisper, 'Welcome aboard, Alicia,' as I gazed over his shoulder at the ocean. *What on earth am I getting myself into?* I wondered, before releasing him. *What wild adventures am I about to share? What new and exciting experiences?*

In Algeciras, Southern Spain, January 1990

A MONTH LATER, WE were on our way to Algeciras. Alain had arranged for the car and trailer to be shipped from there to Conakry in Guinea in a forty-foot container aboard a Maersk cargo vessel, with a one-day stopover in Dakar in Senegal, and he'd booked one of two passenger cabins for the two-week voyage.

'It's a three-bunk cabin,' he explained when I agreed to join them, 'so we're going to have to share. One solo bunk, the others one above the other. You can have the single bunk beside the window with the ocean view.'

Now you tell me, I thought, aware he was watching for my reaction. 'Sounds challenging,' I said. 'Just as well I'm not a prude. It will give me time to adjust to living in close quarters with the two of you.'

'Two brothers with a younger sister.' Tony grinned. 'We'll take good care of you. I'll make sure we've got a good supply of activated charcoal tablets handy to curb the farting.'

'They'd better work,' I said.

As we passed through Seville, Alain took a surprise detour to Écija, eighty kilometres to the east. It was late evening. I was relaxing, half-asleep in the front seat beside him, a *Basic Malinké Grammar* unopened on my lap.

I was thrilled I was so much at ease with Alain in so short a time, as if I'd known him for years. Being together was so right it made me reconsider how it had happened. He had a quiet, observant sense of humour matching my own, and every so often he used an Australian colloquial turn of phrase he'd explain and make me smile. I'd never reacted this way with a man before, never experienced this level of mutual attraction and expectancy generating so much warmth and longing.

Tony was stretched out behind us, his hands over his eyes, resting after driving the first five-hundred-kilometre leg from Bilbao.

'Don't wake him,' Alain said. 'We'll surprise him. We'll book into a hotel for the night in Écija and pay a visit to the most famous horse stud in the country tomorrow. Tony and I are interested in Purebred Spanish horses—dressage and jumping. Both our parents breed them. That's how we met. One of the broodmares at his parents' stud in Gidgegannup is a pure-bred Andalusian. She makes a killing for them, breeding up with Australian Andalusian cross-bred stallions.'

Tony twisted himself upright and looked at Alain in the rear-view mirror. 'Did I hear Andalusian? Are you taking Marabella's name in vain, mate?'

'Sure way to get your attention, Tone. You said you'd like to visit the Cárdenas stud. Well, we can drop in on them tomorrow. Pity to waste the opportunity now we're this close. Besides, we do have a day up our sleeve.'

'I know nothing about horses. Just the front from the back, not the make or the model,' I said. 'Although I used to ride them when I was younger, in the Copper Canyon.'

'You've got a lot to learn, then.'

'So teach me. I'll shoot some candids for you. I've got a fresh film in my Leica.'

'I will. You're in for a pleasant surprise.'

'To put it mildly,' Tony said.

The next morning, with me translating for him at first, Tony explained to Francisco Guardiola, the aristocratic-looking, immaculately dressed white-haired senior overseer who met us at the gates, that when he was a teenager in the mid-seventies, he'd worked at the El Caballo Blanco Andalusian Dancing Horses and stud farm at Wooroloo, near Perth. When he mentioned the stallion Bodeguero and five mares the entrepreneur owner had bought in Spain and transported to Perth twenty years ago, Francisco's eyes widened.

'*Si, recuerdo la venta*. Yes, I remember the sale. I remember it well,' he said, in broken English. 'I was working at the stud in Jerez where they were sold. I helped prepare the mares for shipment. It was the first sale to Australia, wasn't it?'

'I believe so.'

'Three were in foal, and the famous Carmen II was among them, I remember. We did not want to part with her. She had the perfect pedigree. The buyer paid a fortune.'

'He did, and she was worth every cent,' Tony said. 'In fact, I assisted at the birth of her first foal—a charcoal grey filly we named Frasquita.'

Francisco embraced him like a prodigal son returned, slapping his back and confirming he'd give us a personal tour of the estate.

He proved a man of his word.

While I'd never been interested in horses other than Tía Ariché's ponies I'd ridden at Cerocahui, I found myself absorbed in photographing animals of such astonishing power, grace and elegance. I captured some displaying a serene intelligence and curiosity, displaying all their shades of white, dappled grey and bay, and others exhibiting a certain independent fractiousness, showing off the shining strands of their flying manes and lifted tails illuminated by winter sunlight as they paraded past with what seemed casual arrogance.

I was far from bored. I enjoyed listening to the discussion between the three men, translating for them now and again, pleased to witness Alain so engrossed in equine details I couldn't understand. There was something precious to me in sharing the moment with him, in our being together in this place at this time, recording it on the Leica, occasionally catching him and Tony unawares.

I took special care with the composition of everything I photographed. I hoped they'd later bring to life the uniquely Spanish atmosphere of the estate. It took me the morning to familiarise myself with it all, capturing as vividly as possible the rich, sensory experience of our visit. Not just the arched grandeur of the whitewashed buildings and their grounds, but the distinct colours, sounds and smells of the circular arena, the stables, the horses, the bales of fresh hay, the recently mown expansive paddocks of yellowing stubble stinging my nostrils and making my eyes water.

I was particularly struck by the contrasting fragrance of the late-blooming lavender and rosemary in large terracotta pots lining the brown gravelled walkways, and the sweet-scented winter-flowering white star jasmine clambering over the pergolas, trellises and fence posts, their shining leaves and wind-blown tendrils the deepest emerald green.

During lunch in the estate's restaurant, I excused myself, and while looking for the ladies' toilets, I passed the display window of the estate's shop. A poster advertising an exhibition of photographs by Robert Vavra caught my eye. A powerful, pure white Andalusian stallion was captured charging full tilt through the foam of green translucent waves crashing onto a beach, with spectacular sunlit expanses of dark blue sea and light blue sky behind it, joined at the horizon. The name 'Babieca' was printed beneath it in smart black cursive—and '*El caballo del Cid*, the warhorse of El Cid'.

I did not hesitate. I bought it, along with a basket and a white t-shirt for myself, emblazoned with another stallion, a dappled grey, and the Cárdenas stud emblem. I placed the tube in the basket, concealed beneath the t-shirt. A perfect gift for Alain.

I'll find a way of surprising him with it when he least expects it.

Later we accompanied Tony as he filmed several short takes of the horses and different parts of the complex.

'I'm chasing some brief filler frames we might insert into the film,' he told me, 'as diversions or additions to the storyline dynamic. To give the narrative more punch or take it down a notch when we have to take a breather.'

It was interesting to watch his technique: his careful selection of the scenes before he filmed them, his manipulation of the lenses and the light, the way he limited the timing of his shots to save the power of his batteries and maximise his use of film. A single four-hundred-foot reel allowed him ten to eleven minutes of filming, he told me, and at the end of the session, which took him two patient and persistent hours, he had six classic brief shots totalling three and half minutes of running time.

In one take, he filmed the elongated black shadows of three dancing horses thrown onto a whitewashed wall by the afternoon sunlight slanting across the ring in glittering dust-lit rays. 'Plato's cave—don't be tricked into believing everything you see is the absolute truth,' he said, before adding under his breath, 'because there's always more to reality you don't yet know.' He focused back on the three grey horses, their four-beat pirouettes stirring up the sand.

In another, he filmed a ginger cat grooming itself with quiet concentration in a corner of the stables, seemingly safe from passing hooves clattering past less than a metre away—a cat with three legs, we soon discovered, its right foreleg missing below the shoulder. 'Hey, Tripod, looks like you played Russian roulette with a horse's hoof and now you've only got eight lives left, mate,' Tony called out. It stood as if in response, arched its back in a stretching movement, before stalking round the corner out of view.

I was especially interested in the ledger he filled out after the shoot, when we sat in the café before leaving.

'I record what I've done as soon as I shut down the camera,' he explained, 'to keep close tabs on every shoot. I'm worse than a friggin' accountant, but these records are pure gold when it comes to post-production editing. It's the only way to keep a tight grip on the storyline. Otherwise, you can get lost, end up with garbage and waste your valuable time on coils of discarded celluloid.'

He opened the black three-ring binder I'd seen him working on in San Sebastián. 'The blank pages are all the same. They're photocopies of my own design.' He turned the binder around. 'Here, take a look.'

The River of Dreams, the title read, and on the line beneath it, underlined twice, *Not just a Travelogue—A search for insights into human nature.*

Beneath it, the landscaped page was divided into four columns. They were labelled *Facts/Images*, *Insights/Truth*, *Sound/Music*, *Score*.

'Yeah, I know what you might be thinking,' Tony said. 'Pretentious. But I live by it, to be honest. The visual facts are simply what I filmed, what images I've captured in the world around me. The insights or truth list is what I imagine appeals to my viewer in those images, the reactions he or she has to them. Are they memorable? Mysterious? Haunting? What do they reveal about him or herself? Sound or music tells me what's been recorded on the sync sound, or what might work as a future voice-over or as a musical background. And the score at the end? It tells me whether the shot deserves one, two or, best of all, three asterisks. It locates the high points in the storyline and helps me work on the rhythm and pacing.' He stared across at me, eyebrows raised. 'So there you go. Simple, but effective.'

I glanced at a previously completed page and looked back at him. 'It makes good sense to me and I don't find it pretentious at all. But tell me—the three-legged cat. Where does it fit into a documentary recording us kayaking down the Niger?'

'Risk,' he said at once. 'Nature's indifference. Survival—but at what cost? Let's face it, we could die out there on the river. It's a startling image. Unexpected. One to take the viewer out of his comfort zone, one likely to stay in the memory.' He gave a quiet, knowing chuckle. 'As for the horses, both Alain and I have been brought up among Andalusians, as you know, though it turns out he prefers flying.'

'Flying?'

'He hasn't told you? He's a pilot in the RAAF, the Royal Aussie Air Force. He's taken all his leave for the project.

* * *

Three hours later, in Algeciras, we booked into a hotel close to Getares Beach, with adjoining rooms. We left our gear in the rooms and disconnected the kayak trailer before driving through the city and crossing the causeway into Gibraltar to drop Tony off at a friend's house—an English migrant he'd gone to school with years ago at Aquinas College in Perth, now a customs officer there. Alain arranged to meet him at the Maersk Line container terminal the next day for the shipment to Guinea.

'Make sure you're up in time, Tone,' Alain said, as Tony exited the car. 'We'll meet at the terminal at ten sharp. Take it easy on the turps. Don't sleep in.'

'Trust me, Al-ay.' He patted his top pocket. 'I've got the Berocca handy.' He leant down, looked in through the window and grinned knowingly at both of us. 'I've never seen a handsomer couple, I have to say. You two look good together—Al-ay and Al-bee, made for one another. Make sure you do everything I'd do, now you've got the opportunity.' He stood, made the sign of the cross with one hand and tapped the roof of the car with the knuckles of the other as he did so. 'You have my blessing, my children. Make hay while the moon shines. Get it over and done with, because we have months of hard labour looming."

'Cheeky bugger,' Alain shouted as Tony walked away. 'Stay sober.'

Tony gave him the finger and, laughing, scratched his temple with it as we drove away towards the immigration checkpoint and across the causeway back into Spain, with darkness falling.

'I hope you don't feel he's put you on the spot,' Alain said when we reached the city, the dim streetlights brightening.

'I'm getting used to him,' I replied, curious as to how he'd reacted to Tony's pointed suggestion. 'Do you?'

He sighed. 'He's just reminding me it's time I moved on.'

'From what?'

'From what happened last year.'

A cold shiver ran through me and I tensed. 'Which was?'

'A betrayal, I hate to tell you. I didn't see it coming. My fiancée got cold feet. She ran away to Queensland on the day of the wedding and dumped me virtually at the altar. She could have saved me the indignity.' He gave out an irritable grunt. 'My sister Christina told me in the church, just after I arrived for the ceremony. She was one of the bridesmaids. Most guests were already there.'

'Oh, I'm so sorry.' I wondered if he'd pick up on the mix of sympathy and relief in my voice.

'Don't be. She did me a favour, come to think of it.' He gave a quiet, confidential chuckle. 'We didn't waste the food or the booze at the reception. The RAAF boys and I made sure we got a skinful and were off our faces in no time flat. Tony got it all down on celluloid. Two classic scenes he thinks might suit the opening to the story in the doco—the wedding, with me going nuts wondering where the hell she was, and the boozy aftermath. Sure to hook the viewers. So I took a year's leave from the RAAF and planned this trip. Something as far out of left field and close to impossible as I could dream up—to lose myself in it.'

'Tony told me you were a pilot,' I said.

'I'm involved in pilot training at the Pearce air base, just outside Perth.'

Although empathetic, I was relieved to hear the outcome of his story, and despite the irony in his voice, I was dismayed because he hadn't mentioned his fiancée or a wedding before. I recalled him telling me in the Cafe de la Concha that Ben and Tony had been trying to get him paired off for most of this year. *Is he on the rebound, after all?*

'I know what it's like to experience rejection,' I said.

'You too?'

'Six years ago. Like everyone else at some time in their lives, I imagine.'

'Shit happens and the cookie crumbles. I'm over her. I guess she saw the flaws in our relationship earlier than me.' He slowed the car and turned to me. 'Every chance we'd have ended up in the divorce courts anyway, with all the bitterness and recrimination. So it was for the best. And besides, she's already taken up with someone else. Good luck to him.' He gave me an appreciative grin. 'And look who it's brought me.'

I put a hand on his forearm. 'Her loss, my gain—if you're feeling the same… and if you aren't, I'm still your third kayaker for the trip.'

'If?' He reached for my hand. 'Isn't it obvious? Of course I do, and you can take that to the bank.' He lifted my hand to his lips and kissed my fingers, before releasing it as he changed gears.

'Good, I will. I liked what Tony said about us, by the way. We do look good together.'

'Even if I'm the better-looking one.'

'Hah! You think so? That must be why you keep looking at me the way you do, just to make sure.' I gave him a wide smile. 'It feels good, so don't stop. But guess what?'

'What?'

'I'm starving.'

'Something with chilli and lime?'

'Perfect.'

'Shouldn't be hard to find. Keep an eye out for the word "Mexican", navigator.'

I pointed out the *Los Tres Sombreros* restaurant, two streets from the hotel and overlooking Getares Beach. We ordered spicy chicken fajitas served with a garden salad side dressing, washed down with a margarita each, the extra dash of Cointreau we asked for making the occasion more memorable.

'The last supper,' Alain pointed out when the waiter served us the meal. 'We'd better enjoy it. We're going to be living rough on what we can buy along the riverbank for the next six months.'

'This is delicious,' I replied, 'as good as we get at home. So it's going to be goat meat, plantains and tropical fruit salad when we can get it from here on?'

'Pretty much, not to mention rice, millet and maize meal. All very healthy, along with Tony's sangas, of course, when he can wrangle the ingredients from the locals.'

'Oh, yum. My mouth's *so* watering already.'

He lifted his empty glass at the waiter and ordered refills. 'Better enjoy these as well. We'll be drinking boiled water when we're in Africa, laced with Milton's sterilising tablets, to get rid of all the nasties. Especially the Guinea worm.'

'What's that?'

'You don't want to know.'

When we'd finished the meal, 'You've let me in on a secret,' I said, lifting the second margarita and contemplating it, 'It's time I shared one of mine.'

'Uh-oh. Here we go.'

'No, no. Nothing to do with previous relationships recent or otherwise.' I squeezed my slice of lemon into the salt around the rim of my glass and sipped my drink. 'No. It concerns my mother. She died a month after I was born.'

'I'm sorry.'

'No need, but it means I never knew her. I was raised by my father and grandfather and the occasional aunt, one in particular, when I was still an infant. It meant I learned to stand up for myself. To always give as good as I get.'

I leaned back and clamped my mouth shut. I had said something foolish and obvious, and I was struck by the thought, *This is not the time or place to expose old wounds.*

I could see Alain was listening while running his slice of lemon around the rim of his glass. About to tell him what it meant to miss out on my mother's influence, her personal, protective and committed touch and her love, I decided against it. He might have understood without my explaining it, that the men closest to me were my role models. I'd learned to be independent and self-reliant—like them—determined to work out for myself where I fitted in and how to deal with the world. And I recalled that by the time I was eight, I knew from personal experience that life was unpredictable, and it could be shockingly cruel. You tread warily through life at your peril, with your eyes wide open, on the razor's edge between happiness and misfortune, between what you judge to be good and evil.

'Fair warning.' He looked up and grinned. 'I have noticed you can float like a butterfly and sting like a bee when you're in the mood.'

'Only when I need to. Some people have accused me since my adolescence of building a defensive wall between myself and others.' I stroked his cheek. 'I'm glad you've breached it.'

'A defensive wall?' He shook his head. 'It's hardly a disadvantage, surely?'

'Maybe not for a man who doesn't need one.'

There are people who misunderstand me, who tell me I'm aggressive, stubborn and unemotional, even cold. They don't know the real me, the deeper, private self I preserve behind the masks they misinterpret, all of which comes from being motherless, unmoored in the world, deprived, but unwilling to admit to needing anyone for fear of rejection.

'But it is for a woman, especially in patriarchal Mexico,' I went on, 'where you're taught by your mother, if you have one, to be hyper-feminine. To be compliant. To know your place in the kitchen, the nursery and the bed. Bend or break the rules and it's a mark against you. Well, I don't fit the mould.'

He placed his elbows on the table, linked his fingers, leaned his chin on the apex they formed and stared at me, bemused. 'Aren't you overthinking things?'

I shook my head. 'Sometimes, perhaps, but from as far back as I can remember, I've been autonomous. I live my life the way I see fit, not according to the expectations of others. Especially the men.'

He gave a quiet chuckle. 'Look, I like you just the way you are. Give me fair warning when you're about to let fly though, and I'll double my efforts to match you.' He held his hand over mine. 'I look at you and like what I see. You're strong. Self-reliant. Comfortable in your own skin. A successful linguist. And as far as I've observed, happy with the way you interact with the world. As for being cold and unemotional, look at the empathy you showed Ben. You worked wonders for him. You helped him understand the grieving process, calmed him down. I've never seen him respond so openly to a complete stranger before. You even got him home earlier than we expected. Your mother would have been proud of you, I'm certain. As proud of you as I am.'

'Thank you, kind sir.' I was happy and embarrassed at the compliments he'd paid me. 'I should have recorded you for future reference, when a replay would come in useful.'

'Oh, Tony did, trust me. For the doco. He snuck in some long shots of your interactions with Ben when he was filming on the streets of San Sebastián.'

'I thought so, the sly old fox. I caught him at it once or twice, out of the corner of my eye.'

'It'll be interesting to see how that reel pans out. Come on, sweetheart, it's time for us to go.'

'Sweetheart? Twice since we first met, Rick? Now that I like. Very much. Yes, it's definitely time to go.'

About to stand, he resumed his seat. 'Before we do, I have to tell you I think we should take things slowly. I know Tony's given us the green light, after his fashion, but I worry about how the dynamics between the three of us could be adversely affected if we take things to the next level too soon. Especially with us living in each other's pockets for the next six months.'

I lifted the margarita and gazed at him over the salted rim as I drained the last sip. 'Now who's overthinking things? Of course you have a point, but it shouldn't keep us apart, should it? We're adults, after all, but if you believe there's a risk, why don't we compromise and simply sleep together? At least give ourselves something to look back on for the next six months.' He looked directly at me, the lamplight reflecting the gold flecks in his dark brown irises, so much like Papá's. A surge of warmth radiated through me, my connection with him deepening as his expression softened. 'And look forward to forever afterwards?' I asked.

'I hope so.'

'Alright. We might be tempting fate, but it sounds good to me.'

Out on the street, he held my hand and led me across to the nearest street lamp, shining through the silver leaves of a tree planted in the pavement, its trunk whitewashed.

'We've waited long enough,' he said.

A lifetime, I thought, as he took both my hands and held me at arm's length, the pool of light patterned with the shadows of leaves glimmering across his face. I looked into his eyes and saw little else as he pulled me towards him. He embraced me, his right hand on the small of my back, his left cradling my neck as we kissed. Our bodies leaned into one another, our contours matching. My heart beat strongly at my throat as my face became flushed. Delightfully sensual and gentle at first, when the tips of our tongues met through parted lips and we tasted the powerful tang of oranges and salt, I opened my eyes and we simultaneously turned the kiss into shared smiles, our faces lingering cheek to cheek.

We disengaged and he gave an irrepressible burst of laughter, throwing back his head and looking momentarily up through the flickering canopy before reaching out to to me again. 'Now *that* was a kiss with all the flavours of Mexico I will never forget. Let's go down to the beach. I can't wait to taste another.'

And we did, slipping off our shoes and walking at the cool water's edge, stopping whenever the urge for another embrace took us. The lights of Gibraltar flickered across the bay, their glow marking the upper curve of the rock in a halo of light, a blue-black backdrop to the star-scattered sky beyond it.

Back at the hotel, we left the connecting door between our rooms open. I stood at the basin in the bathroom after showering, cleaning my teeth. I spat and rinsed and with the green toothbrush still in my hand, I appeared in the open doorway. I had a white towel wrapped around me, tucked at the shoulder.

'I want you to know that whatever we do, there's nothing I want more than to make love to you right now,' I said. I saw him slowly nod. 'No more feeling each other out. I think we should. It will do us both the world of good. It's been a long time for me and twice as long for you, by the sounds of things.' I tried reading his expression but was unsure. 'I hope you're not going to suggest you don't want the same.'

'Of course I feel the same.'

'Then what?' Still uncertain, I thought perhaps some other obstacle lay between us. I walked across to him. 'Do you want me as much as I want you? It's the right time in my cycle, so it's perfectly safe. We've got days to spare.'

He looked up at me, impassive for a moment, and looked away, his thoughtful expression turned inward and impenetrable. *Is he concerned our developing relationship will jeopardise the expedition? Is he measuring one against the other? Or is it the thought of another commitment alarming him? Doesn't he trust me?*

'That's not the answer I want. It's a yes *and* a no,' I said, with a sigh. 'Alright then. It'll be good just to sleep with someone for a change, as we agreed. I'll get my pyjamas.'

He caught my towel by the hem as I turned and took the first step away from him. The towel unravelled and fell to the floor.

I turned to face him.

'You are lovely,' he murmured, placing his hands on my hips and drawing me towards him. 'Just lovely.'

A surge of excitement overwhelmed me and my throat constricted. *So you've decided.*

'That settles it,' I said, barely able to speak. I leant across, placed the toothbrush on the side table and tentatively kissed him, both hands on his shoulders, before settling into his lap. 'Sealed with the taste of Colgate this time,' I whispered, before giving him another kiss, which he returned, joyful and uninhibited, the physical intoxication of it carrying us both away.

* * *

The next morning, relaxing naked on the windowsill in the first rays of the sun, my skin aglow and my body vibrantly alive, I looked across at Alain. He was still asleep, outstretched beneath the sheet drawn up to his hips. He had his back to me. I marvelled at the regular lift and fall of his muscled rib cage, saw the barely perceptible movement in his wide shoulders and admired his clear, lightly suntanned skin, his sun-bleached hair.

With a shiver of excitement, I imagined him in my arms again, tasted his kiss and felt him making love to me, surprising me with his passionate gentleness. For the first time in my life, I experienced a surge of tenderness deeper and more overpowering than I ever had before, and with it came the unexpected but enticing thought of having his child. It shocked me for a moment. Whenever the urge to have a child had crossed my mind before, I'd laughed it off and ruled it out. Until now, when the idea became an insistent, secret whisper.

I knew at once I could not mention it to him, not right now. Not with the conquest of the Niger front and centre. But rather than curb the flow of my thoughts, I drifted into an almost dreamlike state and convinced myself the child would be a girl. And her name? *Mariposa* came to me at once, a butterfly, shortened to María. I traced a butterfly's wings with a forefinger across the windowpane, a Silver Emperor like those I used to find attracted to Tía Ariché's yellow and orange marigolds in Cerocahui, similar to Mamá's garnet brooch Papá gave me on my birthday so many years ago.

As I did so, I realised the name satisfied the tradition among the Tarahumara to associate a newborn with something from the natural world and I'd chosen the butterfly from deep within my imagination for the beauty and the freedom of its flight, perfect symbols for her soul… for her spirit.

Throughout her life, I'd be devoted to her. I'd give her the mother's loving care I'd experienced myself for one unremembered month so long ago. I'd show her—*shower* her—with the motherly affection I'd longed for all my life.

Rapidly shaking my head to clear it, I stepped down from the window ledge and walked across to stroke Alain's cheek and rouse him.

'Good morning, handsome,' I said as he opened his eyes. 'Wakey, wakey.'

He stretched and yawned, before leaning on his side to face me. 'Hi, what's the time?'

'Time you were up. It's beautiful outside.' I raised my eyebrows and asked with a smile, 'So who's Sandra? You were talking in your sleep. In bed with me, but already dreaming of someone else.'

He leaned on an elbow, focusing on me. 'My God! Surely not! You're joking, aren't you? She's my ex. I don't remember dreaming about her. Or having nightmares, more like. I hope I didn't keep you awake.'

'I slept well, but I woke early, as I always do. You sounded troubled, so I woke you. Do you remember the glass of water I brought in for you?'

'Vaguely, yes.' He glanced at the empty glass on the bedside table. 'Very thoughtful of you. Thanks.'

I walked across to the bed and sat beside him, one leg tucked beneath the other. I stroked his hair. 'When you're good and ready, you can tell me more about her. It sounded like you're still damaged goods.'

'It wasn't easy at the time, but it happened a year ago and I thought I was over it. I *am* over it, for God's sake.'

'I stirred up memories? It's bound to happen when the wounds run deep.' I wrapped my arms around him. 'I had no such worries. Trust me, you ticked all the boxes. So let's get another good look at you.' I stood and gripped the sheet, pulling it slowly from the bed, leaving him naked, with his hands behind his head on the pillow.

'Gorgeous!' Kneeling beside him, I ran my hands down his flanks to his feet and began to drag him from the bed. 'It's time we were up. As I said, it's beautiful outside. Let's not waste it.'

When we'd dressed and were about to go down for breakfast, I placed both hands on his chest to stop him from opening the passageway door. 'Before we go, I've got something to show you.'

I took the poster and my faded blue rebozo scarf from my case in the adjoining room, walked back and blindfolded him. I unrolled the Robert Vavra poster from the tube and spread it across the coffee table, flattening it out with both hands. 'Okay, you can look now. It's something I thought you'd like.'

He removed the scarf, hung it across his shoulders and leant across the table on his extended arms, taking in the striking beauty of the poster. The lucent blues of the sea and sky. The white horse charging through the breaking surf, with mane and tail flying.

'Like it? I love it,' he said at last, reaching for me. 'It's extraordinary.'

'It's a reminder of the first twenty-four hours of this journey we're on together.' A surge of warmth at his response and the pleasure derived from the act of giving welled through me.

'It's perfect,' he said.

He held my face in both his hands and with his thumbs gently wiped my cheeks, wet with unexpected tears I tried to smile away.

In Guinea, West Africa, January 1990

Tony WAS WAITING FOR us beside the closed gates to the Maersk Line container terminal. He had his camera on his shoulder, recording our arrival. Beyond him, lines of containers were stacked along the dock, scurrying yellow forklifts and gliding overhead container cranes partly obscuring a large, light blue cargo ship moored alongside. The name *Louis Maersk* was just visible beneath the bow.

Alain slowed and turned to me. 'Speak of the devil. Be prepared. He's bound to take the mick.'

'Take the mick?'

'Tease. Make fun of us. He won't be able to resist the opportunity. He can be too smart for his own good sometimes.'

'I'm getting used to him. He's so much like Andrés. He's picked on me for as long as I can remember, but I don't mind. I like the challenge.'

Alain squeezed my hand. 'Here we go. We're on *Candid Camera* again. Another chance to win an Oscar.'

I gave Tony a wide, engaging smile as we pulled up, and watched him in the rear mirror as he loaded his camera and backpack in the back.

'G'day Albee,' he said as he climbed in behind me, 'and Alay.' He gave a knowing chuckle. 'I don't have to ask. It's written all over you both. It's a compelling read and needs no censoring. Congratulations, and I'll say no more.'

'You? Say no more? I'll believe it when I don't hear it,' Alain replied.

'It's good to see you both looking so on top of the world, Al. It really is.' He patted Alain on the shoulder. 'Like a honeymooning couple, just tied the knot. I'll respect your privacy and there'll be no walking on eggshells. Trust me.'

'Good to hear.' Alain turned to me, his eyes alight. 'Did you take that down?'

'Word for word.'

'Then we've got him by the short and curlies.'

Tony laughed. 'Better get me a Brazilian, then. Glad we've got that cleared up. Okay, then. Are we all cashed up?'

'No problem. All done earlier this morning. Guinea francs by the thousand and enough US dollars to see us through, at least as far as Benin, I reckon.'

'By the thousand?'

'The exchange rate's seven hundred to one right now—two thousand Guinea francs for a three-dollar cup of coffee. The wad I'm carrying makes us millionaires.'

'Sounds good. So let's get this show on the road.'

The customs officer at the gate inspected Alain's paperwork and allowed us through, directing us towards the row of offices to the right. Five hours later, the car and trailer were in a forty-foot container and on their way aboard, and we were chauffeured to the ship's gangway with stamped passports, carrying our gear for the trip.

The ship's Danish first officer met us on the deck. He introduced himself as Tobias Thorsen—'But Toby will do,'— and welcomed us aboard. 'It's always good to see new faces on board,' he said. 'It's a diversion for the crew.'

'How many of you are there?' Alain asked.

'Twenty-four all up, including three officer cadets.'

He showed us to our surprisingly roomy external cabin, one of two designed for passengers. 'There's an American couple travelling with us in the cabin next door,' he said. 'Schoolteachers both, they tell me, heading for the international school in Dakar.'

The blue-carpeted cabin was two decks up on the mid-ship superstructure, with a double window above my bunk, as Alain had mentioned. It faced forward, with a view across the containers stacked on the foredeck and the sweep of ocean beyond the bow. It had a small ensuite shower and toilet, a bar fridge and coffee-making facilities.

'No probs swinging a cat in here,' Tony said as we entered and he laid his camera on the upper bunk opposite mine. 'Plenty of room to breathe.' He walked across to the fridge and opened it, a jug of water and two frosty glasses upside down on a lower shelf, 'And we won't die of thirst. I should have bought a slab or two.'

'Not allowed, I'm afraid.' Tobias gave him a regretful nod. 'This is a working ship and the *sprut* is strictly rationed. Company policy says no alcohol, but the captain allows us two a day, passengers included. Maximum. The bottles are opened for you by our chief steward during happy hour between six and seven.'

'Heinekens?' Tony asked.

'Wash out your mouth! Carlsberg and Tuborg Gold. The world's best.'

'Second best, don't you mean? Haven't you tasted VB?'

'No chance, my friend. From what I can remember when we were docked in Melbourne, there's no comparison.'

'I'll be the judge.' Tony laughed. 'You don't know what you're missing.'

Alain sat on the lower bunk and looked across at me. 'What do you think?'

'Five stars so far,' I said. 'We will survive.'

Tobias showed us over the rest of the accommodation: the officers' mess where we'd eat and the day room where we'd join the evening card games and karaoke if we wished; the small open decks on either side of the ship beside the lifeboats to sunbathe on and take the air; the bridge at the top, with the monkey island open to the sky above it, where we might be allowed an occasional visit by invitation. The rest of the ship was out of bounds.

The fortnight at sea before arriving at Conakry passed unexpectedly quickly. While it seemed to be over before it began, it gave Alain and I the time and space to establish our relationship at a deeper level, to explore our backgrounds and appreciate one another's views of the world, our likes and dislikes. Opening up as I never had to anyone before was wonderful. It confirmed and strengthened the connection between us I'd sensed in the Café de la Concha.

I also enjoyed several marathon sessions of chess games, using the travelling set Abu Cerrildo had carved for me. I played with Alain, though he wasn't as fascinated with chess as I was; and I took on Terry Wu, a young Chinese-Danish cadet officer, when he was off duty. He was a gifted, relentless and intelligent player so skilled I stood little chance, but his strategic coaching went a long way to developing my game, and I was thankful.

On the last evening before our arrival in Conakry, Alain and I were sitting together on the starboard open deck beside the lifeboat. Bare feet on the rails, we were admiring the sunset, the tin-foil surface of the ocean burnished in every shade of orange from vermilion to fire.

I felt especially fortunate and carefree, and was thrilled when Alain surprised me with a gold-chain pendant hung with a sparkling solitare diamond on a gold clasp.

'A late Christmas present,' he said, smiling. 'Your birth stone. I bought it for you when I was doing the banking in Algeciras, when you were waiting for me in the café.'

Before I could thank him for it, Tony surprised us there. 'Ah, *there* you lovebirds are,' he said. 'Been looking for you everywhere. It's good to see you fitting together like pieces in a jigsaw.' He swung his camera in my direction, and surprised me with, '*Smil... sige "appelsin"* as the Danish say. Smile... say "orange", Alicia.'

Keeping a straight face, I pointed at the ocean. 'Orange,' I said, as Alain clipped the necklace round my neck and I stroked his hand and kissed his cheek.

Tony had been filming the sunset from the monkey island above the bridge, he told us, the shadow of West Africa a serrated purple smear on the port horizon.

'That shot will make an interesting segue to our arrival in Conakry tomorrow,' he said, his voice as passionate as ever when discussing his documentary. I knew how much it meant to him. 'Creative filming gives my existence real meaning,' he'd told me one evening when he showed me the workings of his camera. 'I don't know what I'd do without it.'

* * *

At dawn the next morning, we skirted the Îles de Los, a compact circle of lush green islands off the peninsula of Conakry, and moored alongside the container terminal at nine o'clock.

One of the first Guinean officials aboard was Abdoulaye Camara, the liaison 'fixer' Alain had hired to accompany us on the eight-hour journey upcountry to Faranah.

Tall, straight-backed and solid, his skin a light mahogany, he had at first glance the appearance of a determined boxer. His eyes were faintly bloodshot beneath his initial frown and his lips were compressed, but his expression lit up and he displayed an appealing, pugnacious mix of smiling aggression as he picked us out waiting for him on the deck. Bareheaded, his beard white at his chin, he was dressed in a smart, dark blue, short-sleeved safari suit. A gold medallion on a silver chain hung around his muscular neck, and a gold-winged badge, similar to a pilot's, was attached to the left-hand pocket of his shirt. I read 'GFC' embroidered on it.

He exuded reassuring authority. *He's someone with his finger on the pulse*, I thought.

He shook Alain's hand, 'Good morning gentlemans from Australia, and Mexican lady,' he said, his voice gravelly and his English slightly accented. 'Abdoulaye Camara, *à votre* service. I represent the Guinean Film Corporation. I am pleased to make your acquaintances.'

We've hired a smiling assassin. He may be just what we need, was my next thought as Alain introduced us, Abdoulaye's smile all flashing white teeth.

Alain led us to the officers' day room, which he'd arranged for a conference. He handed Abdoulaye all our paperwork. It took him some time to go through it—the passports and *Laissez-Passer* permits, the yellow fever and typhoid inoculation certificates, bills of lading, ownership papers and licenses for the car and kayaks, and the letter of permission from the Guinean Ambassador in Paris to film the documentary.

He also had an outline of Tony's documentary and read through it. At one point he raised his eyebrows with a sceptical shake of his head, 'The River of Dreams? An expedition kayaking down the Niger River from the source to the sea? C'est trés, trés ambitieux,' he muttered, before gazing at Tony and raising his voice, 'You must be aware several have failed and others died trying—'

'Of course. We've done our research,' Tony snapped.

'So isn't it evident the river is cursed? The spirits guarding it are trés mauvais. They are evil and malevolent.'

Tony smiled dismissively, 'We'll take care. We'll keep our fingers crossed and touch wood,' he said, tapping his temple.

Abdoulaye gave him a direct stare. 'You may smile, but remember, you have been warned,' he said, nodding and pursing his lips. 'In this country, you must expect the unexpected. Especially since you will be travelling close to the Sierra Leone border when you go to the source of the river. It is an unmarked no man's land.'

He went on to explain that there'd been reports of raiding parties of disgruntled striking Sierra Leonians rebelling against the financial crisis in their country crossing into Guinea and pillaging the local farms. In one case Liberian mercenaries who'd crossed the Sierra Leone border to stir up the simmering civil war in that country were among them.'

A rush of dread uncoiled deep in my gut as a sudden premonition of disaster overwhelmed me. I am rarely wrong, so I gritted my teeth as Abdoulaye reached for the other documents and reread them. 'Two days only or perhaps three,' he said at last, leaning back in his chair, 'to offload the car and your canoes. To arrange the official stamps and, naturellement, to pay the customs and other duties. It will cost you, but I will fix it so you pay the minimum.'

He gave us a quick, knowing grin and a sage nod. I caught what I took for a cunning glint in his eye and wondered for a moment if he was being ironic; he'd been educated by the French, after all. And if he was, how were we to judge? 'That is why I am here. A man with much experience, I have my ways and means. You will not regret it. Meanwhile, I will take you to the Novotel Ghi hotel,' he pointed vaguely through the door, 'just over there. Very new and very close. After immigrations.'

Despite my misgivings, Abdoulaye—soon Abdou to us— was as good as his word.

Within two days, Alain had all the necessary paperwork in hand, including receipts suggesting he'd been fairly taxed the right amounts. We also had the car and kayaks in the Novotel compound, adjacent to the container terminal at the end of the peninsula and facing the ocean. When we checked the four hatches in the kayaks—the two smaller hatches in the long, narrow foredeck and the two larger in the wide rear deck behind the seat—we were relieved to find that the camping gear and other equipment for the expedition packed inside them were intact.

Alain had been with Abdoulaye to visit the Rio Tinto minerals exploration office in the city to reconfirm their sponsorship of the project, prearranged in Perth. They agreed to allow us to share rooms for a week in the mining camp up country at Faranah and, critically and generously, for the company helicopter to ferry us for one flight to and from Foroconia. It was the closest village to the Tembakounda spring at the source of the Niger.

They had also visited the principal of *Lycée francais* Albert Camus—the LAC—an international secondary school, to which Alain had decided to donate the Toyota and trailer for their water sports program, once we were on our way down the Niger aboard the kayaks. They agreed to the handover in a fortnight, with Abdoulaye assigned to drive the vehicle back to the school from Faranah when the time came.

On the third and final afternoon, Abdoulaye drove us around Conakry and we watched Tony film two successive scenes.

The first was a sweeping pan of the waterfront Boulbinet fish market. He captured the teeming stalls and barrows glittering with the red and silver fish scales of the day's catch, the bustling and colourful crowds, and the dockside lined with an uncountable number of gaudily painted, high-prowed wooden fishing boats. Some were dragged up onto the narrow beach, others moored in the murky, rubbish-strewn shallows, and everywhere, the tangy sea smell turning rancid. By way of contrast at the end of the shot, he focused on the blue hull and superstructure of the *Louis Maersk*, still moored alongside the container wharves in the distance.

The second was a deep-focus, wide-angle shot of Alain outside the sprawling Madina market in the centre of the city. He was surrounded by eight or nine ragged and rowdy beggars, none more than ten years old. I stood back with Abdoulaye and other locals attending to the smoky street food stalls lining the red gravel walkway behind us, watching the drama play out.

Alain had bought a plastic bag of boiled sweets and he handed them out into outstretched open palms, the beggars clamouring for more until the bag was almost empty.

Suddenly, as if materialising out of the bare ground, a dusty, runny-nosed child of about six appeared, his twisted, crippled legs curled beneath his backside. He shuffled forward for his share, using both long arms to drag himself to Alain's feet. When Alain handed him the last sweet, he took it in one hand and wrapped his other arm around Alain's calf. He pocketed the sweet and asked for another. When Alain showed him the empty packet, shaking it and holding it upside down, the child screeched and showed his temper, reaching out to clutch his leg with both arms, catching him off-balance.

I was horrified as Alain staggered backwards for six or seven steps, dragging the boy across the gravel. When he regained his balance, he shook his leg, before taking several further steps, this time forwards, with the same unfortunate result. The child clung to him with a vice-like grip as he was yanked along, his crippled legs now trailing out behind him.

I heard a ripple of laughter running through the watching crowd.

When Alain at last stood still and looked down, I could see how agitated and perplexed he was. Abdoulaye and I both took a step towards him. Before we could reach him, he went down on his haunches, sat back on the ground, forcibly unlatched the beggar's hands and stood, still holding his wrists. He lifted the child from the ground by his arms and held him against his chest, cradled in his right elbow. With the boy's skinny black arms now gripped around his neck and his legs dangling, Alain murmured what I took for reassurances to him as I followed them from one street food stall to the next. When the boy pointed excitedly, they stopped beside the corncob brazier, where the pungent, smoky smell of charcoal embers and roasting maize filled the air. There Alain lifted him to the ground, selected a cob and bought it for him.

'It's hot,' he said, blowing on it before handing it down, 'don't burn yourself.'

He leant down and held out his fist, and the boy fist-pumped him as Abdoulaye translated, patting the boy on the head.

I watched, deeply moved, as Alain took out his handkerchief and wiped the boy's face clean.

'Nicely done, mate,' Tony said as he shut down the camera. 'That'll make an interesting addition to the doco. I got a decent tracking shot of you both. Every step you took and both your expressions.'

'The last shot with the young fella staring straight down the barrel of the lens must have seemed uncanny,' Alain said.

'You're telling me. He looked like a little jungle alien interrogating me. Made me squirm, especially when I stalked in for a close-up and he didn't bat an eyelid. He was looking straight into my soul, to be honest. My viewers are going to feel the same. It'll stir them up, give them a new slant on their perception of reality. They won't know what to feel about things they've never seen before or been too preoccupied to notice.'

'His image will show them something of themselves?'

'Exactly. They'll find the boy cross-examining and observing *them*, rather than the other way around.'

'They will believe the boy is justifiably questioning the white man's presence in Africa,' Abdoulaye suggested, before adding with a sharp, ironic glance at Tony, 'and warning him about his disbelief in our primitive superstitions.'

It was Abdoulaye who told me the villagers around Faranah spoke the Yalunka dialect and not Malinké, when I showed him my textbook. '*Now* you tell me,' I said, dismayed and annoyed with myself for not researching the Guinean dialects more thoroughly.

'There is a little similarity,' he said, and when he saw how confused and concerned I was, he added, 'but fear not, madame. I'm sure you will find one or two Malinké speakers among them. There is intermarriage everywhere among the tribes, and many wives. And besides, most speak French. You are aware it is the second language.'

* * *

We left Conakry at nine the next morning, with Abdoulaye at the wheel. It was the dry season, the dusty, corrugated and potholed gravel sections between stretches of bitumen barely slowing us down.

During the journey, armed soldiers stopped us at three separate checkpoints. Our papers were scrutinised with shows of overplayed officialdom, before a toll was demanded, and Alain paid. Abdoulaye had warned us about the practice. 'My advice is to pay without argument. Refusing will not be productive. It will result in a hold up,' he'd chuckled at his play on words. 'I will make sure you are not charged more than three thousand francs each, so four or five American dollars at the most. Twenty for all four of us.'

Seven hours later we passed beneath the white wooden archway welcoming us to Faranah, a kilometre from the town. *Bienvenue à Faranah* it read, with the Guinean red, yellow and green striped flag freshly painted on its crown.

When we crossed a cast iron bridge and sighted the Niger for the first time, Alain couldn't control his excitement. 'Stop, Abdou!' he shouted, and Abdoulaye pulled over to the right, on the upstream side of the deck.

Forty metres across, the river was chocolate brown and looked, I thought, deceptively deep and surly, the swirling current breaking the surface in irregular threatening surges as though showing its muscle.

An icy terror ran through me again and for a moment I shivered uncontrollably.

'There must have been a recent thunderstorm up in the headwaters,' Alain said, as he scrambled out, 'though it's partway through the dry season.' He threw his wallet and papers on the passenger seat he'd vacated, handed me his sunglasses, climbed onto the railing and with a triumphant yell, leapt into the river fully clothed, his arms flailing above his head.

Without a thought for his safety or the possibility of crocodiles or hippos, Tony wasn't far behind, and if anything, louder.

They were two crazies out of control, shouting and laughing like teenage boys in their element. I held my breath when they were swept by the current beneath the bridge and into a wild and rocky rush of white water a hundred metres downstream on the other side, where they were able to stagger ashore.

I loaded the camera as they jogged back along the path on the bank, and filmed them as they repeated the leap, this time Alain shouting, 'Beware the candiru! Better safe than sorry!' before he struck the water and disappeared beneath the surface.

'The candiru?' I had asked him when we were aboard the *Louis Maersk* and he was listing the many dangers we faced on the journey.

'The toothpick fish. It's supposed to be able to swim up a man's penis and hook itself into his urethra,' he told me.

'Ouch!'

'Ouch, for sure. I believe it's only found in the Amazon, and its ability to attach itself to a man's private parts is probably a myth—but Tony and I will take no chances. We'll keep our clothes on all the time.'

'That was some christening, by Jeez,' Alain said, shaking the water from his blond hair before he and Tony climbed back into the car, soaking wet.

'Sure was,' Tony agreed.

'It's in the can,' I told Tony. 'All the action of the second jump.'

Half an hour later we registered into the mining camp. It was a collection of six white modular transportable huts, which Alain told me were called "dongas" in Australia. One of them housed the showers and toilets, another the mess hall and the kitchens. After a well-deserved long hot shower, I found the self-serve rice and spicy goat stews satisfyingly filling.

When I settled down for the night, Abdoulaye's foreboding warning, "Expect the unexpected," echoed in my apprehensive mind. I could not shake my dread. My only consolation was the thought that whatever terrifying or deadly challenges lay ahead, Alain and I would be facing them together. I fell asleep spooning him, hoping his pragmatic and cheerful Australian optimism would prove my premonitions wrong... and woke the next morning wondering what destiny held in store.

* * *

By twelve o'clock on the following day, we were in the village of Foroconia, a two-hour helicopter ride from Faranah. Abdoulaye remained in Faranah, manning the two-way radio and watching over the car and kayaks.

I will never forget the ride, my first in a three-passenger helicopter. I had a window seat. I found the spectacular Fouta Djallon Mountains similar to the *barrancas*, ravines and canyons of the Sierra Madre Mountains I was used to at home, but on a far smaller scale. We flew between numberless imposing grey pillars of rock and through mountain valleys, their lower slopes covered with what looked like a rampant and impenetrable jungle, the canopy a quilt of sunlit vivid greens. I saw streams and waterfalls everywhere as we swept close to the rocky outcrops and low to the ground, almost grazing the treetops.

I found it both exhilarating and terrifying.

Alain sat beside me shaking his head at one point. We were wearing earmuffs against the helicopter's noisy rotors and weren't able to converse, but he told me when we landed he was wondering why the Tembi River's spring at Tembakounda had been selected as the Niger's authentic tributary and source.

'Why the Tembi, with so many springs and streams to choose from across the watershed?' he asked as we walked towards the village. 'And why decide it's a sacred site, protected by the spirits of a mixed bag of ancestors?'

A worrying thrill of alarm ran through me. 'You haven't mentioned it's a sacred site before.'

'So they say. And not just watched over by ancestors. By royal figures as well. Legendary warrior heroes. You name it, even Moslem holy men.' He chuckled, 'Not to mention the odd malevolent bandit with a cutthroat reputation.'

'To keep working-class Bogans like us well away, as Abdou suggested?' Tony asked.

'Could be.'

'Let's see them try.'

'Too right. So much for superstition.'

'Me, I'm not so sure.' I hesitated, not wanting to sound naïve. 'We Mexicans believe it's wise to tread carefully where the spirits of the dead are concerned.' My thoughts flashed back to Tía Ariché's maid, Ofelia, who had laid the miniature dry-stone wall of magic crystals on Mamá's ofrenda altar to keep her safe from evil spirits and other devils who might want to cause her harm in the afterlife so many years ago.

'Ah, we will, sweetheart,' Alain said, an arm around my shoulder. 'Don't worry yourself. As Tony said, we'll touch wood and keep our fingers crossed. Of course we will.'

'And I'll toss a pinch of salt over my left shoulder,' Tony added with a dry grin.

'You better had,' I said. 'Don't forget we're also going to have to appease the genies living in the Niger later. You don't want to get into their bad books.'

Alain laughed. 'Especially them. We'll treat them with the respect they deserve.'

We arranged for the helicopter to return in three days to pick us up, and then set up camp in a large open hut in the centre of the village. The *du tii*—the village chief—offered it to us once we'd paid him. A Yalunka man called Ibrahim, who spoke French and broken English, translated for us.

We settled in surrounded by curious villagers and a mob of shy and inquisitive children, their timid faces serious and filled with uncertainty at first. But not for long. During the afternoon our interaction with the villagers—especially the children—was something I will always treasure. Their generous hospitality. The chattering laughter. And the food they offered us that night. They slaughtered a goat and made a peanut stew with cabbage and manioc spiced with chillies. Eaten by hand, with a side serving of rice-like fonio millet, it was delicious. The thought of it brings back its mouth-watering smell and makes me yearn for more.

Tony spent hours entertaining the children, once they'd satisfied their curiosity about our white skin, the younger ones stroking and rubbing our forearms to make sure it wasn't black beneath a veneer of white. At first, Tony used a Polaroid camera he'd brought with him—magically producing images of them out of thin air. 'How do you like them apples?' I heard him shout at one point, the children around him screaming with delight as their images gradually appeared on the film he held on the palm of his hand.

Then he filmed them for his documentary, showing off their prowess with handstands, impromptu dance steps across the red dust, and whirling airborne somersaults, their gleeful shouts and excited screams echoing.

And the dancing. Oh, the dancing, to the rhythmic drums! I can still hear them and feel the stamping feet and drumbeats vibrating through my bones whenever I recall it.

During the dancing, a senior woman, Ayisa, to whom I'd been introduced on arrival because she spoke Malinké, gave me her necklace of miniature African beads when I admired it. She immediately insisted I accept it, and despite my embarrassed reluctance, placed it round my neck herself as we took a break from the dancing. The tiny beads were threaded in a zigzag pattern of primary colours, red, yellow and blue, connected by streaks of green. She assured me the beads would bring me good fortune in the future. I can remember her blessing and hear her voice as if it was yesterday, "*Alla i la kanda*, Alicia," she said, "*Ka sewa. Sinin di fisaya bi di*, May God protect you, Alicia. Be happy. Tomorrow will be an even better day than today."

* * *

The next day, Alain and Tony set off with two paid guides. One was Ibrahim, who was carrying the camera, tripod and battery belt, the other a young teenager, Baboucar. They intended to walk to the nearby village of Bakando, where they'd have to negotiate with the official *ji tii*, the guardian of the Tembakounda source, for permission to visit the spring and remove a thermos flask of water.

'I'm going to tip it into the Gulf of Guinea at the end of the trip,' Alain said.

Before they left, one of the village elders took Alain aside to warn him he had to be extra vigilant on the trek to Bakando and back. With me translating, the old man explained that the nearby border with Sierra Leone wasn't marked, and he may inadvertently cross and re-cross it, depending on the paths he took. There had been recent cross-border raids by large gangs and many, many goats and baskets of fonio millet and rice had been looted from surrounding villages.

'We appreciate the warning,' I translated for Alain, 'and we will keep a sharp lookout there and back.'

'You must,' the old man replied. 'And put your trust in Christ and Allah.'

I stayed back in Foroconia to man the two-way radio, keep an eye on the campsite and keep in touch with Abdoulaye in Faranah.

'We'll be back this evening,' Alain said as he kissed me. 'That's a promise, sweetheart.'

He reported in to me every hour.

They reached Bakando at eleven, and he told me they'd had no trouble locating the guardian. He was an aristocratic white-haired Yalunka man who struck a hard bargain for the permit, before offering one of his younger sons, Modou, as a guide to lead them to the spring.

His price required more negotiations and the further emptying of Alain's wallet. When Alain refused to make a further payment, Ibrahim stepped in to calm the situation.

'You should pay, monsieur Alain. He has to make a sacrifice to the N'iena, the spirits guarding the springs… we call the practice the Barinkiina.'

Alain shook his head. 'I don't believe it,' he said. 'I've come unprepared for so many payments. He's seen how much I'm carrying and he's cleaning me out.'

Ibrahin nodded and smiled. 'It is the common practice. He will not let us go unless you comply.'

The old man nodded shrewdly as Alain emptied his wallet and handed him the last of his notes. He licked a forefinger, deliberately counted out the money, and then, with a raucous cackle, reached for Alain's wallet and stuffed half the notes back into it.

Ibrahim smiled again. 'It is another common practice, monsieur. Une échange équitable. He is making sure you do not leave empty handed.'

I found Alain's reports of their progress to the source fascinating. It was a hard two-hour slog. They followed a series of faint wet paths slippery with moss, mud and rocks across steep ridges and through dense and towering bamboo thickets. Fallen trees and ankle-deep snake vine ground cover impeded them before they descended the slope of a saddle to a shallow clearing opening up at the base, carpeted in coarse grasses and clumps of moss-covered rocks.

Modou, Ibrahim and Baboucar halted halfway down the slope. They sat and refused point-blank to approach any closer.

'De peur d'attiser les démons—les N'iena—qui gardent cet endroit,' Ibrahim admitted to me over the radio when Alain handed him the set and I translated. 'Nous ne pouvons pas prendre le risque, pour le bien de nos familles, For fear of stirring up the N'iena who guard this place we cannot risk approaching it, for the sake of our families.'

Alain told me it was Tony who found the source of the spring in a steep-sided, semi-circular hollow at the far edge of the clearing. Cold, crystal-clear water was pouring into a shallow pool, three metres across. It flowed from a rocky crevice in the rear embankment thickly interlaced with tree roots, streaming like a tap turned partway open. They drank from it, splashed it over themselves and gave each other a solemn mock baptism before Alain ceremonially filled his blue RAAF thermos flask.

He described Tony setting up the camera on the tripod and taking a series of shots of the two of them standing beside the pool and cavorting around it, before recording their reflections mirrored in the pool's silvery surface, distorted by the furrows spreading across it from the splash of falling water.

He changed reels and handed the completed one to Ibrahim, who pocketed it.

At the far end of the pool, they discovered a streamlet running into the undergrowth, the beginnings of the Tembi River, a major tributary to the Niger.

Alain's next radio call reached me late in the afternoon. He confirmed they were on their way back and scaling a steep incline up to the escarpment.

'By Ibrahim's estimation we're an hour or so away,' he said. I could hear him panting. 'I will see you very soon, sweetheart.'

* * *

Night was falling when the screaming started at the western edge of the village. It spread rapidly towards me from hut to hut.

I sprinted towards the hysterical crowd and saw Ibrahim, his arms across the shoulders of two senior women, his feet stumbling behind him. He was drenched in blood. Part of his left ear had been severed and a deep machete wound had torn his shirt open and sliced through the thick pad of muscle in his shoulder from bone to bone.

Stunned, a frantic question tore through my mind, W*here are Alain and Tony? Where are they?*

I froze. I had no idea what to do, before forcibly controlling my panic. My heart pounding. I sprinted back to the hut, grabbed the two-way radio, my hands trembling. I checked the channel and fumbled with the "talk" switch before depressing it. 'Alain!' I shouted hoarsely into the microphone. 'Alain! Come in! Come in!'

There was no reply. The snakelike hiss of static was so terrifying and otherwordly, the feelings of dread so crushing I felt I was about to black out.

'Alain, if you're receiving me, come in!' I yelled, over and over, ending desperately with: 'Tony! *Anyone!* Please come in.'

Again, there was silence, underscored by the ominous hiss.

Then, urgently switching channels and quivering with a rush of adrenaline that spread like fire through my chest, I contacted Abdoulaye. I could barely speak as I described what I'd seen.

'Arrange for the helicopter to come down to Foroconia first thing tomorrow morning,' I shouted, relieved when he complied.

Then I hurled aside the two-way and rushed back to the crowd pressing around the door to one of the huts. I wrestled my way through, but was held back by a group of women. After a frantic argument they released me and I burst in. Ibrahim was semi-conscious, spread-eagled and groaning on a bare wooden table. Asiya and another two women had cleaned him with warm water and were applying padded cloths to his shoulder and ear under pressure, binding them in place with a roll of black electrical tape.

Shocked, my mind in turmoil, I sat back to watch.

I'm not sure why, but their practical skills and the calm, efficient way they went about it both surprised and settled me down as I fought to curb my impatience. I'm not sure what concoction the old *basi tii*, the village medicine man, prepared for Ibrahim moments later, but drinking it seemed to work wonders for his pain and subdued his groaning. He was conscious and coherent within ten minutes—and then he saw me.

He struggled to sit up, but Asiya took him by the shoulders and forced him to lie still.

'I am very sorry, madame,' he said as he lay back, his voice slurred. 'I have to tell you monsieur Alain and monsieur Tony, they have been murdered. We were ambushed and I am the only one who escaped.'

I gave out a despairing, unearthly scream, '*No! No! No!*"

The moment seemed surreal as the room whirled around me. Filled with horror, I put my head between my knees to catch my breath and avoid fainting.

I barely heard him as he explained in French that Modou had returned to Bakando, leaving himself and Baboucar with Alain and Tony to make the return journey.

'We were passing through some trees on the escarpment about five kilometres from Foroconia when we walked into an ambush. There were fourteen or fifteen men in the gang. I'm not sure who they were. Two had rifles, the rest were armed with double-bladed machetes and scythes. We were surrounded. We did not stand a chance.'

I forced myself to look up as he spoke and concentrated on piecing together what had happened. At first, it looked like a robbery gone wrong, with Alain and Tony offering up their wallets, the camera and tripod Ibrahim was carrying, and the radio. The wallets were almost empty, infuriating the leader. He flung them aside and screamed at Alain in Krio pidgin English when Alain explained they were Australian.

'I do not care where you are from. Sierra Leone is a black man's country and you have no privileges here. You crossed the border without permits and I have every right to hold you hostage for as long as I want.'

When he went on to mention the word "ransom", a man who may have been his second in command stepped up to Tony. He said he did not like the way Tony was looking at his leader, leaned in, and spat into his face. In a swift reflex action, Tony ducked, stepped sideways and swung his right arm wide and violently upwards. He hit the man across his open throat below his jaw with the rear of his straightened palm with all his power. He crushed his trachea and felled him as if he'd struck him with an axe.

The reaction of the rest of the group was savage and immediate. They butchered Alain, Tony and Baboucar in a melee of flashing machetes.

Ibrahim had been standing at the back of the group. When they charged at the two Australians, he turned and sprinted through the trees. A single blow glancing from the left side of his skull wounded him. There were gunshots, but he was not hit, felt little pain, and did not stop.

'No one followed me.'

He was further from home than he thought. He made it back to the village on the verge of collapse. He was fortunate to have escaped.

He said the end must have been quick for the others.

The stunned silence that followed was unbearable. An uncontrollable wave of white-hot rage tore through me as the silence lengthened. Then I leapt to my feet and rushed blindly from the hut. I ran through the village, across a field of millet and into the trees, swiping aside anyone who stepped forward to bar my way or comfort me.

There, I collapsed to the ground at the base of a tree, leaned back against the trunk, buried my face between my knees and howled, before subsiding into a series of gut-wrenching sobs. I have no idea how long I was there, venting my unbearable pain and outrage into the darkness. Late into the night, when I felt so washed out sleep was all I wanted, I heard for the first time the communal wailing of the village women. I took it to be their grieving process for Baboucar.

Exhausted, I staggered to my feet and walked back towards the huts. It was without a doubt the longest walk I'd ever taken. The stalks of millet whipped at my legs as I stumbled across the stubble and pebbles, conscious of their treacherous roughness through the soles of my sandals, once or twice thrown off balance.

When I reached the edge of the village, the sound of the villagers crying out around me was despairing. Two of the senior women, who I didn't realise had been watching me, stepped to my side, linked their arms through mine and led me with gentle purpose to Ayisa's hut. Weakened with fatigue, I was too tired to protest.

'Come in and join us in the *haus krai*, Alicia,' Ayisa said, inviting me in and showng me to a bed. 'Allow your grief to take you over. It will help you deal with your loss.'

Overcome with anguish, my confused emotions tearing me apart, I allowed the wailing to wash over me. Its hypnotic effect eventually allowed me to drift into a dazed, uneasy, broken sleep.

* * *

The following morning, Ayisa shook me awake. 'The helicopter is here,' she said. 'Ibrahim is ready for the flight. I have prepared a breakfast of Akwadu and hot Osang tea for you. I assumed you'd like it with sugar... two spoons... and brown. It's all we have. You must eat and be strong, Alicia. You have much to do.'

Still half-asleep, I sat up slowly as she spoke. When I swung my legs from the bed and stood unsteadily in the shadows of the hut, I was filled with dreamlike images of the afternoon and night before—and then the painful echo of Alain's last promise, 'I will see you very soon, sweetheart,' struck me so deep in the heart I could not hold back the crying.

Her arm around my shoulders, Ayisa led me sobbing to the table where she'd laid out a plate of sliced and baked bananas topped with honey and grated coconut, coupled with a cup of black, steaming tea. She squeezed half a lemon and orange over the dish, before leaving me alone in the hut.

I noticed the the dark stains of Ibrahim's blood like bruises in the timber of the table, despite Ayisa's scrubbing.

Then I leaned forward for several intense moments resting my forehead in my hands, my elbows on the table, as the sobbing eased. I had to face the reality of the situation. I had to be practical. I had to shut down Alain's project and pack up all the gear, sorting out what to return to Alain and Tony's parents in Australia. And I had to assist the authorities with whatever investigation was about to begin.

I dug deep and summoned all my resources, before sitting up and taking a series of deep breaths with fresh determination. I ate several mouthfuls of the Akwadu, the sweet, hot tea burning my lips as I washed it down. Then I went out through the door, pausing to wash my face and run my fingers through my hair at the water barrel beside it. As I made my way back to our hut, I shook hands with several women who reached out with an empathetic murmur to express their sorrow, clicking their tongues as they did so. I recognised one of them as Baboucar's mother, and I gripped her hand and pulled her towards me to embrace her.

I was grateful for the opportunity to occupy myself by contacting Abdoulaye on the two-way to relay what had happened, before packing up the gear—including the priceless can of film Tony had given to Ibrahim for safekeeping—and tearfully thanking and farewelling the villagers before leaving.

Half an hour later Ibrahim and I boarded the helicopter for the flight to Faranah. Once in the air, we flew towards an out-of-control bushfire a kilometre or so inside Guinea and not far from Foroconia—a swirling column of black smoke with orange flames raging within it. I was surprised we hadn't seen the smoke from the village.

We circled it, and once Ibrahim got his bearings, he confirmed it was the place where the ambush had taken place. The pilot made a wide sweep across the border, flying over three villages inside Sierra Leone. We saw nothing unusual there, no crowds, except for villagers scrambling out of their beehive thatched huts to watch us fly overhead, and many children, some half-dressed and others naked.

When we landed back in Faranah, Abdoulaye was at the airstrip to meet us.

'I am so sorry, madame,' he said, shaking his head and embracing me in a hug so sorrowful I had to stifle another upsurge of tears. 'You have my personal apologies on behalf of GFC... and my country.'

'It's not your fault, Abdou,' I gasped. 'You're not responsible. Neither is your Company or country. The boys were unfortunate. They were in the wrong place at the wrong time. It can't be undone.'

'Words are inadequate,' he said as he released me with an intent look, the muscles in his jaw taut. 'Now we must do everything we can to rectify the situation.'

Once we were back in the mining camp, he drove Ibrahim to the local hospital for stitching and review, before he was flown to Conakry for the surgery he needed.

'You must prepare yourself, madame,' Abdoulaye said when he returned. 'This incident has made the international news, as you can imagine. The camp administrator has contacted the Australian embassy in Accra. They are organising your flight to Australia and sending someone to assist you. It will take a day or two.'

I was shocked and wondered if I had misunderstood him. 'What do they expect me to do, Abdou? Stay here in Faranah and wait for them? For days on end? I couldn't bear it.'

'No. They have instructed me to drive you down to Conakry. I have booked you back into the Novotel. We will leave when you are ready. A shower first? A meal?'

We were back in Conakry by late evening. It was a relief to lock myself in the silence of my room and sit on the balcony staring at the sunset over the Atlantic, my mind empty and relentless surges of grief overwhelming me. I surrendered to it this time, as though I was drowning in a bottomless pool of impenetrable blackness. When I was drifting at last into a light, uneasy sleep, I recalled Alain's smile that had me begging for more, and was convinced I heard his voice, 'We'll *always* have Zurriola Beach. Someday you'll understand.'

* * *

Two Australian officers arrived in Conakry within two days, flown in from Ghana. Paul Murray was a member of the Australian Federal Police—the AFP—and Ian Carpenter, a smart young liaison officer on the embassy staff.

They stepped in at once and shielded me from the worst of the publicity and the paparazzi. They arranged my flight to Cape Town aboard an Ethiopian Airlines flight departing the following week, and an onward flight to Perth aboard South African Airways. Ian told me the Leroys had guaranteed my flights. I was grateful and felt indebted to them.

Paul was lean, sharp-featured and middle-aged, well over

six feet tall and noticeably pot-bellied. His hair was white and cut short, his jaw square and his blue eyes disconcertingly piercing. I was struck by his blunt, conversational style. Everything he said seemed always to the point, with no shades of grey.

The day after he arrived, he joined the Guinean military and police gendarme unit sent to Foroconia to investigate the incident. Tense and barely able to speak to him on the day he left, I asked him to collect some of Alain and Tony's ashes, if possible.

On his return three days later, he told me unseasonal thunderstorms had put the bushfire out.

'We buried what was left of the bodies where they'd fallen,' he said, as he handed me two small, sealed Nescafé cans. 'We had no choice, but I did as you asked.' He nodded down at the cans, his expression wry. 'As you can imagine, I'm not sure who is who.'

'Thank you,' I said, my voice shaking as I accepted them. 'So the bodies weren't recognisable?'

'No. I'm afraid they were mutilated and burned beyond recognition. All three of them.'

His words sent a shockwave through me. I stared at him aghast. '*Mutilated*?'

'I don't like to think about it, either. It was tragic and horrifying,' he said. 'We erected wooden markers for them. I understand the Leroys are going to put something more permanent there sometime in the future. They discussed it with the embassy when they were told the bodies were not going to be repatriated. Ian can fill you in.'

'Did you recover anything else from the site?'

'Apart from the photographs we took? Yes, just one thing, this thermos flask,' he said, reaching into the basket he was carrying and handing it to me. 'The photographs you do not want to see.'

The fire had charred and buckled the thermos, but it was still intact. I had trouble unscrewing the cap and Paul took over. Unbelievably, we found it full of spring water, filled to the brim. It came as a surprise. I wasn't sure what to do with it at first. Drink it, as Alain and Tony had done at Tembakounda? No. Tip it into the Atlantic off Conakry? That didn't seem appropriate either. In the end, I decided to take it with me to the Leroys in Perth.

Abdoulaye and I delivered the Toyota and kayaks to the *lycée français* Albert Camus two days later. We parked the vehicle and trailer on the central concrete sports arena, where the principal had arranged a school assembly for the three hundred secondary students.

Abdoulaye filmed the proceeding on the last of Tony's blank reels.

After a brief speech outlining Alain's project and describing what had happened to end it, I handed the car keys to the school captain. Then we joined the audience as they milled around us, admiring the kayaks, which they hadn't expected, shaking our hands and requesting autographs.

I know Alain would have approved of the handover. At one uncanny moment I felt he was standing beside me on the stage, just as I had with Mamá when I sensed her running with Andrés and me in the Urique cemetery. I like to think I saw him gazing down at me when I sat back down after speaking, and believe I heard him say, 'This is real, sweetheart. Trust me,' with his familiar smile, his eyes alight, before fading from view.

Am I hallucinating? I wondered as he disappeared. *Did Abdou capture him on film?*

In Perth, Western Australia, February 1990

PAUL MURRAY ACCOMPANIED ME back to Perth, the formal report of his findings at Foroconia in his cabin baggage. Apart from my personal belongings in my backpack, I loaded aboard the things I'd prioritised: Alain's documents, including his two green hardcover diaries for 1989 and 1990, a selection of his clothes, his thermos of spring water, Tony's nine completed cans of film and ledger, and of course, their ashes. The rest of the gear Alain had accumulated for the project was air freighted and due to arrive in Perth a month later.

We arrived at four in the morning on Friday, 9 February. We faced a barrage of flashbulbs when we cleared customs and entered the airport concourse, several microphones and camcorders jammed in our faces. I refused to speak to anyone as Paul held my elbow and steered me past them. Formal interviews could come later, when I'd recovered enough to face them.

When Paul left me, I walked to the baggage carousel, where Don and Eva Leroy stepped forward to greet me.

I was worn out and my nerves were on edge, but I composed myself, uncertain how such a charged first meeting between us would develop, and wondering how much Alain had told them about me.

Eva was elegantly striking for her age. She was tall and slim in a loose-fitting royal blue halter neck jumpsuit, her snow-white hair set in a sharp bob cut. Her face was small, delicately featured and beautifully proportioned. The fine lines in her skin were barely noticeable at first, as if she'd been moulded in porcelain, and her eyes were such an astonishing grey I sensed the unexpected glow of an immediate connection as our eyes met.

The next moment she surprised me. The initial gravity in her expression gave way to a light-heartedness I hadn't expected, as she shook my hand and spread her arms to give me the gentlest of embraces. 'My dear Alicia,' she said, her voice surprisingly mellow and her accent echoing Alain's. 'Welcome to Perth.'

Is she being cheerful on my behalf? Is it a show of empathic stoicism?

'I'm glad to be here,' I said, as she stepped back. 'It's good to meet you… and I'm so, so sorry about Alain.'

She immediately reached up and put a forefinger to my lips. 'I know, and thank you, but we can talk about it later. Right now, this is Don,' she said, stepping across to let him shake my hand, the rayon in her jumpsuit swishing.

'I know Perth's not Mexico,' Don said, 'but we want you to feel it's no different.'

He had the forearms of an experienced woodchopper and the hand I shook was powerful and calloused. I could see him out in a paddock on horseback, someone attuned to hard work, someone you could rely on to roll up his sleeves and get on with it.

'*Gracias*,' I replied, my tiredness causing me to respond awkwardly in Spanish, and then, realising my mistake, I recalled the moment I'd welcomed Alain in the Café de la Concha when he'd ordered coffees and quickly went on, '*De las descripciones de Alain, estoy segura de que lo encontraré en casa lejos de casa.*'

His face broke into a half-smile. 'Beg yours? Come again? I didn't quite catch it.'

'From Alain's descriptions, I'm sure I'll find it a home away from home.'

'We'll do our best,' he said. 'Alain warned us about you. He said the first time he met you he knew you were a shiela with the smarts.'

Shorter than Eva, barrel-chested and thick-set in his worn denim shirt and jeans, he looked out of place in the glaring lights of the airport. His face was square, his white hairline receding and his brown eyes beneath thick dark eyebrows calm and faintly questioning... but when he smiled, he looked as though he was about to burst into laughter and I thought at once of Alain.

I looked back at Eva and saw that though they may be physically opposites, they seemed perfectly matched. They were clearly aware of my distress and their mutual empathy and understanding eased my tension.

Don picked up my two Adidas carry bags when they arrived on the carousel and he led us out to the carpark, while Eva and I talked about my flight and the brief stopover in Cape Town when I changed planes.

'The city must have been buzzing,' she said, 'with the release of Nelson Mandela in two days' time.'

'Yes, that's on Sunday. You're right, the atmosphere among the staff in the hotel was electric. And on the streets. I wasn't sure what was going on until one of the housemaids filled me in. She told me Mandela had been moved from Robben Island to the Victor Verster prison two years ago and they were going to open the gates for him there.'

'What a moment for the country,' Eva said, before adding, 'and for the world.'

'She was so excited,' I said. 'She told me she was taking the day off to go and watch him walk out. It was a sixty-kilometre bus ride, apparently, and she wasn't going to miss it. The city was packed when we left. They're expecting well over a hundred thousand at the city hall when he gives his first public address.'

'Now that will be interesting. Reconciliation with the white population, do you think? Or revenge?'

'Oh, reconciliation. The country can't afford to be vengeful.'

'Unless they take matters into their own hands,' Eva murmured.

Sensing a touch of bitterness in her tone, I glanced at her, wondering if what she'd said reflected her feelings about Alain's murder.

'I doubt it,' I said. 'The atmosphere on the streets was euphoric.'

'For now. Maybe time will tell.'

Half an hour later, with dawn breaking, we drove to the end of Range Road in Millendon, where Don turned into the long gravel drive bordered by white-fenced paddocks sloping up to the house. I saw no horses.

'They're in Gidgegannup at the moment,' Don said when I asked. 'Seven of them. They're in foal at the Drummond's stud. At Tony's parents'.'

Their home was a striking white, ranch-style, single-storey house with a high-pitched, corrugated iron roof and surrounding pillared veranda. It was set on a levelled terrace cut into the foothills of the Darling scarp, rising steeply behind it.

Alain's sister, Christina, was standing on the veranda as we pulled up. She was a younger version of Eva at first sight, but without the fragility, and her bright brown eyes reminded me of Alain. She had dyed her hair a luxurious copper red. Combed back in a long ponytail, it gleamed in the sunlight as she came down the steps. She wore a white t-shirt and hippie-style tie-dye patterned maroon dungarees matching her hair. They suited her perfectly.

'Hello, big sister,' she said, giving me a close, firm hug, before stepping back to look at me appraisingly, her eyebrows raised. 'No wonder Alain fancied you. He had good taste.' She gave me a wicked grin. 'In your case, that is. We won't mention any of the others.' She took my hand. 'Come on in. The coffee's on, I've beaten the life out of the eggs for the omelettes, prepared the bacon and peeled the mushrooms, and the bottle of wine is breathing and ready to pour. Give me ten minutes and we'll serve you a gourmet West Australian welcome.'

'Wine? For breakfast?'

'Pinot Gris, the best. For the toast.' She laughed. 'Because we've run out of bread, and you've arrived.'

Still holding my hand, she showed me through the house: the open plan, airy and light-filled lounge-dining room leading out through glass sliding doors to the rear alfresco pergola at the back running the length of the house, the spacious kitchen, the darkened theatre to one side, and the two wings, where there were several bedrooms.

I was struck by the magnificent white grand piano in the lounge. I stopped to admire it, the lid up and a Schubert musical score open on its musical rack.

'Who's the pianist in the family?' I asked.

'That would be me, classically trained by Mum. She insists I've overtaken her technically, but I'm not convinced. I'm better on the violin.'

I looked down at her right hand holding mine and spread her long fingers across my palm. 'You sure have the hands for it. The fingers.'

'Pure luck. Take a look at Mum's and you'll see where I inherited them from. I play with the West Australian Symphony Orchestra now and again, so I have to keep my skills up. You're going to have to turn a deaf ear on me pounding away or plucking the strings at all sorts of odd hours.'

Eva appeared and showed me to my bedroom in the corner of the house at the end of the right-hand wing, with wide windows facing a sunlit wooded view of the scarp. When she opened the window to air the room, I was startled to hear an alarming maniacal cackle echoing in the nearby trees. I rushed across to the window as the barking laughter died away.

'That's one of our resident kookaburras,' Eva said. 'There are a few around. You'll get used to them, or you better had, because they sound off on most days around this time. Like clockwork. Beats setting your alarm.'

I leaned across the window-ledge beside her, 'Where is it? I've never seen one. Are they well-camouflaged?'

'Sort of. Imagine a bug-eyed, obese pigeon with a white chest, large head and prominent beak. Its tawny wings speckled in flecks of blue. They seem to like the clump of Marri trees, over there to the right. The ones in flower. See them?'

A faint sweet peppermint smell coupled with resin reached me. 'Oh, yes. Is that their scent?'

'It is. Eucalyptus and honey. You'll get used to that too. It gets stronger next month when they're all in full bloom. You don't suffer from hay fever, I hope. Or asthma?'

'Neither, as far I know.'

'Right, then. We'll see you at breakfast in five. You know where the patio is at the back?'

'Christina showed me on the way in.'

'We'll see you there. And Chris prefers Chris, by the way.' She gazed at me as she turned for the door. 'Make sure you make yourself comfortable here, Alicia. Don't be backward in coming forward.'

'*Gracias*,' I said.

'We can talk about Alain and all your adventures once we've eaten.'

All our adventures? I wondered when she left the room.

How much has Alain told them about me? When did he have the time? We were only together for two months, after all.

* * *

After breakfast, with the table cleared, I unpacked Alain's diaries, his clothes and papers, and Tony's nine reels of film and his ledger, and carried them out to the pergola. Unsure about displaying the cans of ashes and the thermos, I left them in the bedroom.

A cold sense of shock ran through me when Eva, without a word, placed a box of tissues beside the stack of films. It seemed so clinical, so practical. I took one to ease my rising tension, folded it up and scrunched it in my hand as a distraction. For some reason, the memory of the men and women in Foroconia formally and loudly expressing their grief throughout the night of the massacre came to me... and here we were, about to do something similar.

'So,' Don said, checking the items on the table, 'I know we're all grieving, but perhaps the easiest way we can talk about Alain is for me to start by admitting how bloody hard it is for a father and mother to lose a son while we're still alive. It should happen the other way around, but what's done is done. We thought his goal of getting the best of the Niger was foolhardy, but we understand why he decided he had to do it, and we admire him for trying.' There was a catch in his throat. 'Better than not making the attempt.'

I saw his eyes fill as Eva placed an arm across his shoulder, and Christina, sitting beside me, reached across and put both hands over his, which were on the table, fingers interlaced.

'What makes it unbearable is to know how he died and that his remains have been buried where he fell. In Guinea, of all places. May as well be on the dark side of the moon. We don't have anywhere to grieve and we haven't said our goodbyes.' He turned to me. 'The AFP told me they'd managed to gather together some of his ashes, along with Tony's. They said you'd be bringing them with you.'

'Yes, I have them. In the bedroom. Shall I get them?'

'Please.'

I left the table and retrieved the two cans. I'd had the sense to label them in Cape Town so there'd be no confusion, even though Paul Murray had been uncertain of their identities. I knew I'd have to confess at some stage what I'd done.

I took them back to the table, with the thermos.

Christina broke into a spasm of sobs when she saw the cans, thrust back her chair and ran into the house, with Eva following her.

Don picked up the can labelled 'Alain' and held it in both hands, examining it for a full minute. I wondered where his thoughts were taking him as he shook his head. 'Nescafé… we can do better.'

'I have to tell you we weren't able to differentiate the ashes after the fire, Don. The labelling is arbitrary.' I spoke in a tense and breathless rush.

'I know. We've been forewarned.' His voice was shaking. 'We'll keep them labelled as they are and I'll make two Jarrah urns to show the boys some respect.' He looked across at me as Eva emerged from the house and sat in Christina's seat beside me. 'And the thermos? What's the significance?'

'Alain filled it from the spring at Tembakounda. It's still full.'

He picked it up and unscrewed the cap. 'So it is. How extraordinary.' He dipped his forefinger in, tasted it, looked thoughtfully across at Eva and after a long silence, raised his eyebrows and nodded. 'Here's what we'll do, darling. We'll bury his ashes up on the scarp where he had his treehouse as a boy. We'll plant two or three olive trees there for him and we'll water them in with his spring water. Plant a lawn there, too. How does that sound?'

Eva nodded. 'I like the idea. It crosses the 'T's and dots the 'I's.'

'In fact, we can bury both urns there, if Colin and Lyn agree. The boys used to play together up there, after all. I'll find a decent-sized moss rock for a headstone and get two plaques made.'

He tightened the cap and put the thermos back alongside the cans. 'Okay, now then. If you feel up to it, Alicia, perhaps you can fill us in on how it all went down.'

A sudden unexpected wave of grief rushed through me. It took my breath away and made me gasp, as if someone had punched me in the solar plexus. Eva poured me a glass of water. I thanked her and stood, unsure what to say and shivering with what I felt was lack of sleep. I took the glass and walked the length of the pergola and back, sipping it, regaining my composure as I stepped across the intricate sunlit patterns the leaves of passion fruit vines overhead were throwing across the the paving.

'Before I start,' I said when I sat back down, 'I want you both to know how much I cared for Alain. He was very special to me.'

'We know,' Eva said. 'He said the same about you in a letter he wrote us. Virtually word for word.'

I spent the rest of the morning describing what had happened, from the time I first saw Alain beside the Aldabide waterfall to the moment Abdou and I handed the Toyota and kayaks to the school. It was draining and painful, interspersed with emotional pauses when I became so overwrought I couldn't continue; but in the end, I was relieved. It proved cathartic.

Although wrung out by the experience, when I woke after a sleep that afternoon, I knew I could now gather the strength to face the burial of the ashes.

The next day, Don took the cans of film, the ledger and Tony's ashes to his father Colin in Gidgegannup. I was shocked when he soon returned with everything he'd taken, along with a can of film Tony had shot in Perth before moving to Spain.

'Complete change of plan,' Don said in the lounge, handing me the cans and the ledger. 'Colin's flat out with the stud right now. He can't spare any time for the documentary, but he has contracted Western Cinematics in Midland to develop them all and kick off the post-production editing. They are the technical experts. He believes it'd be a good idea for you to oversee the process, Alicia, since you were so close to Tony's filming. We presume you're familiar with his intentions.' He raised his eyebrows in a glance edged with what I took for humorous intimidation. 'I must say, I have to agree, don't you?'

I was beginning to recognise that look—it suggested he wouldn't take no for an answer. I nodded. 'Of course. That makes sense, even though I know nothing about editing.'

'You don't need to. Cinematics will provide the equipment and the expertise. You'll be in the driving seat, the one with the storyline and the vision.'

'It'll be an interesting distraction for me.' I said, wondering how arduous task of putting together Tony's documentary would be. 'We'll be bringing Alain and Tony back to reimagined life.' Then I pointed at Tony's ashes. 'I see you've brought his ashes back.'

'I have indeed. Colin has agreed to have them buried here, alongside Alain's.'

* * *

Within three weeks, Don had levelled a circular clearing and placed a large granite moss rock headstone on it on the slope at the rear of the house. Beyond it stood a gnarled and spreading white-and-grey barked eucalypt Eva told me was a Wandoo tree, the platform of Alain's boyhood treehouse propped across its lower branches. A rope ladder dangled from it.

'We built it for him when he was eight,' Eva told me when we were inspecting the site. 'He was so wild at that age. Such a bush basher. I don't know how many times we thought we'd lost him up in the ranges, him and Tony... and Ben, when he was here. We had to somehow rein him in and the tree house helped. Kept him close to the house. When he was in his teens he removed the upper structure but kept the platform you can see up there. He liked sitting on it as he got older, birdwatching or reading. It's got a view right across Millendon, as far as the Olive Farm vineyards way down there.' She looked at me. 'I often think that may be where he first developed his love of flying.' She peered up at the tree, her expression sombre. 'Not to mention his decision to kayak down the Niger.'

'I'll have to check it out.'

'You must. Chris goes up there sometimes, with her violin. I don't know how she makes it up the ladder, for goodness' sake. I don't like to watch her climb it one-handed. Her playing attracts the magpies like you wouldn't believe. She has her own private choir—the "Collingwood Choristers", according to her.' She gave me a bemused look. 'Collingwood's a football team nicknamed the Magpies because they wear black and white. Her playing puts the heebie jeebies up the twenty-eights, though.'

'Heebie jeebies?' I asked. 'Twenty-eights?'

'Frightens them off, the ring-neck parrots. You'll see them here at times. In pairs or flocks of around a dozen. Brilliant green, they are, with a blue-black head and yellow frill neck. You can't mistake them. They've got a cheerful call to die for when you're feeling down. *Darlmoorluk*, the local Noongar Aborigines call them.'

'Darlmoorluk. I must remember that. And Noongar.'

Don and Eva organised an intimate private burial ceremony when the two plaques were anchored in place a fortnight later. Tony's parents attended, along with several of Alain's RAAF friends. Ben was unavailable. He was in Melbourne, rejoining the Monash University Faculty of Law, but he intended visiting in April.

A young, low-key RAAF chaplain from Pearce air base moderated the proceedings, and once the urns were buried together at the base of the rock, Don and Colin planted three olive tree saplings in a semi-circle around the site. Christina and I shared the Tembakounda spring water in a jug each and watered them in, before Don soaked them with the hose.

Next, Christina played two pieces of music on the violin. I'd heard her practising them before the ceremony and found them deeply moving. I asked her what they were. 'The first is the andantino movement of Camille Saint-Saëns's Concerto number three for violin,' she told me. 'The other I'm sure you'll recognise. It's Neil Young's "Harvest Moon". Alain loved them both.'

I held myself together during the ceremony. It wasn't until later I broke down, when everyone except Christina and I had returned to the house. Seeing the miniature colour portraits of Alain and Tony on the plaques, and reading their epitaph, a quotation from the poet Rumi, tore me open and I wept, as did Christina beside me, our arms around our waists.

What is the body? the epitaph read. *Endurance. What is love? Gratitude. What is hidden in our chests? Laughter. What else? Compassion.*

* * *

During the next three months, I drove Alain's black and silver Peugeot 505 to Midland to assist with the edit, often with Christina. During the weekends, we explored the cities of Perth and Fremantle and the surrounding hills and beaches beneath clear blue skies and a blazing summer sun that reminded me of Mexico and made me unexpectedly homesick. I found the strange, new freshness of it all-absorbing, especially the wildflower everlastings surviving beside the roads and carpeting in pastel colours the clearings beneath the Banksia trees alight with upright orange and yellow flowers along the scarp, Christina pointing them out and naming them.

Imagining Alain with me and showing me around helped me through the occasional moment when I was struck with grief.

By early March, the technicians at Western Cinematics had developed all the films and were ready to run the celluloid frames through the flatbed editor. We had over two hours of running time at twenty-four frames a second. I found it intriguing, running the sequences backwards and forwards across the viewing screen, intently monitoring the scenes with one of the technicians, cutting and splicing to suit the storyline and maintain the rhythm and pacing Tony had established during the filming.

The first reel though, filmed in Perth before the Niger project was underway, was so heart-rending and unexpected I could barely stand to edit it. Tony had filmed Alain's wedding day scenes at St Joseph's Church and Caversham House. He'd begun with a sweep across the church car park, with groups of wedding guests arriving for the ceremony. Alain was the last to arrive, his car driven by his best man, Ben. Tony filmed them entering the church, but before he followed them in, he was disturbed by a taxi. It accelerated to the door and Christina emerged, running. She was wearing a flowing magenta bridesmaid's dress and was barefoot, a coronet of roses in her hair, her pink high-heeled shoes in her hands. Breathless, she sprinted past Tony filming her.

'She's gone,' she said as she passed him, her hoarse voice caught on sync sound. 'Sandra. She's done a bloody runner. She's on her way to Queensland. Where's Alain?'

Another shot inside the church showed Alain turning to face the guests, the priest standing to his left. 'Good afternoon, everyone,' he said. 'As you've all no doubt guessed, I've been dumped at the altar. God knows why. It's the last thing I expected. But just because I haven't kissed the bride, it doesn't mean the wedding ceremonies are over and you've wasted your time. Far from it. It means we can kick off the reception at Caversham House earlier, like right now. I want to thank you all for coming, and I hope you'll join me there and help me drown my sorrows.'

When I saw his face and heard his voice a burst of emotion doubled me over, as if I'd been stabbed and had the dagger twisted within my chest. I stumbled away and it took me several minutes to recover.

Once we'd processed the rest of the take at the reception, I packed the film back in the can and taped it shut. It had no place in the film, even though it may have contributed to Alain's decision to undertake his quest. I knew it would distress Eva and Don.

A fortnight later at dinner I turned to Eva and said, 'It looks as if we'll end up with a film running for just under three-quarters of an hour. It's like I'm giving birth to a baby, but with birth pains of a different order. I'm watching it take shape as it grows, hoping my parenting skills are up to the task as it develops its own personality.'

'We have every confidence in you,' Eva replied. 'Chris says you're doing fine. She thinks the whitewater scenes in Catalonia just after the opening have caught the moments they were training there beautifully.'

'Well, I wasn't there, so I had no preconceived ideas about those particular scenes, but Tony made it easy for me. His ledger helped, and the scenes were so full of life they virtually organised themselves. All I had to do was look at each sequence, feel the energy driving it and select the most outstanding moments to maintain the tension or lessen the suspense.' I gave her a quiet chuckle. 'Believe me, I've had Tony whispering in my ear, "Don't you mess it up, Albee, or I'll have your guts for garters."'

Don gave a loud clap of his hands. 'Way to go, Alicia! "Guts for garters"! We'll make an Aussie of you yet.'

'Alain taught me well,' I said. 'Trust me, I'm the full bottle.'

In the following silence, my mind ran over the opening scene Christina and I had selected. Tony had set up the camera on a tripod under the pergola and auto-filmed Alain, Ben and himself seated at the table, their voices recorded.

A large survey map is spread open in front of them, the Niger River snaking across it from the Guinea Highlands to the Bay of Benin. 'Look, it's never been done before,' Alain says, running his hand the length of the river. 'No one has kayaked from the source to the sea, but that's beside the point. Bugger *The Guinness Book of Records*. What I'm after is doing something so far out of left field it puts me on the spot. Have I got the smarts to organise a project so outlandish? Am I up for the challenge once I'm committed to it and can't turn back? Do I have the persistence? The patience? The sheer dogged stubbornness? And when things do go wrong, as they're bound to, how will I react? It's me I want to discover the truth about, not the Niger.' He looks around at the others, his eyebrows raised. 'Are you both with me?'

Tony points up at the camera and taps the map with a forefinger. 'Me? Sure am, mate. I've got a film to make, a job to do. Part travelogue, looking at this map, and part feature film, listening to you. I can smell a good story in the making—three Aussies risk death to find themselves. I can't wait to get started.'

'And you, Ben?' Alain asked.

'I'm in it for the ride because you are, and for the novelty of it, not to mention filling in most of my gap year from Monash Uni. Like you, it'll be good to learn something about myself I'm not already aware of.'

'Good. That's it, then. We're all singing from the same song sheet, so I'll start the ball rolling. Sponsors. Finances. Equipment. Logistics. The works. If I need a hand, you'll hear me shout.'

By the end of May, we had the first working version of the film completed. I found the landscapes and the kayaking action on the rivers in the mountains of Catalonia and the Basque country mesmerising—including the brief scene where I was running past in Gorbeia Park—and I was eventually happy with the meticulous cutting and splicing of the succeeding scenes with which I was familiar, through to Abou's filming of the conclusion, the handover of the Toyota and kayaks in Conakry.

Ben was with us for a week at the end of April. The cadence of his quiet, baritone voice-overs for the opening scene, the whitewater kayaking and the treks to and from the Tembakounda spring perfectly matched their atmosphere and tone. We trimmed back his voice-ver of Ibrahim's description of the ambush though, removing his reference to Tony's reflex defensive action triggering the massacre, to save Colin and Lyn the pain of hearing it.

Christina worked wonders with the background music. Her violin and piano arrangements melded with the narrative, matching and reflecting the images and highlighting the varying moods of the silences.

'I don't know how you're doing it,' I said one afternoon, partway through a recording session. 'I love it, Chris. It's brilliant.'

She smiled. 'Hard work and hanging onto the coattails of a master. That piece is based on Arvo Pärt's *'Spiegel im Spiegel'* and the one before it his *'Tabula Rasa'*, the second movement. I'll be working on the same Saint-Saëns's Concerto I played at Alain's burial next. It'll offset the scenes in Foroconia perfectly.' Her smile widened. 'Except for the drums for the dancing, of course. Tony's sync sound recording doesn't do them justice. I'll look for something to add some zing and bring the house down. Stanley Sackey's group Kukurudu, perhaps.'

We held the opening night in the theatre in the house, with Don running the projector. The only other guests were Colin and Lyn.

My pulse was beating painfully in my throat during the opening title sequence. The suspense was gripping as the camera panned for twenty silent seconds across the canopy of trees on the Darling scarp in the misty pre-dawn light. Then Christina's haunting opening soundtrack, a recording of Loreena McKennitt's 'Samain Night', which we'd been granted permission to use, gathered volume as the camera settled on the platform in the eucalypt and the house beyond it, the title *River of Dreams* and the opening credits appearing.

Ben's first intimate monologue followed, introducing the narrative theme with a quotation from Viktor Frankl's *Man's Search for Meaning*. 'This is the story of three friends who set out to kayak down the Niger River in West Africa, from the source to the sea. They are searching for the truth about themselves. One can best describe their mantra in the words of the famous psychotherapist Viktor Frankl. "Ultimately, man should not ask what the meaning of his life is, but rather must recognise it is he who is asked. In a word, each man is questioned by life; and he can only answer to life by answering for his own life; to life he can only respond by being responsible." Two of the friends pay dearly with their lives in the quest. We dedicate this film to them.'

The opening scene beneath the pergola with the chart of West Africa on the table then segued to a scene showing Alain receiving the seagoing kayaks in Norway and next settled on the mountains of Catalonia—and the film was underway.

The showing took forty minutes and ended with the handover in Conakry.

I held my breath as the lights went on.

The emotional silence lasted, broken at last by Lyn's gasping sobs. No one spoke until Don switched off the projector, walked down to the screen and spread his arms. 'There's only one way to deal with this,' he said. 'Come on, let's have a hug. All of us.'

I will never forget the moving communal embrace that followed. It lasted for several minutes, six of us leaning together with our arms about our shoulders, the deeply shared emotion so intense our tears flowed.

When Colin and Lyn had left, I joined Don and Eva under the pergola. We could hear Christina in the background on the piano, playing a highly complex piece I'd never heard before in an astonishing repetitive cascade of notes, as if wringing out her pent-up emotions across the keys, the wizardry of her technique dazzling.

'It's Debussy's "Fireworks Prelude",' Eva said when I asked her. 'One of the most testing pieces she's mastered. It's taken her years.'

'I have to say Colin was right to leave the post-edit in your hands, Alicia.' Don said. 'Thanks to you, we've got a remarkable record of the boys' quest. You've done us proud. Congratulations.'

'Thank you, but as I've said all along, Tony's skill with the camera made it easy for me. He knew exactly how to bring the story to the screen. Let alone Chris's soundtrack.'

'After watching it,' Eva said, 'I don't feel so empty. So bereft, with Alain gone. So lost. Watching his story unfold gave me insights into the innermost workings of his being I'll treasure for the rest of my life. I'll never forget the compassion he showed the little crippled beggar. I'm so looking forward to watching it again.'

'I know what you mean,' I said, so deeply moved by her reaction I could barely speak.

* * *

During that time, I did not mention to anyone that the stress I went through in Guinea and the emotional tensions in piecing the film together caused me extreme fatigue and unexpected medical problems. I missed my March and April periods and was experiencing nausea and occasional abdominal pains so severe I went privately to see a specialist gynaecologist.

Her physical examinations put to rest my fears—and dashed my hopes. Ultrasounds and extensive blood and urine tests confirmed I did not have cancer and was not pregnant. On hearing my backstory, she suggested the stress on my psychological and hormonal systems, along with my imagining having Alain's child in Algeciras, had triggered a rare case of phantom pregnancy.

'Pseudocyesis,' she told me. 'You have most of the somatic symptoms, and as you've seen, all our tests suggest it.'

I was both shocked and unsurprised. 'So what do I do?'

'Firstly, you relax. You treat yourself very gently, and you both understand and accept that you aren't pregnant. Meanwhile, we treat you with hormone therapy to induce your periods.'

By the end of May, my period had returned and the pain and nausea had eased. Relieved that I was recovering, I went for my first short run up the scarp… yet I was strangely torn. It took me some time to accept that María, fathered by Alain, was a dream too far. To ease my sorrow, on an impulse one afternoon, I had a small Silver Emperor butterfly strikingly tattooed inside my right wrist. It was alighting on three marigold flowers, and María's name was written in black cursive beneath it.

With the film completed, I'd reached another fork in the road. My funds were running low and I knew I could no longer be a burden on Don and Eva's hospitality, despite them insisting I was welcome to stay.

During the first week in June, I contacted the School of Indigenous Studies at the University of WA and was advised that Darwin University was looking for linguists to work on a project researching the Yolngu dialects in the homelands in Arnhemland, commencing early in September. I contacted the faculty there and when I formally expressed my interest they told me they'd add me to the list of applicants and come back to me.

When I researched the Northern Territory, an article on the mango-growing industry caught my eye. Working in the orchards picking fruit until September struck me as a workable idea. Sunlight, fresh air and regular exercise appealed, after months of sedentary work in front of a viewing monitor in the post-edit laboratory. And if the job in Arnhemland didn't materialise I could fall back on teaching Spanish.

I began running again, determined to regain my fitness and

build up to the frequency and intensity with which I'd been running last November in San Sebastián. While jogging up the scarp one early morning it struck me I should do as Alain had done—set myself a quest. Test myself, by hitchhiking to Darwin, and face the hardships and setbacks it might entail.

And so, in mid-June, after an emotional farewell from Don and Eva, Christina drove me for seventy kilometres out among the rolling foothills to Gin Gin and parked at the turnoff to the town on a straight stretch of the Highway north.

She stayed with me for twenty minutes, until a caravanning couple pulled up and offered me a lift to Geraldton.

'Make sure this is not the last time we see you, big sister,' she said, as we embraced. 'It's been a joy, and thanks a ton for bringing Alain back into our lives.'

'Of course I'll keep in touch, Chris,' I said, regret coupled with anticipation rushing through me. 'You can count on me. And when you get around to it, I want a CD of the film's soundtrack you're preparing.'

LENNARD

In the Pilbara on the Great Northern Highway, Western Australia, June 1990

A DAY LATER, I was at the Exmouth turnoff in semi-desert country. I found it surprisingly hot for a midwinter afternoon, but Christina had forewarned me. Everywhere I looked, red sand spiked with tussocks of spinifex and feathered with clusters of pink and mauve Mulla Mulla flowers stretched to the horizon.

Fortunately, there was a stunted, solitary tree with a canopy of glossy leaves standing at the junction a few metres from the bitumen. I sat in the shade, leaning against its gnarly grey trunk, grateful for the rough bark digging into my back, keeping me awake. I couldn't afford to miss my next potential lift to Darwin. Since midday, they'd been few and far between.

I selected the black queen from Abu Cerrildo's travelling chess set lying open beside me. I was partway through a game. I held it up and inspected it—a copper-coloured Aztec queen with a headdress of feathers and a flowing gown intricately carved from silicate crystal. I held it up towards shafts of sunlight shimmering through the leaves and turned it this way and that, its facets glinting. *La Malinche.* I shook my head as I recalled Abu describing her to me. *A woman of words— interpreter between the Aztecs and the Spanish. A woman after my own heart.*

I studied the remaining pieces. *Three moves to mate.* I replaced the queen, displacing the remaining white conquistador, the knight, before toppling the white king. *So long, Hernán Cortés. Suck it up. Get down on your knees in front of Montezuma and take what's coming to you. A flayed heart, probably. Like mine.*

I closed the set and glanced up through twisted branches and quivering leaves at glimpses of the cloudless sky awash with pale blue light.

How long before the sun arcs beneath the tree canopy and shines directly into my eyes? An hour perhaps, at most? It's already lighting up the white flowers dangling like lanterns in the scrawny Mexican Thornapple weed I recognise beyond my feet, identical to those in the Sierra Madre.

I gazed southwards down the empty road and groaned, banging the back of my head three times against the trunk of the tree. Just the three, I remember, because I laughed out loud and spoke to myself, as I sometimes do, 'Oh, come on now, girl. It takes time and patience. When you hit the reset button on your life, you've got to stay in the moment and adjust to the changes.'

I leaned back and closed my eyes, grateful for my sunglasses. Sunlight flaring red across my eyelids seemed to throw up shadowy images of the unforeseen, making me think I was watching black and white stills in the countdown before the start of an action film.

I wondered what was coming next.

Then I was alerted by the sound of a motorbike. I recognised the thump of a Harley Davidson. You can't mistake it. I sat bolt upright and saw the sun flash for an instant, perhaps on the rider's visor or a piece of chrome. I watched the intermittent reflections gliding closer along the road stretching southwards to Carnarvon. It looked like a diamond glittering on a ribbon of black silk.

I straightened up and took a deep breath to calm the pulse beating in my throat. I checked my watch—it was 4:15—and watched the rider's shadow distort and vanish and reappear in the heat haze rising from the road.

I walked out into the sun, dusting myself off, bending to flick a black and speckled grasshopper from the knee of my jeans. I stopped at the road's edge, hands on hips, before leaning forward and waving both hands as the motorbike swept past.

I assumed the rider was a man. He left me in a swirl of sound and I saw him glance over his shoulder. He slowed and circled back, red dust and gravel flung from the verge. He accelerated towards me before turning again towards the north, where the highway disappeared between the crests of low dunes on the distant horizon.

He switched off the engine, removed his helmet releasing a mop of wiry hair, and looked across at me through green-lensed Aviator sunglasses.

I took two steps back.

His eyes were hidden behind the Polaroid lenses and I was surprised to glimpse myself reflected in the curving sweep of the desert and the sky. I saw a tiny portrait of myself framed by his skin and, for the briefest moment, I imagined what he was seeing—my face pared to the bone with a new hardness to it I had lately found disconcerting. It was weird, as if I was someone else standing in the glare of the sun with a friendless arrogance about me. A stand-offish stranger I disliked. Which is not what I was like at all, in spite of everything I'd been through. It must have been a result of the grieving process and the mourning.

I took off my sunglasses and looked directly at him. For some reason, I was deeply self-protective. Unyielding. Speculative and on guard. With my right hand raised against the sun, I wondered if he sensed my defensiveness and I was annoyed he hadn't removed his sunglasses, as if he was keeping himself concealed from me.

Dark-skinned, his hair and coarse black beard were streaked with silver and dusted red, his bulk zipped up in a black leather riding suit with a white panel across his broad shoulders, powdered with grime and flecked with insect spatter.

'How're you going?' he said, his voice deep and resonant. 'I'm Lennard Currie. I almost missed you. You're the last thing I expected. Out here… in the middle of nowhere.'

I studied him in silence, my hand still raised. He tilted his head towards me as the silence lengthened. '*Nyinda wangginyina, malyu*? You do speak, sister?'

'Hi. I'm Alicia. Alicia Serrano. Thanks for stopping.'

'What're you doing? Did you fall out of the sky? Miss your bus?'

'Something like that.'

I looked at him, suddenly relieved. Clearly, he hadn't seen the TV programs or read the local newspaper reports five months ago. Or if he had, he didn't recognise my name or my face—and before I could suppress the memory—*Alain*. My mind was pierced by the vision of a pall of black smoke with lurid orange flames raging within it. For one dizzying moment, I was back in Guinea that dreadful night, waiting for Alain. Fighting for self-control, I looked back at the tree as if to check on my backpack. I hesitated for several moments before I clenched my jaw and turned back to face Lennard.

He waved a hand across the wide expanse of scrub. 'You look like a *wanamalu* waiting for the tide to turn.'

'I look like a what?' I heard my voice shake.

'Like a *wanamalu*. A shag. On a rock. *Nyinda wanamalu nyinangayi barldalyila.*'

I searched his face, refusing to smile, uncertain about his language.

'Cheer up,' he said. 'Now I'm here, you know you're not alone in the world. You and me, could be we're the only two left alive.' He balanced the helmet on the petrol tank and crossed his arms. 'You want a lift? Or have you called a cab?' He gave a quiet chuckle—I sensed it edged with sarcasm. 'Or maybe you're waiting for Godot?'

'How far are you going?' I asked.

As always, when I first start talking to an Australian I've only just met, I wonder if he or she may have misplaced my accent. *Perhaps he thinks I'm from the southern states rather than Mexico, and that's why he believes I may be wary of his dark skin.*

'I'm Mexican' I said. 'I've been in Australia since February.'

He squinted up at the sun before replying. 'I was wondering. That makes sense... so how far's far enough?'

I did not reply.

'I'm heading for Bandilngan Gorge—Windjana Gorge on the maps,' he said, and quietly added, 'I'm on a pilgrimage. To lay a ghost among the ghost gums. That's how my Rosalie would have put it.'

'You're on a pilgrimage?'

'On a walkabout, yes. It's personal. What about you?' he asked. *'Nyinda yanmanha yaburru?* You going the same way I'm going? Up north?'

His voice was expressive, his accent broad and the cadence clipped and foreign to me. His reference to Beckett surprised me. And the word *wanamalu.* To my mind, it sounded Samoan. Or was he Aboriginal?

'I'm on my way to Darwin,' I said. 'I've been told it's mango-picking season. There may be work available up there.'

'So you're looking for some easy pickings? Isn't the season in October, but? Maybe they're coming in early this year, just for you, *malyu.* By about three months.'

There was an easy-going quality to him, yet I was suspicious of the apparent teasing in his grin, the way he looked sideways at me, inclining his head. I've seen black solitary eagles in the Sierra Madre Mountains do it before plummeting, claws drawn, towards a victim rattlesnake or ground squirrel deep in the canyon below.

'If so, I'll look for a teaching job when I get there. I teach Spanish,' I said, and when he waited for me to continue, 'among other languages.'

'How many do you speak?'

'Fluently?'

'For starters.'

'Five.'

'What, all at once?'

I granted him the ghost of a smile. 'Otherwise, I may head across Arnhem Land to Yirrkala. To study the *Yolngu* dialects spoken there.' I took a breath. 'I'm a linguist, you see. I have a PhD.'

He studied me coolly. 'Have you now? And you're going to Yirrkala to doctor with their languages? Now you're talking. So you want to see that good country?'

'Yes, I'll go there anyway.'

'In which case I can take you as far as Fitzroy Crossing. I'll be heading back to Perth from there.' He uncrossed his arms and ran his fingers through his beard. 'Listen, I can leave you at the Nanutarra roadhouse if you like. It's roughly two hours' ride away. I'll be staying there overnight. You're welcome to travel with me through the Karijini Mountains tomorrow, if you're game. I'll be taking a diversion through the national park. It's my mother's country and I have some special sites to visit. To pay my respects.'

So he was Aboriginal. I asked him what dialect he was speaking.

'It's Malgana. It's spoken around Gutharraguda—Shark Bay,' he pointed westwards with a wide sweep of his left hand, 'down that way, by the coast. *Was* spoken, I mean. It's almost extinct. Three old aunties in Northampton are the only ones left who remember it, and one of them is dying, of cancer. Annie Morgan. She's our last fluent speaker and she's helping us resurrect it, but we're running out of time.'

I looked at his broad face, his hair and beard sparsely wired with silver surrounding it. He was solid, thick-necked. Powerful. Dangerous, I thought. I noticed his strong-wristed hands now gripping the handlebars. A builder's hands. I recoiled from the striking image. *They could wield a bloodied machete!*

'Come on, take a risk,' he said. 'This may be the only chance of a lift you'll get for hours. *Ngayi bandi?* What's your worry? *Gurra wayangudhayinyina ngadhangu.* Don't let this face frighten you. I'm not Mad Max… and I won't eat you. Not enough *guga*, not enough meat, by crikey.'

I gave him a quick nod and turned to retrieve my backpack from the shade.

He reached for the backpack, the rolled-up sleeping bag strapped beneath it. 'This feels light,' he said as he laid it across the seat behind him. 'Feels like half a roll of toilet paper and a *Teach Yourself Swahili*, at a guess. You keeping your *marnda* clean and making sure you can communicate with us Aboriginals in darkest Australia?'

'*Marnda?*'

'Your backside. Your *matha*. Your *u'ru*.'

'That's a lot of words for it.'

'Maybe because the *wajbala* think us lazy blackfellas spend too much time sitting on it. What other books have you got in here? A *Lonely Planet* so you know when you're lost?'

'As far as I know, they haven't written one for the boondocks of Guinea yet,' I said, adding so quietly I could see he barely heard me, 'or one telling you how to escape from Sierra Leone when you're desperate.'

He leaned forward and pulled out a black helmet from the pannier. On the front was a green capital letter 'R' in a worn plastic transfer, bubbling like shed skin. He turned the helmet over and folded back the lining to show me a set of wires and felt-covered earphones taped to the shell.

'It's a radio intercom. We can talk while we're travelling or we can listen to the radio when we're within range, but not for a while. The next station's in Karratha, hours away.'

The helmet didn't fit. I fumbled self-consciously with the straps before he made the necessary adjustments.

'You ever ridden pillion before?' he asked.

'Once or twice, a long time ago.'

'Then you'll know there's nothing to it. Was it on a Harley?'

'No, it was my brother's Honda.'

'I can promise you a better ride.' He patted the seat behind him. 'Slower maybe, but a lot more comfortable. You can park your *marnda* here.'

The scarlet petrol tank gleamed where his knees had cleared patches in the rime of dust. I heard the sharp crack of expanding chrome and metal and smelled hot oil as I climbed aboard, awkwardly long-legged. He reached down to my ankle and guided my right foot to the footrest. The uninvited pressure of his fingers on my flesh, the casual presumption of it, unnerved me.

'Remember, you've got to trust me. Lean with me when we take the corners, even if you think I'm cutting you off at the knees and we're about to go *marnda* over *bibi*. We've got a couple of hairpins up ahead, otherwise the highway's almost all dead straight.'

He spread both arms out, miming a balancing act. 'Don't fight the bike upright on the curves, if you get my drift. Like I said, lean into them and leave the rest to me.'

The bike whined back to life at the turn of the key.

'*Nyinda ngugurnu? Ngali yananganhawe.* You ready? Here we go.'

Straddling the bike, he walked the bitumen for several strides before settling into the seat and accelerating, the stationary roadside scrub slowly moving past, before blurring as we gathered speed.

He looked back over his shoulder. 'Okay, we're off. You comfortable?'

His crackling words were drowned in the engine's roar as he changed gears.

I was confused by the sudden heat of the exhaust on the inside of my right calf and the unfamiliar sensation of high speed; things over which I had no control. I was unaccustomed to this awkward dependency, but I was caught in the moment and knew I must resign myself to it. I redoubled my grip on the seat, wedging the backpack against the riser as I imagined falling—the horror, the tearing agony, the bike spearing end on end across the bitumen and red gravel. *Why did I join him? Why didn't I consider the risks more deeply? Just because this is my first chance in hours to resume the journey?*

As we rode on, I gradually relaxed. *It's too late to change my mind.* I was unexpectedly exhilarated at the rush of the slipstream and the hypnotic flash of white lines beneath the wheels... until Lennard began swooping and zigzagging between them without warning.

'This'll get you used to the feel of the bike,' his voice echoed scratchily across the intercom, distorted by the swerving bike's juddering vibrations.

I clutched at the seat beneath me, my fingers numbing as I followed his instructions, leaning with him to the left and right, torn between cooperating and asking him to stop. The steady hammering of the engine softened to a purr, giving me the impression I was going deaf. The wind brought tears to my eyes and they coursed down my cheeks. Some of them, I knew, were from the deep well of my grief.

Over his shoulder, I watched the lines in the road rushing towards us—black, white, black, white—my body tensing with each change in direction as he weaved between them. And then, for the first time in a month, a familiar tearing sensation stabbed me deep within my abdomen, forcing out a grunt of pain. I was distraught. *Not again. Not now. Not now, for God's sake!*

'How's it going back there? You feel like you're riding in an armchair?' he asked. 'There's no better place for your first ride on a Harley than up the Great Northern Highway.'

I could barely decipher his muffled words.

'Do we *have* to?' I asked, unable to control the tension in my voice.

He slowed, threw me a quick glance, levelled up the bike and then accelerated smoothly down the left lane. 'Better?'

'Thank you.'

The next moment he barked a sudden warning as he braked and swerved around a kangaroo bounding across the bitumen from the roadside scrub on the right. It twisted violently in midair to avoid the collision, narrowly missing the rear tyre. I looked round to see it skid on its haunches before it somersaulted across the bitumen and regained its feet, stunned. Lennard slowed and we watched it leap wildly away down the embankment.

'That was close,' he said as he accelerated again. 'She was almost roadkill. Serves me right for talking too much. We have to look out for them. They're always on the move this late in the afternoon.'

Moments later, he gave a dry laugh ending with a sardonic snort. 'I've got a riddle for you, *malyu*. Want to hear it?' Before I could reply, 'What's the difference between a kangaroo and an Aboriginal roadkill?'

An Aboriginal roadkill? I had no answer. Taken aback, I was on edge.

'Give up?'

'Yes.'

'The skid marks in front of the kangaroo.'

'What? That's shocking. It's not funny at all. It's cruel.'

'No. It's not funny, but it tells you everything you need to know as a newcomer to Australia about the racism we face in this country. Us blackfellas, we're at the bottom of the pile, the butt of jokes,' he said, before adding forcefully, 'or so they think.'

I was unsure what to say, concerned I might enflame what I sensed was an underlying rage he hadn't displayed before.

'I haven't noticed yet,' I said. 'I haven't been here long enough.'

'Oh, you will. It's culturally ingrained. I've been fighting it all my life. I'm a glass sculptor and it's inspired my sculptures ever since I started working on them way back when. Confirming we've been here for sixty-five thousand years— we've survived colonisation and our culture is more or less alive and well. I'm pushing shit uphill most of the time, but. We deserve respect, not the discrimination and abuse we cop most of the time from the privileged majority who consider us fair game. As if we've just come down out of the trees.'

'That's terrible.'

'You got that right.' He peered briefly round at me. 'Especially now we're contributing to all forms of culture across the country. I might sound like a blowhard, but we're punching well above our weight. Art, dance, film, theatre, music, literature… and *sport*, by crikey. You name it. Our comedians, even. We're breathing life into Australia's contemporary culture and the national identity.'

He slowly shook his head and alarmed me by releasing the handlebars. He raised both hands above his head and waved them, fingers spread in a dramatic gesture of ironic self-mockery. 'Hah! And when we do succeed, when we break the mould, what do we hear? "You're one of the good ones." I kid you not, *malyu*. It's a bloody insult to the rest of us.'

He gave a burst of dry laughter in which I sensed outrage coupled with regret. 'There you go, I've said my piece. That's me, running off at the mouth. Getting it off my chest. Enough with the politics. Time for me to zip it.'

Then he shouted a curt, 'Hang on!' as a gigantic blue and yellow Kenworth road train prime mover roared towards us down the bitumen in the other lane, its trailers swaying wildly from side to side. I ducked as the monster aluminium bull bar hurtled by above my head, the driver blasting us a welcome twice on the horn. The powerful drag associated with each of the three trailers packed with sheep struck us violently as they thundered past, the momentary stench of ammonia, wet hides and diesel fumes so overpowering I turned my face away.

After a long silence, I heard him ask, 'So you've only been here in the west for five months, *malyu*?'

'Yes. I flew in from Conakry in February via Cape Town,' I leaned into the backrest, stretching until the piercing cramp eased to a dull ache I could bear.

'Is this your first visit to Australia?'

'It is.'

'You mentioned Guinea before. What were you doing there?'

'Looking for the source of the Niger River. We were planning to kayak from there to the Atlantic.'

'And Sierra Leone?'

'We crossed the border by mistake.'

'I thought Sierra Leone was a hot spot. Isn't there a civil war?'

'There is. Or the beginnings of one.'

'So how did you get on?'

I shut him down at once. 'I'd rather not talk about it.'

He was silent for several minutes before continuing, 'Sorry. I don't mean to pry. Listen, if you stick with me, I'll take you to the Eighty Mile Beach. It's out of this world. When the moon's right, shoals of queenfish and threadfin salmon come in with the tides in water so shallow they swim on their sides with their fins in the air. They're so thick I swear you could walk across them without getting your feet wet. I have a ball spearing them when I'm up there doing the tribal thing.'

I concentrated so I could catch his words. They were almost unintelligible above the bike's vibrations. I heard him describe a series of crystalline salt flats extending towards a row of low dunes and a rocky foreshore fronting the never-ending beach, beyond which, he assured me, the sea and sky met in what he called 'the seamless weld' of the horizon.

'At certain times of day when the tide's in, it's a blue void. It's all one colour and empty space in every direction. It gives you the illusion of infinity. And freedom. Not to mention sunsets like you've never seen. It inspires me as a glass sculptor.'

'The illusion of infinity. I like that.'

'It's deadly. It gives you the impression you're so important you're at the centre of the universe. At the same time, it's so vast it cuts you down to size. Stick with me and find out for yourself.'

He told me he had a vivid recollection of a moment when he was a teenager and he stood among the shoaling fish, flashing silver as they turned and twisted in the sun. They turned the sea to silver, as if light itself had come alive in a current of quicksilver streaming beneath the water's surface, and as they passed him by, they touched him to the quick.

I could hear the passion in his voice even though it was distorted by the intercom. His descriptions were so striking I was uncertain if I'd heard him correctly or interpreted his words to suit myself and added colour of my own. Straining to understand him, I was unusually alert. *What's coming next?*

'It's deadly how the memory works, don't you reckon?' I heard him take a deep breath, or was it a sigh? 'Those echoes from the past. They overtake you when you least expect them. Like they're haunting you.'

'Hauntings,' I said at once. 'I know what you mean.'

Moments later, he raised his arm and pointed towards a dense coppice of white-trunked eucalypts appearing half a kilometre down the road on the right.

'The Nanutarra roadhouse is coming up. *Ngamarribala*, just across the Ashburton River, the *Bilyabilyanku*. I'm starving. We'll call in for a bite and book a room each for the night. What d'you say? Stretch a leg and take a shower?'

'Sounds like a good idea.'

'Right now, I feel like a steak and eggs burger with chips and salad. They serve up the best in the west right here.'

I let out a long, relieved breath as the bike rattled onto the bridge, the girders echoing.

A cluster of white buildings and a number of parked cars and trucks were sheltered among trees on the far side of the sleek brown river. Its wide, roiling surface eddied around the concrete pylons beneath us as we crossed, transitory whirlpools spinning lazily downstream.

The persistent ache settled within my abdomen like a dark bruise. It would be a relief to stretch my legs and relax.

* * *

I booked a room while Lennard registered for his. When I'd picked up my key, he led me to the line of dongas at the back, pointing out the café on the way.

'Time to settle in and shower before we eat,' he said. 'Meet you in the café when you're done.'

Half an hour later, we bought our meals and he showed me to the nearest wooden table beside the river, its surface stained to a tan sheen by years of dust and sunlight. It stood with others, shaded by smooth-trunked white-flowering Coolabah trees along the riverbank.

He placed a blue plastic bucket on it. Two Coca-Cola cans gleamed within a slurry of melting ice.

He brushed away fallen leaves and the carapaces of tiny

seeds from the bench. 'There you go, *malyu. Nyinda nyiniyan.* Take a seat.'

I leaned across and set down a tray carrying two wrapped steak burgers and paper cups filled with chips. I unfolded the greaseproof paper and placed the burgers on it, rearranging the shredded lettuce spilling from them.

We sat facing the river.

'There's a decent breeze out here, and no *wilyara*, no seagulls ripping you off like they do in Freo,' he said. 'Not many *warrari*, either; just a couple so far. We'd better get this into us before the rest get a sniff of what's on offer.' He waved a hand across the burgers, disturbing two or three persistent bush flies.

'That's a relief.'

'We've got half an hour before the sun goes down and the mozzies come out in droves.' He removed his sunglasses and pointed with them at the brown reflective water, before reaching for a burger. 'The *Bilyabilyanku*, she's in full flood by the looks. We can watch it flowing down to Onslow while we eat… and wait for the next paddle-steamer that won't arrive.' He turned to face me. 'Now I've got the sunnies off, take a gander at the *guru*. At the eyes.'

I gazed at him, wondering at the uneasiness he'd stirred in me at first. *Has he touched the suppressed memory of an imminent threat in a forgotten face similar to his? A fearful moment when I was a child? Or is it the nightmare in Sierra Leone I can't bear to think about?*

Then I noticed his irises. The left was dark brown, the right a startling electric blue, lit from beneath, it seemed, by a flare of sapphire light. I thought at once of ice and intellect, its liveliness complementing the gentler brown of the other as he smiled.

'You ever seen the likes? One brown eye, one blue?'

'They are striking. Who did you inherit them from?'

'Long story, but I'll give you the short version. A Dutch cargo ship—the *Zuytdorp*—was caught in a storm on the way from Middelburg to Batavia in 1712. It was wrecked on the cliffs north of Kalbarri, on the border of Malgana country. There were survivors. We believe they integrated with one of the local clans,' he gave a burst of laughter, snapped a finger. 'Assimilation in reverse—and here I am. Your brindle rabbit drawn from Nature's magic hat. How's that for a throw of the dice? I reckon I've got long-lost relatives in the Netherlands who have no idea I exist. Yet.'

'Yet?'

'They will when I get round to writing my biography. I've done a lot of research chasing down my ancestry. Years of it. Here and in the archives in Zeeland in the Netherlands. As well as Cape Town. I've got files full of notes, charts and photographs. I've narrowed it down to one likely candidate, the senior carpenter aboard—Gerrit de Waal. All I have to do is prove it.'

'You've got a name for him and you know his eyes were blue?' I gave him a sceptical smile. 'Pull the other one, why don't you?'

'At last. *Nyinda mandarriniya*, it's good to see you smile. I figured you might be *gooninye*, unhappy for some reason. Broken.'

I thought of Alain running towards me across the sand on Zurriola Beach and felt my heart lurch. 'I've had my ups and downs,' I said. 'Mostly downs lately.'

'I thought it might be me.'

For the first time, I laughed aloud. 'With a face like yours? I don't usually judge a book by the cover, but I admit I was uneasy at first. Now you've showered, though…'

'Hah! I'll take that as a backhanded compliment. Might even cancel my next appointment for the facelift.'

'So tell me, why do you think Gerrit what's-his-name is your man?'

'Like I said, there were survivors. My mother found some relics on the cliffs in an old tobacco tin. It had his name etched on the lid.'

I stared at the water as I listened, distracted by iridescent blue dragonflies veering across the surface on transparent wings, alighting on their reflections and leaving circled imprints on the water as if a gentle rain was falling. Beyond the trees the sky was on fire, the sun sinking into distant purple hills.

I glanced back at him when he said, 'She gave me this when I turned eighteen. She found it in the tin. I've worn it ever since.'

He withdrew a black leather thong strung around his neck. He lifted it over his head. There was an oval abalone shell pendant dangling from it. He laid it face up on the tabletop between us, rotating it so that I could examine what seemed to be an albatross carved in cameo within it. The fading light glinted on the whorls of greens and blues. I looked enquiringly at him, and when he nodded, picked up the shell and held it at an angle, highlighting the outstretched wings and the elongated head and beak. I found the carving primitive, precise and mysterious.

'It's beautiful. It looks like a sailor's scrimshaw. Is it an albatross?'

'By the looks, yes. A *banduga*. It brings me closer to Gerrit, somehow. Puts us in touch. When I tracked him down in the Middelburg archives and got to know him, I sussed out two things about him I like to think I've inherited—he was a master craftsman and a survivor. So I've adopted him.'

'And the colour of his eyes?'

'My bet says they were blue.'

'So you're a gambling man.'

He gave me a long, thoughtful look, before breaking into a meaningful smile. 'I know a sure bet when I sense one. Not often I'm wrong.'

'Oh, yes? Me, I prefer to make sure the odds are stacked in my favour.' I placed the pendant on the table between us. '*Banduga*, I like the sound. I'll record it. It'll be the third Aboriginal word in my vocabulary.'

'The third?'

'I already know *akubra* for a hat and *kaarak* for the red-tailed black cockatoo. I learned them when I was eight. Back in Mexico City.'

'How so?'

'My brother taught me. He had an Australian friend.'

'I didn't pick you for a Mexican at first. It came as a surprise. A pleasant one, I have to say. I thought you were American when you spoke.'

'I'm a Mestiza Mexican—part-Spanish, part-Tarahumaran Indian. They were my first and second languages.'

'Interesting, *malyu*. Us blackfellas, we're going gangbusters recalling and preserving all our languages and dialects. Across the country. Something like two hundred and fifty of them, would you believe? If not more.'

'I know. That's why I'm hoping to head for Yirrkala.'

'Like I told you, my language is Malgana and we're resurrecting it. Giving it mouth to mouth, you might say.' He pulled a can from the bucket, tore off the ring pull and handed the can to me with a sudden blazing smile. 'Hey! Come to think of it, if the mango-picking doesn't work out you can always come back to Geraldton and lend us a hand. You with your PhD.'

I looked out over the river, its surface tugging at the trailing leaves of an overhanging branch, the stippled water agitating white and green reflections. 'I thought the three old aunties you mentioned had it under control,' I said.

'Always room for one more. Every little helps. Just saying.' He rotated the ring pull on his finger with his thumb. 'Besides, like I told you, one of the old aunties is dying. The big C. We have to act fast.'

'Oh, I'm sorry.'

He gave me a sideways nod, carefully lifted his forearm, held it steady and slapped at a mosquito, flicking away the red smudge of its black corpse before reaching for a can for himself.

A car approached, towing a large, dark blue twin-hulled Shark Cat fishing boat, *Police Rescue* printed in large white letters along the hull. It rattled over the bridge before pulling into the parking area behind us. Doors slammed and the excited chatter of children carried, their voices fading as they disappeared into the roadhouse.

A moment later, two blond children, a boy and a girl who looked to be twins about ten years old, sprinted from the roadhouse down the embankment to the river's edge. Our presence silenced them and the girl disappeared back up the path. The boy sorted through the pebbles at his feet, found one that suited him and skimmed it self-consciously out into the river. Dragonflies darted in alarm as the stone flicked the surface several times and sank. The nearest paired ripples spread and joined in an unexpected, expanding figure of eight.

Lennard pointed out the pattern. 'The illusion of infinity,' he said.

'Very fleeting,' I said, as the rings converged and collapsed into random turbulence.

The image stirred the memory of one of my favourite poems and I quietly quoted, '"Exultation is the going of an inland soul to sea, past the houses—past the headlands—into deep Eternity—bred as we among the mountains, can the sailor understand the divine intoxication of the first league out from land?"' I took a sip of Coca-Cola. 'Emily Dickinson. I love the way she links the abstract words intoxication and exultation with eternity in the context of a first step taken on life's journey.'

He raised one sceptical eyebrow and looked sideways at me. 'That's deep. Bit too deep for a simple blackfella like me. It's deadly, but.'

He picked up the shell and replaced it around his neck as I gave the boy both thumbs up. He returned a diffident grin before stooping to select a second stone.

Lennard slapped at the back of his hand again. 'Mozzies have arrived, *malyu*. Time to duck for cover. Why don't we head for the café? Or better still, your donga or mine—they've both got chairs and coffee-making facilities. We can yarn until lights out. Tell each other our life stories.'

'You want to hear my life story?' I was suddenly concerned. He may have seen the reports on TV or in the newspapers after all.

'I do. I want to know how you ended up on the side of the road in God's own country the same day I'm on my way to the Kimberley. You, of all people. A Mexican girl and a linguist, who already knows three Aboriginal words. Just the person us Malgana are looking for, by crikey!' He gave out a breathy laugh. 'There's nothing more mysterious than a meaningful chance encounter.'

As we walked up towards the dongas, I was confused.

He wants to know how I've ended up with him here in Australia. There's no way I can tell him about Alain, is there? The memories are far too raw. I won't be able to talk about him without breaking down. What, then? Everything else, when I was a girl or university student? Hardly. What would be the point?

I turned to face him at the door to my cabin. 'Be honest with me, Lennard. How come you haven't recognised me?'

He looked puzzled. 'Why? Should I have?'

'Does the name Alain Leroy ring a bell?'

'Leroy? No. Hang on, yes. Don't they have something to do with training racehorses?'

'Dancing horses. They breed Spanish Andalusians.'

'Oh, okay. So what?'

'Alain was a friend of mine. We were in the national news five months ago. In late February.'

'I was in the States from New Year until April this year. Exhibiting my glass sculptures and lecturing in Seattle. I just got back—in May,' he said. 'So I missed the gossip. Not that I ever listen to it. What did you two get up to? Rob a bank?'

I hesitated, frowned and looked at him expectantly for a full minute.

He has no idea what happened to us. Either I tell him about it and relive the memory, or I wish him goodnight and we go our separate ways. If I do tell him and break down, at least he'll be gone tomorrow and I'll never have to face him again. It might do me good to try. Like going to a counselling session. Or to confession and offloading my survivor guilt.

He read my expression. 'So it was that bad?' he said. 'Now I'm all ears.'

'Worse.' I made up my mind as I reached for the door. 'Look, I'm exhausted. The last thing I feel like doing right now is telling anyone my story.'

'I understand. Some other time, perhaps?'

'Some other time.'

'No pressure. I'll be leaving early. Set the donga's radio alarm for five, if you decide to join me, but you may not hear it if the butcherbirds are singing.'

'Butcherbirds?'

'Best songbirds in the world.'

'How rough are the roads where you're going?'

'Rough, some of them. Graded gravel, others. Sand. Cross country in one place. Very little bitumen. It's been a year, so I can't say for sure. There's obviously been rain. It churns things up.'

'In which case I'll have to give it a miss, I'm afraid.'

'Oh, shame. I did notice you seemed to be in pain at one stage this afternoon.'

'Yes, I was.'

'Grumbling appendix?'

'Maybe,' I lied. 'It started a couple of months ago.'

'Okay, then. It's been good meeting you, *malyu*, even if I may never find out what happened at the source of the Niger.' He paused, held out his right hand. 'The offer of work in Geraldton still stands.'

'Thank you, Lennard. I appreciate the offer and the lift. Here, let me show you how we Tarahumara farewell each other.' I took his right hand with my left, bent my fingers and ran my fingertips gently across his palm in a single swift movement, as his did the same to mine. 'It means goodbye this time, until we meet again soon.'

'The sooner the better,' he said. 'Don't forget to listen out for the butcherbirds.'

'I will, and if I'm awake, I'll come out to see you off.'

'Crack of dawn.' He gazed at me for several long moments. 'I may be Lennard, but my friends call me Ace.'

I watched him as he walked away. He raised his right hand and waved me goodnight. 'Sleep well and sweet dreams. Catch you when I catch you.'

'Same to you, Ace. I'll make sure I come and see you off.'

* * *

I woke while it was still dark, the whine of Lennard's

motorbike starting up next door dragging me from sleep. I dressed in a rush, the scrunching of blue metal and purring motor carrying to me as he rode away towards the petrol bowsers.

I burst open the door and dashed barefoot down the path carrying the Leica, hoping to catch him filling up. When I reached the apron at the front of the roadhouse, I was too late. The arc of his headlight was slicing into the darkness on the main road. He turned right and accelerated northwards as I sprinted towards him, shouting, hoping to flag him down.

He filled up yesterday evening when we arrived, I recalled as I came to a halt, the red taillight disappearing down the road. I watched the headlight beam rise skywards up the long slope before dipping over the crest and disappearing, the rear light flicking out and darkness descending.

I stood on the bitumen for several further minutes until the thumping of the motor faded, surprised at the extent of my disappointment and the change in my mood. I shook my head and gave a violent outbreath. *Why do I care so much? It's too late now. Put it down to experience. Al mal tiempo, buena cara*, when things go wrong, look on the bright side.

I glanced at the roadhouse and saw through the plate glass front window a waitress in blue and white serving breakfast to two early customers in the otherwise empty neon-lit restaurant. I focussed the camera and took the shot from three separate angles. *Nighthawks*, I thought, as I took them. *I've captured Edward Hopper's image of existential loneliness, this time in the Australian outback.*

Lennard's disappearance had left me feeling abandoned. I was unsure why. And then, somewhere in the darkness above me, a solitary unseen bird broke into bursts of song, the exquisite sweep of notes so complex, so flute-like and enthralling, it held me entranced. Others in the nearby trees and the air responded, their haunting chorus echoing the tuneful calls. The butcherbirds! I was transfixed, and my heart cracked open. The stark, unwelcome image of the pajarero's songbirds came to mind—the five slate-coloured solitaire thrushes trapped in the cone of the helicopter's searchlight at Tlatelolco during the massacre, and a rush of grief overwhelmed me.

I sprinted for the sanctuary of my cabin. I settled into a chair with my head between my hands for several minutes, weeping, before consciously relaxing my core and breathing deeply, pulling myself together by immersing myself in the moment. I'd taught myself to do so since my pre-teens, learning to fend for myself a lot earlier than the girls around me still reliant on the comfort derived from their relationships with their protective mothers... although the technique hadn't really helped me in Foroconia.

Over the years I believed I had developed the resilience and strength of will enabling me to cope with the loss of Mamá. I thought I'd achieved something resembling closure, and discovered meaning in my independence and the shaping of my life. But Alain and my achingly beloved María? I knew losing them was of a different order. I gave myself over to my grief again, let out a long, hoarse wail of frustration and anger as if purging myself of such dark emotions, and reached for my backpack on the coffee table.

I withdrew Alain's two green hardcover diaries bound together with a rubber band from an outside pocket. I separated them. The first had 1989 embossed in gold on the leather cover, the other 1990. I walked across to the bed, propped up the pillow, stretched out and opened the first at the bookmark.

I stared down at Alain's neat, dark blue handwriting with its right-handed lean and strong downward strokes. I ran the

fingertips of my right hand across the page in a gesture of
recognition and began to read it once again.

*Sunday, 26 November—Zurriola Beach. Ben is
devastated. The last thing he expected was a call from
home at one am this morning with the unfortunate
news. He's got a week to make it back to Albany for
his father's funeral. Vale Edward. Killed in a car
accident. It's a big ask and it's going to be tight. All
that paperwork and organising flight schedules.
Now, then. Looks as if we may have found our
replacement—Alicia Serrano. She turned up at the
beach after all, which is a lookup for the books. In the
rain. And she was game enough to join us in the surf
in Ben's kayak; an even better sign, even though her
white-water experience is limited to the Chatooga
and Kanawha Rivers, she tells us. She surprised us.
She managed the surf without any dramas and only
missed one of her practice rolls in the rip. Swam like
a fish in the recovery and caught up with the kayak
before it was well out into the bay. Being the athlete
she tells us she is, serves her well.
Her assignment at the University of the Basque
Country ends in a fortnight so she'll be free as a
bird. No boyfriend. No ties. Family in Mexico. A
convenient coincidence. She has accepted our offer. Not
that she jumped at it. Took her two days. She was busy
translating for Ben and using her contacts to organise
his flights home via Madrid and Singapore.
She has an appealing way about her, even if a bit on
the shy side so far. Tony approves, but you know him.
Has anyone ever heard him disapprove of a woman?
So we welcomed Alicia to the team. Yesterday a
waitress in the Café de la Concha, tomorrow a*

*member of the Aussie assault on the Niger from the
source to the sea! Got to beat everyone else to the punch.
We'll be the first. The pathfinders.*

I turned the diary sideways to read a note scribbled in
pencil along the left-hand margin.

*Just an afterthought—we'll have to make sure taking
on a woman doesn't have a negative effect on team
morale and mateship.*

I put the diary face down at the page and walked across to
make a coffee.

Bit on the shy side so far? An upwelling of sadness tempered
with pleasure radiated through me. *That didn't last long, did it?
Your next entry three days later said I'd come out of my shell, that
I had an answer for everything and was slotting into the team like
a foot in a shoe that's a perfect fit. If anyone was on the shy side,
it was you, Alain. It took me until Algeciras to turn you around.
Remember? I do and I'll never forget it. And as for team morale
and your Aussie mateship, don't get me started.*

* * *

I took the coffee, the packet of Anzac biscuits that came with
the coffee-making facilities and the 1989 diary out to the
table beside the river in the half-light.

I was surprised to hear two children chanting between
bursts of laughter. *The butcherbirds must have woken them early
and they've come out to investigate.*

When I turned the corner of the cabin, I saw them
engrossed in a game of elastics. Legs apart, the boy was
straddling one end of a broad elastic band around the
back of his knees, the other end anchored around the legs
of one of the benches, the lengths between them taut. The
girl, with her back to me, leapt across it, her feet landing in

a complicated sequence of steps in and out of the band as she danced to the rhythm of her breathless chanting, over and over, 'Queensland, Queensland, New South Wales. Inside, outside, puppy dog's tails.'

The girl took no notice of the boy's warning whisper as I approached. He gave an embarrassed grin and nodded as I settled on the bench.

The girl redoubled her efforts, her feet thumping as she sped up the rhythm and altered the chant, the elastic band riding a little higher up the boy's thighs. 'Harbour Bridge is falling down, falling down, falling down. Harbour Bridge is falling down, my fair lady.'

At last, she slammed her feet down on the band, triumphantly pinning both lengths of elastic to the grass, before she bent to gather her breath and looked around at me, arms crossed, her face flushing, as much from exhaustion as shyness.

'Hi,' I said. 'That was excellent. You're an expert.'

'Thank you. I'm not that good.' She stood with her hands on her hips, panting.

'Oh, I think you are. I used to play elastics when I was your age in Mexico and I wasn't nearly as good.'

'Are you from Mexico?' the boy asked, stepping out of the band and approaching his sister. 'You sound American.'

I gave them a wide smile '*Quieres que demuestre que soy mexicano? Eso es fácil. Este soy yo hablando español como lo hacemos en Chihuahua.*' I spoke as rapidly as I could, exaggerating the accentuation. 'Are you happy with that?'

Both children laughed. 'You made it up,' the boy said. 'You were just yabbering.'

'Yabbering? I haven't heard that one before. Is it Aussie slang? If it is, you're proving you're an Australian. I was talking in Spanish, as we do in Chihuahua, proving I'm from Mexico.'

'What did you say?' the girl asked.

'I said, "You want me to prove I'm Mexican? That's easy. This is me talking Spanish like we do in Chihuahua."'

'I liked the sound of it,' she said. 'Can you say it again?'

'*Quieres que demuestre que soy mexicano? Eso es fácil. Este soy yo hablando español como lo hacemos en Chihuahua,*' I repeated, slower this time.

'How do you say hello and good morning?' the boy asked, sitting at the table opposite me. His sister joined him.

'*Hola, y buenos días.* "*Hola*" is hello, "*Buenos días*" is good morning.'

'*Hola,*' the boy said. '*Hola.*'

'*Buenos días,*' the girl echoed.

'*Hola,* you two,' I replied. 'I'm Alicia. What are your names?'

'I'm Sean. She's Siobhan, but we call her Shiv.'

'We're twins,' Siobhan said. 'The O'Brien twins.'

'I can see that. You've both got the same green eyes. The same blond hair. And the same noses.'

'His is longer. We measured them once.'

'Is not.'

'Is. By three millimetres, remember? Where are you going?'

'To Darwin. I'm hitch-hiking.'

'We're going to Broome,' Siobhan said. 'I can't wait to get home and see my friends.'

'Me too. It's so boring on a long drive with nothing to do,' Sean said.

'Except play Uno and Snap.'

'And get car sick like you do, looking at the cards.'

'I can't help it.'

'Yuck. Up comes breakfast, lunch and dinner.'

'It's not that bad.'

'It is for us,' Sean said, momentarily pinching shut his nose.

'If it's any consolation, Shiv, I used to get car sick too, when I was your age,' I broke in. 'Which of you is the oldest?'

'Him, by seven minutes. So he thinks he's the boss.'

'I am the boss.'

'Says you.'

I gave a burst of laughter, memories of the banter Andrés and I exchanged running across my mind. 'You remind me of me and my brother Andrés,' I said, 'but he's ten years older than me. So in a way, he *is* the boss, but I always give as good as I get whenever we disagree, if not better.'

'I do the same,' Siobhan said. 'Did you ever play elastics with your brother?'

'No, with other girls at school. He wasn't interested. He thought he was too grown up for it. He was more of a runner.'

'I'm a runner too,' Sean said. 'In Little Athletics. But I don't mind playing elastics when Shiv hasn't got a partner.'

'It takes three to play it properly,' Siobhan said. 'Would you like to have a go, Alicia?'

'Not right now.' For a sudden despairing moment I was struck by how cruelly indifferent life could be, the thought racing across my mind, *This could have been me and María enjoying each other's company had she existed... perhaps even playing a game of elastics.*

'Later, perhaps. My coffee's getting cold.'

'Later? After we've had breakfast? Will you still be here?'

A slender blond-haired woman in a red dress appeared at the corner of the cabins and called out to the children.

'*Hola*, Mum,' Sean shouted back. 'We're coming.'

I stood to help him lift the bench and release the elastic band.

'Will you still be here?' Siobhan asked as she rolled up the band.

'Possibly.'

'I hope you are. How do you say goodbye?'

'*Adiós.*'

'Oh, I know that one. *Adiós*, Alicia. I'll look for you later.'

'*Adiós*, Shiv. *Te veré luego*, I'll see you,' I replied.

'*Te veré luego*,' Siobhan called out, her broad Australian lilt evident, as she chased after Sean across the grass and onto the gravelled path.

* * *

I sipped my coffee. I opened the diary to a later date and began to read the entry once again, my right elbow on the table, my forehead leaning on my splayed fingers.

> *Wednesday, 29 November, Bilbao airport. Went to*
> *see Ben off on an Iberia flight to Madrid. Same-day*
> *connection Malaysia Airlines to Singapore and Perth.*
> *Virgin Oz to Albany where his sister Helen will pick*
> *him up. He'll make it home with three days to spare.*
> *Passport, paperwork and packing all in order—*
> *gracias, Alicia. She has worked wonders for him,*
> *especially with him in such a bad way. She has a great*
> *sense of empathy to which he responded, which was*
> *good to see. She has that quality in spades, by the looks.*
> *Talking of looks, there is something about her. Call*
> *it charisma plus self-deprecating charm and that*
> *unmistakable Mexican Indian face you'd see on the*
> *cover of* National Geographic. *Remember that*
> *famous Afghan girl? Change her eyes from startling*
> *green to amber, remove the fear, enlarge the cheekbones*
> *and you're looking at Alicia.*
> *It hasn't taken her long to come out of her shell. She*
> *seems to have an answer for most things, which will*
> *be interesting down the track when things get hairy.*
> *She mentioned that Mexican women were expected*

to be the retiring type, their place in the kitchen, barefoot with a broken leg, under the thumbs of their patriarchal macho men who rule the roost. Obviously not with our Alicia. Not so far. In only three days, she's slotting into the team like a foot in a shoe that's a perfect fit. We shall see.

She's already working on the Mandingo language spoken in Guinea, checking on the Malinké dialect used in the Fouta Djallon Mountains where we'll find the source of the Niger. It's in her line of study, so hopefully, we have our interpreter. She says she thinks of herself as La Malinche, the woman I've never heard of who translated for Hernan Cortes and his conquistadors way back when. Must look her up. She's Alicia's heroine, apparently.

All okay with the ship from Algeciras to Conakry on Sunday, 7 January, arriving Guinea 22–23 January. Should be in Faranah on 24 January at the latest. Rio Tinto chopper ok'd Friday 26. T-Day! Tembakounda Springs, here we come—the source of the Niger! I have my thermos ready to fill with your spring water we'll carry to the delta and pour into the Atlantic. What a moment that will be. Our goal achieved! Can't wait.

I looked across at the Ashburton, the brown water in full flow swirling past, and the thought crossed my mind for no logical reason, *You never step in the same river twice. Just the once. Just the first time...* e ir con la corriente, *and you go with the flow.*

Slowly shaking my head, I dunked another biscuit, took a bite.

Our goal achieved? Aunque más no sea. *If only.*

* * *

An hour later, Siobhan reappeared, holding her mother's hand.

'Hola, Alicia,' she said. 'This is my mum.'

The blond woman in red was petite, her attractive features delicate and her skin pale and lightly freckled. She was carrying two takeaway cups of coffee, Siobhan a handful of sugar sachets and a wooden spatula.

'Hi, I'm Fiona,' she said. 'Do you mind if we join you? We've got half an hour before we take off. Shiv was concerned your coffee was getting cold. She thought you could do with a fresh cup.' She placed the cups on the table.

'I didn't know if you take sugar or not,' Siobhan said, spilling the sachets and spatula beside the cups.

'Thank you, Shiv. That was thoughtful. I take one sugar.' I stood to shake Fiona's hand. She was several centimetres shorter. 'Hi, I'm Alicia. Please join me.'

We sat facing one another across the table. 'I can see where the twins get the colour of their eyes.'

'All my own work. Conor's are black and tan. Not a speck of green to be seen.' She gave a quick laugh. 'And the twins are both blond, even though his hair and beard are bright ginger in true Irish fashion; a heritage he's proud of, even though he's a dinky-di Australian.'

'Dinky-di?'

'Genuine, through and through. True blue.'

Siobhan giggled. 'Yes, that's right. They even call him "Bluey" at work because of his red hair. Bluey O'Brien. It sort of rhymes.'

'Aussie slang. I've got a lot of catching up to do. You have a very considerate young girl here, and an expert at elastics.' I reached out and held Siobhan's forearm as she blushed. '*Nunca dejes que un cumplido bien intencionado te avergüence.* Can you guess what it means?'

'I don't know.'

'Never let a well-meant compliment embarrass you.'

'We're proud of her, but she hates the limelight, especially when she's being talked about and she's sitting right there, listening. It makes her squirm.'

'I know how you feel, Shiv, but it's another way of saying how much I like you.'

'I like you too.'

'Now we've got that out of the way,' Fiona said, 'I have to be honest, Alicia. I have an ulterior motive for wanting to meet you. I don't mean to pry, but is your surname Serrano by any chance?'

I stared at her, before slowly nodding. *It had to catch up with me sometime.* 'Serrano it is. Now you're going to tell me you've heard it before?'

'Not me, so much. Conor. He's in the police. When the twins told us you were Mexican and your name was Alicia, he put two and two together. I hope you don't mind. I'm so sorry.'

My heart sank. I found the thought of bringing up what happened once again depressing. 'He's given you the details? Conor?'

'Some of what happened, yes. The Leroy family are well known in the state. All those dancing horses. They're in the public eye. What happened to you and Alain was tragic and it was big news at the time.'

I nodded and looked away across the glinting river. I didn't need reminding. Sick at the thought of talking about something I'd rather forget, I didn't wish to seem rude. I steeled myself and looked back at her, 'I know. I stayed with his parents on their horse stud in Millendon until last week. It was time to move on before I outstayed my welcome.' I offered the biscuits around and reached for one for myself but changed my mind. The two I'd already eaten would do for breakfast.

'How far north are you going?'

'To Darwin to begin with. I was thinking of picking mangoes until I get settled, but I've been told it's too early in the season.'

'Shiv tells me you're hitch-hiking.'

'I am, actually, for the distraction. I wanted to test myself, after all the water that's gone under the bridge. To make sure I'm ready to face the world again.'

'So you don't have a lift?'

'Not yet.'

She placed a hand over mine. 'Well, you do now, or at least the offer of one, if you'd care to join us. We're going as far as Broome. We should be home by eight tonight. We're towing the new rescue boat, so we'll be taking things easy.' She gave a quick laugh. 'There's room in the back with Sean and Shiv if you can stand their company.'

The idea appealed to me at once. I found the liveliness and curiosity of the twins appealing, a breath of fresh air, but wondered how they'd feel about having an adult with them in the back. 'You're very kind, but I'll need the okay from the twins. What do you say, Shiv?'

Her face lit up as she beamed. 'Oh yes, please! I'd love it.'

'Do you think Sean would mind?'

'I'm sure he'll agree. He's sick of playing Uno and Snap and Happy Families with me.' Her grin widened. 'You could teach us more Spanish. Hola! Adiós!'

'Anything for a change,' Fiona said, 'and it might help you with your car sickness, Shiv.' She raised her eyebrows as though a sudden thought had crossed her mind. 'We've got a spare bedroom if you need one for tonight, Alicia. Or even a couple of extra days, if you'd like to break your journey in Broome? Conor will be taking the boat out on trials for a marine survey the day after tomorrow. We'll be joining him. It'll be quite an adventure, and two days' break might be just what the doctor ordered for you.'

I gave a burst of laughter. 'Not another convenient coincidence! There have been so many since I left Mexico I've lost count. Of course I'll join you for the ride. It'll be a pleasure. I'll think about the extra days on the way.' I turned to Siobhan. 'So what Sean said about you feeling sick when you're looking down at the cards was true?'

'Yes.'

'I might have an old Basque fisherman's remedy for that. I'll need your sunglasses, if you have a pair, so I can adjust the handles. Or a pair of pointy matchsticks.'

'Matchsticks? What for?'

'To apply equal pressure behind your ears and stop your inner ear balancing system from sending confusing messages to your brain.'

'Does it work?'

'It does for me. Like I told you, I used to get car sick all the time when I was your age. Not anymore. You never know till you try.'

In Broome, Western Australia, June 1990

I STRETCHED OUT ON the bed in the spare bedroom in Broome that night, restlessly facing the window, curtains drawn and moonlight seeping through them. I was exhausted, so worn out and overtired I was unable to sleep.

I'd spent the evening after dinner with Fiona and Conor on the balcony of their house overlooking Town Beach, the twins asleep at last. We'd watched a full moon rising from the horizon like a gigantic blood orange, casting reflections across the blue-black satin of Roebuck Bay, laying down a shimmering stairway across the ocean.

The journey from Nanutarra had taken twelve hours, as Fiona had predicted. The twins had pestered and cajoled me into teaching them the Spanish words for a wide range of everyday objects—body parts, animals, the landscape we were passing through, the colours of passing cars and the numbers on their registration plates.

They'd also asked me to translate the first two chorus lines of their favourite songs played incessantly on Conor's tape recorder—'Eagle Rock' by Daddy Cool and Men at Work's 'Down Under'. After more or less learning the words, they'd hilariously sung along to the tapes in what sounded like childish gibberish. Fiona and Conor had occasionally joined in.

Siobhan had not been car sick, for which I claimed the credit with the tightened handles of my borrowed sunglasses she'd worn, but Fiona was convinced the two Dramamine tablets she'd bought in Nanutarra had done the trick.

I relaxed, slowed my breathing. Tried to empty my mind. As I did so, my thoughts veered back to my earlier conversation with Fiona and Conor, when I'd replied to his questions concerning Alain, the expedition to the Niger and his murder. Unsure of Conor, I'd been reluctant to respond at first, even though he assured me he didn't want to seem intrusive. He was interested from a forensic and policing perspective, he'd insisted.

I was defensive and resentful at first, unwilling to revisit the traumatic climax of that time in my life as if I were facing another unwelcome interrogation. But as my story had progressed and I'd found myself relaxing and opening up, I discovered to my surprise and eventual relief that talking through what had happened, as if talking to myself, became easier and the memories sharper. *Easier?* I never thought I'd use that word to describe discussing what had happened.

'I once thought I'd have the strength and tenacity to cope with anything I had to face,' I told them as I stood to leave. 'It shocked me to discover that wasn't the case when I reacted the way I did to Ibrahim's story. How easily I broke down and panicked. How deeply I felt the loss of Alain. How long it took me to pull myself together.'

'No, it's understandable,' Fiona said, standing and laying a hand on my arm. 'It's very clear to me. It's called love, even if you haven't used the word in all you've told us. I would have done exactly the same.' She gave me a hug. 'Thank you for telling us everything. I know it hasn't been easy. You are truly, truly remarkable.'

I was uncertain how to acknowledge the compliment she'd paid me. I didn't feel I deserved praise for the way I'd handled the tragedy, though what she said touched a nerve... perhaps I'd reacted as any woman would under the circumstances.

It took me another hour before I fell asleep.

* * *

Late evening two days later, Conor slowed the police rescue boat after a day out at sea, where he'd performed some startling manoeuvres for the marine surveyor. The delighted shouts and screams of Sean and Siobhan had been piercing above the whine of the twin outboards accelerating to top speed, turning in circles and figures of eight. The rooster tails of spray behind us were spectacular, a fine mist settling on my exposed and sunlit skin.

As he steered towards the ramp to join the queue of incoming craft, I reached for the binoculars. Without questioning my motives at first, I swept them along the shoreline, examining the faces of people walking their dogs, jogging or cycling past, and others leaning on the jetty bollards, watching the incoming craft being winched back onto their trailers.

Lennard isn't there. I gave myself a mocking smirk as my thoughts raced. *Why am I looking for him? Because he proved such an attentive and considerate listener when we swapped stories? Because I don't have the photograph of him I wanted to take at Nanutarra? Because I need him to give me a deeper understanding of his endangered Malgana language? No, no and no. Then why? To know that he reached Broome safely? To let him know I was grateful for the lift he gave me and I appreciated our conversations? No, I already did so.*

It struck me how impatient I was, how urgently I wanted to continue my journey northwards. I wanted to get away, to resume my journey to Fitzroy Crossing as soon as possible.

I should have accepted his offer of a ride through Karijini, I thought, *in which case we'd be in Bandilngan Gorge by now. I'm treading water, wasting time. Lennard said he'd reach Roebourne the day after visiting Karijini, in which case he'd have travelled up the highway today, while I was out on the bay enjoying the sun, the wind, the sea and the company of the twins.*

When I replaced the binoculars, Siobhan turned my right wrist over. She examined my small, eye-catching tattoo. She looked up admiringly. 'I love it,' she said. 'I'm going to have one just like it when I'm old enough. Who's it for? Who was María?'

'It's for my mother, Shiv,' I lied. 'Mariposa means butterfly and I've shortened it to María.'

Siobhan stroked the butterfly's wings. 'What sort is it?'

'It's a Silver Emperor. You find them all over Mexico. The flowers are marigolds and those butterflies are attracted to their colours and scent.' I laughed. 'They also like rotten fruit, so I used to rub the inside of my wrists with an overripe banana and sit beside the marigolds very patiently when I was little. They used to settle on me and open and close their wings as they tasted the banana. They tickled my skin until I gently blew them off. It was magical. That's why the tattoo is where it is.'

'Oh, I'm going to try that. I recognised the flowers. My grandma grows them in her veggie patch in Kalamunda. They're beautiful. I like the smell and the colours too.'

'That's why we Mexicans put them on people's graves when they die.'

Her eyes widened and she looked horrified. 'On their *graves*? Is your mother dead?'

'Yes, she is. When I was your age, and even now, we put marigolds and sunflowers on her grave every year, and sometimes in between. We use marigolds because we believe the smell will guide her spirit home and sunflowers because they were her favourites.'

'Did she die when you were young?' Sean asked across the table.

'Yes, I was just a month old.'

'Wow. You were just a baby. So who looked after you?'

Fiona placed a hand on his shoulder. 'You're asking very personal questions, Sean. Alicia may not want to talk about it.'

'No, that's fine. I don't mind.' I said, uncertain whether Fiona's warning was an apology for his persistence or a hint that she'd prefer me not to continue. 'Death is death, and in Mexico, we don't mind talking about it.' I turned back to the twins. 'My mother, Suré, died on Mother's Day, would you believe, a month after I was born. And her sister, my Aunty Ariché, looked after me.'

'On *Mother's* Day?' Siobhan asked, her shocked expression deeply sympathetic, her widened eyes shining. 'That's *terrible*.'

'It's what you call an irony, the opposite of what you expect. So we celebrate her life by celebrating her death on that day.'

'It sounds weird,' Sean said, 'two celebrations in one day. I'm glad we don't have to do that.'

The twins were quiet for several moments before Sean reached for a slice of homemade fruit cake Fiona was cutting on a plate on the retracting table. He climbed onto the coaming to walk up to the bow rail. Siobhan did the same, but she turned to me before she left and said through a mouthful, 'I'm still going to have one when I'm older.' She swallowed. 'Like yours, in the same place. That way I'll always remember the word "Mariposa", like you do.' She looked back as she balanced along the coaming. 'I'll always remember you, too, but didn't you just say your mum's name was Suré?'

Thankfully, she didn't wait for my reply.

I looked across at Fiona when the twins had gone.

'I lied,' I said, a rush of shame radiating through me. 'I *hate* lying.' My eyes filled against my will. 'I know it sounds strange, but María is my daughter, Fiona. My imaginary daughter, the one I'll never have now Alain's gone. I call her María, named for Mariposa, the butterfly.' I was barely able to continue. 'I never mentioned it to Alain, but he was the first man I ever dreamed of having a child with. I don't know what he would have thought.' I took a deep breath, feeling torn. 'I got the tattoo in his memory, actually. If we'd had a child, he would have lived on through her. It was one of the first positive moves I made in rebuilding my life. This is the first time I've mentioned María to anyone. I'm not sure how reliving the experience of dreaming about her and thinking of Alain as her father is going to affect me.'

'Not too adversely, I hope,' Fiona replied. She stood and clutched my shoulder as she staggered to regain her balance when Conor drove the boat up onto the trailer.

* * *

The next morning I was combing my wet hair after a shower following a run to Gantheaume Point and back when Sean knocked at my door.

'I was on the trampoline just now when a man asked if you were living here. He knew your name. He was Aboriginal. He told me to give you this,' he said, handing me a note.

I felt a stab of shock. 'What did he look like?'

'I don't know. Old. Tall. He was Aboriginal and all the old ones look the same to me. In thongs and a yellow t-shirt. With a beard. Oh yes, I remember, he was wearing green Ban-Rays, just the same as my dad's, and his t-shirt had the sleeves torn off.'

'You mean Ray-Bans? Is he still there?'

'No. He's gone. He said he was coming back to see you later.'

'Was he on a motorbike?'

'No. He was walking. In thongs, like I said.'

Shock turned to a flood of relief, coupled with uneasiness. *I'll be on my way again at last, but at what cost?*

'Thanks, Sean. That sounds like my friend Lennard.'

'Oh, okay. Shall I keep a lookout for him and let you know when he comes back?'

'That would be great.'

I unfolded the note.

Good day, malyu,

If you're still interested in the ride to Fitzroy Crossing via Bandilngan Gorge, I will be out the front at nine sharp—or thereabouts—you know me; I'm on Aboriginal time. Good to know you made it to Broome in one piece before I did.

See you then,

Godot.

PS, I have some good news for you.

When Lennard arrived on the Harley, he was forty minutes late. He was in his leathers. He'd hosed them down and scrubbed them clean.

He greeted me with a beaming grin as he glanced at his watch. 'Circular time, like I warned you. I see you've caught the sun since I last saw you.'

To conceal the rush of pleasure overtaking me, I turned away and pointed at the trailered boat alongside the house. 'We were out on the water all day yesterday… and part of the day before.'

'That's how I tracked you down. Way back there on the highway, my friend Wally Macarthur at the Sandfire Roadhouse told me he remembered these two blonde kids singing, "I Should Be So Lucky" in some foreign lingo out by the petrol bowsers, and a woman who looked like you was in the car towing the police rescue boat. I put two and two together. All I had to do was find the red-headed bloke driving. No problem. Turns out my cousin-brothers here know "Bluey" O'Brien, and his new boat's been in the news.'

'So I've got Wally Macarthur to blame for you finding me again?'

He gave me a dry chuckle. 'You sure do. Just as well he's a nosy old bugger whose memory's in good nick.' He raised his eyebrows. 'So are you coming with me? Or have you got cold feet?' He gave me his familiar predatory sideways look I recognised, as if I had to answer yes.

I gave a burst of laughter. 'How can I refuse? My backpack's inside. Why don't you come in and meet Conor and Fiona before we take off? Do we have time for a coffee?'

'Sure we do. It's four hours or so to Bandilngan, so we're fine.'

'Before we go in, what's the good news?'

'Ah! Something for you to mull over. I contacted my mum down in Balline last night. When I told her about you, she was over the moon. She said to tell you there's a job going for a linguist at the Yamaji Language Centre in Geraldton. Permanent. Right now, working on a bilingual Nanda dictionary and school syllabus with audible tapes and all the bells and whistles. That's the language spoken just south of us. It's no longer as endangered as Malgana, which they'll be concentrating on next, bringing it back to life, like we talked about. They're both long-term projects.' He looked at me, his expression serious. 'She told me not to let you slip through my fingers or she'll skin me alive, by crikey. And she always keeps her word. Trust me. You can't let that happen.'

I was taken aback. I struggled to hide my confusion as I opened the front door for him. 'I appreciate the offer, Ace. I do. I'll give it some thought between here and Fitzroy Crossing. I'll make my mind up there.'

It's already made up, I thought. *I'm on my way north to Darwin and Yirrkala, testing myself. Without diversions. I need to be sure I'm coping and back in the world of the living before I settle on anything else. I can't compromise.*

He patted my shoulder as he stepped around me. 'You take your time.' I suspected he'd picked up on what I was thinking from my expression when he added, 'You know me. There's no hard feelings either way.'

While enjoying our coffees on the upstairs balcony, Lennard described his trip through the Karijini National Park and beyond, fascinating the twins. The gorges gouged deep into the red sand plains, their vertical walls of red and yellow banded ironstone, dolomite and jasper, with occasional glints of tiger eye and quartz. Some with freezing rivers running through them. The spring-fed *Yarnda Nyirra* Fortescue waterfalls where he swam. The sacred forty-thousand-year-old petroglyphs gouged on the rock walls of Secret Pool. The tiny, darting rainbow-coloured gudgeon fingerlings in *Yurlburr* Python Pool he caught and released in his cupped palms when they swarmed around his legs, nibbling at his flesh.

As he and I rose to leave, he responded to Sean when he asked about the sleeves torn from his yellow t-shirt.

'You're an observant young fella,' he said. 'I'm now a member of the Sandfire Sleazy Sleeveless Shirt Club. When old Wally Macarthur told me he remembered you two twins singing in Spanish with Alicia in the car, I was so pleased I took off my leather jacket and ripped the sleeves off my yellow t-shirt. How's that for a celebration? Both sleeves are now nailed to the ceiling beams at the roadhouse with all the others. Hundreds of them. I hacked the first sleeve off and donated ten dollars to the Flying Doctor, then I ripped off the second one and got an eight-dollar discount off my lunch. I'd call it a bargain, wouldn't you?'

'I've seen all those sleeves,' Sean said excitedly. 'I wondered what they were doing up there.'

'Now you know. See if you can recognise my yellow sleeves among the others next time your dad's filling up there. I bet you can't.'

'I bet I can, and if I've got any pocket money, I'll nail mine up there and give some to the Flying Doctor, too.'

'Over my dead body,' Conor said.

'I love the tame peacocks there, don't you?' Siobhan asked. 'Alicia took some photos of them.'

'I'll send you some prints when I've had them developed, Shiv. I promise,' I said.

'What's the Spanish word for peacock?'

'It's two words actually: *Pavo real.*'

'*Pavo real*… it sounds beautiful.' Siobhan's face lit up. 'I might decide to have a peacock tattoo on my other wrist when I get your photographs.'

'You let me know if you do when the time comes.'

'I will.'

Fiona laughed. 'I'll know who to blame when my daughter comes home with her skin covered in tatts and we can read her like a comic book.'

Later we gathered in the driveway to say goodbye, and after a round of hugs, Siobhan clung to me impetuously, preventing me from mounting the motorbike. She was crying when we disengaged and she ran back into the house. Fiona gave me a wave and followed her in. Deeply moved and filled with a rush of gratitude for the generosity and friendship they'd shown me, I peered around at Sean and Conor, my arm raised until we turned the corner and accelerated away.

* * *

Two hours later, we passed through Derby and headed north for the Gibb River Road intersection, where Lennard wheeled right onto the gravel Leopold Downs Road. He stopped at the turnoff, removed his helmet and looked back at me. 'How are you travelling so far? Your appendix is not giving you curry, is it?'

'I'm fine so far.' I took off my helmet and balanced it on my thighs. I looked doubtfully at the gravel road ahead of us. 'It looks a bit rough from here on, though.'

'It could be, depending on when the graders last came through. I'll take good care of you. Trust me. We'll get there in an hour or so. Let me know if you want me to take things easier on the way.' He nodded. 'We'll pull in to the Lillimooloora ruins before we get there. I want to tell you Jandamarra's story. Long as I don't bore you shitless.'

'If you do, I'll let you know.'

'He's one of our legendary heroes of the Frontier Wars. When you see the quartz rock in the gorge, you'll understand why I want to use it as the model for a glass sculpture—a cenotaph—to commemorate Jandamarra and others like him. The rock's especially significant to the Bunuba people, and to me, so it makes sense to copy it.'

'A cenotaph?'

'Exactly, *malyu*. A memorial in Perth or Fremantle to all our mob who died in the frontier wars. It's overdue. It'll be one of the first in the country.'

I recalled what he'd said the day we met at the Exmouth junction. Now it made sense to me. 'So that's why you're on the pilgrimage you mentioned the other day?'

'Among other things, yes.'

'Other things? You mean Rosalie? You mentioned her as well, I remember.'

'I did. She was my partner. I'll tell you about her when we reach the gorge.'

'Okay. I'll hang on tight.'

I adjusted the helmet and surprised myself by leaning forward without hesitation and gripping his waist again. Doing so was safer and left me comforted in a way I hadn't expected.

For the next hour and a half, he manoeuvred the bike across the worst of the corrugated and potholed sections, guided it carefully over the cattle grids and through the sand traps threatening to slide us sideways. I was relieved when we eventually pulled into the ruins of the Lillimooloora Police outpost, close to the turnoff to the gorge.

We dismounted and Lennard showed me around the site.

Once a pair of small buildings, it was now a collection of head-high sandstone ruins with scattered flagstones in the driveway. As he did so, he pointed out the probable locations where Jandamarra, a police tracker, and Bill Richardson, his English friend and fellow policeman had sat, slept, cooked and eaten when they'd spent five extraordinary days there in late October 1894.

'They had a third policeman with them,' he said, 'Coogiair, an Ngadju man from Esperance, who'd been transferred up there from Roebourne. His nickname was "Captain" and Jandamarra was known as "Pigeon". They had rounded up and arrested seventeen of Jandamarra's fellow Bunuba tribesmen for spearing sheep. They had them chained at the neck and the ankle around a tree. They were on their way to Derby when Richardson came down with a fever. He was asleep in the bedroom recovering.'

We sat in the shade of a silver cadgebut tree beside the ruins, leaning against the trunk, drinking water from a shared bottle Lennard had bought in Derby.

'This tree here,' Lennard patted its trunk, 'could be the original tree around which they were chained. Jandamarra's uncle Ellemarra, a senior lawman, he was among them, along with other relatives. His *wadu*, his brother-in-law, Lilamarra, him too. And Byabarra, Wingerarry, Luter, Merrimarra, Muddenbuddin, Tulbarra... and Bundajan, if I remember rightly. As well as eight more whose names I don't know.'

'You've got quite a memory, Ace.'

'Lest we forget, isn't that what they say? We have to remember them for their resistance to the invasion. I've seen dozens of photographs taken in those days of nameless tribesmen in long lines, chained at the neck, walking to Derby or waiting on the docks for shipment south to Rottnest prison. All half-naked. In the blazing sun. Treated like animals. Worse than.'

He gazed at me and slowly shook his head. 'Makes you wonder, *malyu*. I sometimes reckon most whitefellas these days believe it's not lest but *best* we forget.' He took another swallow from the drink bottle and pointed across at a section of the ruins. 'Right there, that may have been the bedroom in which Richardson was lying asleep when Jandamarra shot him. Can you imagine it? What a moment. His indecision. His doubt and confusion. He was trapped between two worlds—like many of us blackfellas are today—until he aimed the rifle, held his breath and pulled the trigger.

'He must have been ripped apart—torn between his loyalty and friendship for Richardson and his tribal connections to Ellemarra and the others. I believe they'd convinced him to commit the murder and release them. I can imagine him walking up to the outstretched figure sleeping or half-awake in the bed, the loaded rifle in his hand. I can see him hesitating, measuring his guilt and shame at this act of treachery under white law against his terror at facing his own death by *makurndu* spearing under black law. I reckon his fellow tribesmen would have threatened to spear him in payback at the first opportunity for his betrayal if he didn't do it.'

He peered around deep in thought, as if searching for the words, and then, 'I reckon they'd also promised to forgive him for breaking Bunuba law if he did do it. I can almost hear their voices. He'd previously broken his skin taboo by running away and living with Mayannie, a woman forbidden to him under tribal kinship rules... which is why he'd been exiled from the tribe in the first place and joined the police.'

'What about the other Aboriginal policeman you mentioned?' I asked. 'What was his reaction?'

'Yes, Cooigair, he was up to his neck in it. He had no choice. When he heard the shot, he did the sensible thing.

He went in and emptied his revolver into Richardson's body as well. And so it all began.'

He looked across at me with a wry grimace, his lips compressed. 'I can hear the cheers from the prisoners as Jandamarra emerged through the doorway, can't you? Ellemarra—chest-scarred senior lawman and elder—yelling his approval as Jandamarra unlocked the chains.'

'What happened next? Did they take to the hills?'

'No, no. Even better, by crikey. They laid an ambush. Ten days later, the next cattle herd arrived at the gorge for watering. They were heading for Plum Plain Station. They shot and speared the two white drovers, Billy Gibbs and Frank Burke. They stole their horses and their supply wagon, which was several miles back down the trail. Apart from food, it was loaded with Schneider and Winchester rifles. A shotgun, even. And four revolvers and boxes of ammunition. The records say there were four thousand cartridges and a barrel of gunpowder in there.

'And there was young Freddie Edgar. He was on a horse leading the supply wagon. He raced back to Derby to raise the alarm with police sub-inspector Drewry.

'A week later, they fought their first battle at the mouth of the gorge. It was the start of a three-year guerrilla war. Can you imagine it? Armed Bunuba tribesmen terrorising the European settlers and their herds of sheep and cattle. Keeping them out for that long.'

Lennard stood and pulled me to my feet. 'Jandamarra became a hero to his people. Still is, and some. With a reputation for being a spiritual *jalgangurru*, untouchable and bulletproof.'

'You say the war lasted for three years?' I asked as I put my helmet on.

'It did. It took another Aboriginal trooper to end it. On 1 April 1897, at Tunnel Creek. The police brought in Mungo Mick, a Yindjibarndi tracker from Roebourne, to hunt him down. Mick cornered Jandamarra just down the road in Tunnel Creek and shot him dead.'

'You want to know something really surprising, Ace?' I asked moments later as I mounted up behind him. 'When I was eight years old in 1968, my brother Andrés pointed out Jandamarra's name written into the concrete at the base of Meadmore's sculpture "Janus" in Mexico City. In Mexico City, Ace, of all places. Two continents away. I took a photo of it. And now here you are, telling me you're going to inscribe it onto your glass cenotaph. Such synchronicity. Isn't it strange?'

'It's deadly, *malyu*. You know his full story now,' he gave a quiet laugh, 'like you were always meant to after all this time.'

'Not only that. The "Janus" sculpture is an abstract form symbolising the god of doorways, who could look both ways at once. Into the past and into the future. Isn't that what Jandamarra did? Look into his people's past, the rich history of their ancient culture, and simultaneously foresee the disastrous future steamrolling towards them?'

'Well put, *malyu*. Steamrolling. You could say so, but right now, with the cenotaph, it's a matter of acknowledging the past and drawing on it to work together towards a better future.' He gave another burst of laughter. 'What do you know? Here I go again. Mouthing off. What's the word that describes me?'

'Moralising?'

'Moralising, exactly. Up on my soapbox.'

'There's nothing wrong with moralising when what you're telling is the truth.'

The truth? It seems the essence of Australia's Aboriginal history is gradually revealing itself and I am on the verge of a deeper understanding, I thought.

'Time we hit the road. Let me introduce you to Rosalie and the *Jula Bandilngan Rarrgi*, Jandamarra's Rock itself. Enough with just talking about it.'

We soon glided into the official campsite at the mouth of Windjana Gorge. We dismounted and Lennard stood the bike in the shade of a corrugated iron shed. He removed his sleeping bag and some netting from a pannier and shoved a can of insect repellent into his back pocket.

I slung my backpack and sleeping bag across my shoulder and followed him along the rocky track towards a gap between the one-hundred-metre-tall sandstone cliffs, the setting sun now burnishing their summits a deep red gold. I glimpsed the jade ribbon of the river to my left between the trunks of overarching paperbarks, fruit bats roosting among the upper branches like inverted black velvet bags.

Lennard stepped onto the spit of sand beside the river, disturbing a flock of white corellas. They erupted in a coordinated mass, the undersides of their wings flashing pale yellow and their complaining shrieks deafening until they settled on the opposite riverbank.

Jandamarra's rock stood in the middle of the river just as I'd imagined it when Lennard had described it to me—an imposing two-storey block of gleaming white quartz. It was so eye-catching I understood at once why he'd selected it as the model for the gigantic glass cenotaph he'd told me he intended to make.

'There it is,' he said. 'The cenotaph. I've chosen it not only for its impressive shape and dimensions but also for its cultural significance to the Bunuba people.'

He selected a spot close to the water's edge and laid out his sleeping bag and roll of netting before walking back up to the trees and dragging back a dead branch. He broke it up for firewood and built a mini-pyramid, dry grass inserted as a firelighter at the base.

'It's against the rules,' he said, 'but there's no one here but us and the ranger won't be checking in until tomorrow. So we can make ourselves at home with the sandflies and the mozzies.' He pulled out the can of repellent and stood it on the sand. 'This'll help and the net will do the rest. I'll rig it up later, like I used to for Rosalie and me. You can park your sleeping bag next to mine to share the net,' he sent me a mischievous grin I was beginning to recognise, 'long as you don't snore or have any plans to molest me, *malyu*. Otherwise, you can hang out over there and let the wildlife carry you away.'

'Nor you me,' I said, 'but the snoring? I can't guarantee it.'

'No chance of either, for me. I'm here to mourn. It's an extra special place and I'll stay awake.'

'I guessed as much.' I unrolled my sleeping bag next to his and settled on it.

'I'll get the fire going later and we can share a can of Irish stew I've saved. And we've got the second bottle of spring water I filled in Dales Gorge to see us through. We can take off first thing tomorrow. At the crack of dawn. You'll be woken by the butcherbirds if they're singing.'

'I heard them in Nanutarra the day you left. Just after you'd gone. You're right. They are mesmerising.'

'Best songbirds in the world. Then we can have breakfast at Fitzroy Crossing before I drop you off. How's that sound?'

'Fine,' I said, unsure what the night ahead held in store. While I'd got the better of my earlier fears and he'd surprised me with his consideration and gentleness until now, he was still an unpredictable man I had yet to get to know... and I hadn't forgotten the outrage he displayed for a moment when he asked me the riddle about the roadkill.

He removed his leather jacket and withdrew a plastic photograph holder from an inside pocket. He flicked it open and handed it across to me.

'Meet my Rosalie, Alicia. She was the love of my life, even if some people deny there's such a thing. She's sitting on the rock. She climbed it without realising she shouldn't. I hadn't warned her that the *muwayi*, the country here, is sacred to our Bunuba brothers. I didn't spot her climbing it in time to stop her. I took the shot of her anyway, before she came down.'

I gazed at Rosalie seated on an upper ledge. She was smiling down at Lennard. Her classic green-eyed beauty, striking cheekbones and tanned oval face was framed by auburn hair with copper tints to it, flowing across her shoulders. She was tall and slender, with a black pearl on a fine gold chain at her throat, her swimming costume white. Her arms were wrapped around her knees, her feet bare. She was bathed in mellow light similar to that filling the gorge around us, the cliffs behind her painted the same deep rust and ochre. Their reflections shimmering on the river's surface were so still you'd swear you could step across them.

She was beautiful and looked self-assured. And mysterious, I thought, but was there a hint of teasing mockery in her smile? A knowingness? Is that what had attracted him to her? Out of nowhere, a rush of unexpected envy spread through me and I suppressed it.

'No wonder you loved her, Ace. You must have taken the shot around this time in the evening?'

'Yep, almost to the day and hour, twenty-seven years ago.'

'I'm glad I've met her,' I said, handing the wallet back to him. 'I can see why you brought her here. There is something special about this place.'

'It is special. Very.'

He turned away and stared at the rock in thoughtful silence for several minutes. I did not disturb him. When he turned back to me, his expression was so intense it shocked me. Our eyes met and I held his gaze, uncertain what he was about to tell me.

'Rosalie was shot here on 14 June 1987,' he said at last. He was talking fast, either because he wanted to get it over with, or he was struggling with the emotion. 'You won't remember the German tourist who went berserk up here at that time. I believe Rosalie was his sixth victim, but the police were doubtful at first. They didn't recover the bullet that killed her so they couldn't prove it.' He inhaled deeply and let out a heavy sigh. 'We were swimming in the deeper pool at the time.' He pointed, 'Over there, beside the rock.'

He raised his left fist to his mouth and exhaled a loud breath through his clenched fingers and thumb. 'So anyway, she was badly wounded. I carried her out across the river and tied her behind me on the bike for the ride to Derby Hospital. You can imagine how difficult that was, especially on the gravel.'

'It must have been horrendous.'

'It was. When I got to the bitumen, I came across a tourist operator in a Toyota Land Cruiser, who took us the rest of the way. She died in the Emergency Department at ten that night.'

I squeezed his forearm. 'I'm so sorry, Ace.'

'Yes, well. Nothing else I could do, except bring her ashes up here a month after her funeral and spill them across the pool, which I figured she would have wanted.' He glanced sideways at me, sending me a wry smile. 'That was some trip. The grieving wasn't easy. In fact, it's never easy. It's a shapeshifter, varying in intensity, is all. Strikes when you least expect it.'

I felt a rush of empathy, recognising what I was experiencing with Alain's death. 'I know exactly what you mean.'

'I've come back each year ever since at this time, to mourn. This is my third pilgrimage. I'll never stop if I can help it.'

I realised how difficult it must have been for him to share so intimate a memory with me. 'Thanks for letting me share the privilege.'

I sensed him relaxing. 'If you feel like a swim, by the way, steer clear of the freshie Johnstone crocs in the water here,' he said.

'Freshwater crocodiles?' I sat bolt upright, shock settling in my gut like a block of ice. 'And you two swam here?'

'There are usually some around, but they're shy. Leave them alone and they'll do the same for you.'

'That's reassuring. Thanks for the warning.' I cut short a laugh. 'Swimming's definitely off my agenda.'

'I'll be going in. I always do.'

'Be my guest. Just don't expect to be rescued.'

* * *

I woke at two o'clock the next morning and sat up, immediately uneasy. Lennard was not in the sleeping bag beside me.

The gorge was awash with pale moonlight, the full moon past its zenith. Through the net, I saw the blue-black sky blazing with a brilliant trail of stars, as if someone had flung handfuls of shattered glass across it.

The fire was still lit, the crackling underside of a new log thrown across the glowing embers giving out wisps of smoke and the smell of burning resin.

I saw Lennard sitting motionless at the water's edge. He was facing the rock, cross-legged, straight-backed, his hands palms upwards on his knees, grounded in the scene. He was a dark brown lightning rod in that extraordinary light, his backdrop the rock, an iceberg of glass lit through by moonlight. The towering cliffs behind it glinted like obsidian.

To his left, not ten metres away, two dark shadows were outstretched on the sand. One made a barely perceptible movement and the bright red flash of a pair of eyes glowed in the firelight. Horrified, I froze, holding my breath. The freshwater Johnstone crocodiles he'd warned me about. Shy, he'd said, but aggressive if provoked.

For twenty nervous minutes, I sat and absorbed the scene, prepared to scream a warning at Lennard if I needed to.

Looking out through the net, I suddenly became eerily detached, as if I was someone other, separated from reality by the finest veil, as if a swirling, multi-dimensional hologram was transforming around me. I seemed to be on the verge of passing out, unable to grasp the mystery unfolding in front of me, as if losing my sense of self and descending into a fearful void. It was threatening. I thought I was milliseconds away from losing my mind and being enveloped in some terrifying ecstasy.

I lifted my right hand and struck my left shoulder hard to disperse the vertiginous sensation of disconnection from reality... or connection with something uncanny, infinite and unreal.

The sound of the slap must have disturbed Lennard.

Without looking round, he stood and walked barefoot knee-deep into the water, his jeans rolled up. The crocodiles, disturbed, spun around and hurtled towards the pool, one or both emitting low-pitched growls of warning. They splashed beneath the surface, their thrashing tails leaving a trail of foam and an expanding arrowhead of ripples, the triangular scales along their backs visible until they submerged and the pool resumed its calm.

I watched, disbelieving, as Lennard walked further out until only his head was showing and he swam towards the rock before disappearing behind it. He did not reappear. I waited for over half an hour before relaxing and sinking back into an uneasy sleep.

I woke late for once, the calls of the corellas disturbing me. When I opened my eyes and squinted, I discovered Lennard leaning over me, blocking out the sun. He nudged me with his toe.

'Time we were on the move, *malyu*,' he said, giving a dry chuckle. 'It's a wonder you slept through your snoring. You were like a steam train once you got going.'

'Thanks for the reminder,' I said, hauling myself out of the sleeping bag. 'I never heard the butcherbirds.'

'No. The corellas did the trick.'

I looked around and discovered he had removed the net and his sleeping bag and he'd cleared away all signs of our having spent the night there. 'You've been busy.'

'I got rid of the evidence while you were snoring.'

'What happened to you last night? The last I saw of you at two this morning you swam behind the rock and disappeared.'

'I do that sometimes.' He grinned. 'Vanish into thin air like a *kadaitcha* medicine man, leaving no trace. I was checking the proportions of the rock on the other side for the cenotaph. Took me a while before I came back. I got an extra couple of hours of sleep before dawn, would you believe, so I'm good to go. It's time we made tracks.'

An hour and a half later, we reached the bitumen of the Great Northern Highway.

'I usually turn right here and head south, back to Perth,' Lennard said, as he turned left instead, 'but I've promised you breakfast and I'm starving, so we'll head for Fitzroy Crossing. I can drop you off there once we've fed.'

'Sounds good to me.'

Forty minutes later we were enjoying Marty's Specialty of the Day in the Homestead Restaurant at the Crossing Inn—a thick omelette quiche with the lot, mushrooms and all, washed down with hot coffee. It was a meal to die for after last night's can of Irish stew.

The Fitzroy River—a wide brown slick of gliding water—was visible between the trunks of flowering river red gums, their discarded flowers a white carpet spread across the sparse lawns.

'So,' Lennard said, when we'd finished the meal, 'let's talk about the elephant in the room. Is there any point in me giving you one more pitch to join Annie Morgan and the others giving CPR to our endangered Malgana language?'

I glanced out across the river, my thoughts racing. Return to Perth within a week of leaving? After spending so long building up the determination to escape everything there that reminded me of Alain's tragic death? No. Definitely not.

I turned back to him. 'Look, it's difficult for me, Ace. I appreciate the offer, I truly do.'

'Oh-oh, that's what you said before. Here we go. Here comes the Dear John.'

'I know we haven't talked about it since Broome, but I have given it a lot of thought. The idea of working on the language is extremely tempting and learning more about the Malgana songlines you mentioned is something I'm keen to do. But as I explained, some things have happened this year I haven't yet come to terms with.'

I raised my hand to prevent him from responding. 'I have to pick myself up and get myself motivated. I have to turn what's happened to me into something positive. I told you that's why I'm on this journey and doing it the hard way, hitchhiking. Testing myself by travelling to Darwin and Yirrkala. They're my goals right now. My mind is set, and the best way for me to keep going *is* to keep going. I need to be sure I'm coping and back in the world of the living before I settle on anything else.'

'So that's it?' He raised his eyebrows, thoughtful disappointment reflected in his eyes. 'I can't convince you there's testing and there's testing, and you've done well to get this far? I can't get you to come back with me and take the next step up from the bottom rung in Fremantle?'

'I don't think I can compromise, Ace.'

'You don't think or you can't?'

'I can't.'

He leaned across and patted my shoulder as he rose. 'All right. Like I said, there's no hard feelings, *malyu*. Make sure you visit me if you're ever back in Perth. And I know the Geraldton language centre will always welcome someone with your expertise.'

'Of course I will.'

'Make sure you do.' He gave me a wide, frank smile. 'You know what they say, drink the water up here and you'll never leave, and last night you drank the water from Dales Gorge. Now you're a goner. You'll be back. I simply have to count the days, by crikey.'

We rode through the town and he stopped beside a coppice of towering ghost gums three hundred metres north of the outskirts.

'This looks the goods,' he said. 'You've got some shade and it's a long straight stretch, so you'll stick out like a dog's.'

'That's one Australian slang phrase I do know,' I said, laughing as we dismounted, 'but I wish I'd never heard it. It reminds me of my brother Andrés's dog, Geronimo, and it's completely changed my image of him.'

'Sorry about that,' he said, flicking the motorbike stand out with his boot and propping it up. He shook his head, his expression filled with regret. 'So this is it, Alicia. Mission only half-accomplished, as far as I'm concerned. But at least you're on your way.'

He stepped forward, put a hand on my forearm and attempted to kiss me, but I dropped my backpack and turned my face away. His beard grazed my neck and ear as he took a quick backward step. When I looked at him, I realised I'd both surprised and hurt him. I felt terrible.

'Please don't get me wrong, Ace,' I said. 'That's not how we Tarahumara farewell each other. I showed you how we do it. Remember?' We held out our right hands and our fingers stroked our palms. 'Now we're bound to meet again.'

'Sooner the better,' he said. 'If you do come back to Perth, you'll find me in the glassworks on Bathers Beach in Freo. You got that? Bathers Beach.'

'Goodbye, Ace. Thanks for the lift. And everything else. I appreciate all you've done for me.'

He mounted the bike and turned southwards, towards the town. He lowered his visor. 'See you when I see you,' he said. 'Hopefully sooner than that, to be honest.'

He accelerated down the road and didn't look back.

As he disappeared, somewhere in the tree above me unseen birds broke into bursts of song and an electric jolt of excitement raced through me. Butcherbirds again! Others in the nearby trees echoed the fluted trills and calls. I listened, spellbound, as a wave of grief welled through me and I was back in Windjana Gorge, looking through the net at Lennard meditating at the water's edge. He was so integral to the landscape I experienced the pain of my exclusion from it.

And from him, I suddenly realised.

I'd rarely felt so isolated, my deepest vulnerabilities exposed. I had an aching need to connect with the sense of mystery in the world around me that Lennard seemed somehow to be in touch with. I had so much to learn... and so much to give linguistically.

Before I could stop myself, I sprinted across the road and ran along the verge, following him, waving desperately and screaming at him in the growing distance. He didn't respond at first, and then I saw him bend to peer into his rear-view mirror, before coming to a stop and twisting around to look back at me.

He turned the bike and rode back, the thumping of the engine changing tone as he approached, sunlight flashing from his visor—a diamond glittering on a ribbon of black silk once again.

I took a deep breath to calm the pulse beating in my throat and I was unexpectedly conflicted, my excitement tempered by sadness close to deep despair at seemingly betraying Alain's memory so soon.

* * *

It wasn't until I met Annie Morgan two days later that I forgave myself and was filled with gratitude as I anticipated the changes in my life's direction.

Lennard introduced us when we passed through Northampton.

She was sitting with two friends on her front veranda beneath sprays of purple bougainvillea. Their animated conversation reached us when Lennard switched off his Harley and we dismounted. It sounded as though they were bickering and squabbling good-humouredly at the tops of their voices, intermittent bursts of laughter carrying to us as we approached.

They were silent as we climbed the steps. The whirring of their battered Panasonic tape recorder greeted our arrival, before one of them—Susie Kelly, I soon discovered—switched it off and the rollers squealed to a stop.

'Afternoon, Aunties,' Lennard said. 'Let me introduce Alicia Serrano.'

With an extended forefinger he pointed out Annie Morgan, Susie Kelly and Molly Sanderson in turn, before explaining, 'I picked Alicia up on the side of the road at Exmouth, hitch-hiking to Darwin—'

'*Darwin?*' Molly interrupted him. 'You lost your bearin's, sister? Aren't you headin' in the wrong direction?'

'No, Aunty Mol. I've convinced her to join us. This is where she belongs right now. Where she's needed. Alicia is the linguist we've been looking for.' Then he grinned. 'With a PhD.'

In the silence that followed, the three old ladies looked up at me bright-eyed, dawning appreciation evident in their collective, '*Aaaah.*'

'Just what the doctor ordered,' Annie Morgan said, patting the seat beside her. 'Never mind Darwin. Make yourself at home right here, 'Leesh. Next to me. Tell us all about yourself.'

Although her sunken eyes were bright and her strong, dark face appeared cheerful beneath a red-chequered scarf that concealed her skull, her wheezing cough told a different story.

When I sat beside her she took my right hand in both of hers and stroked it, without a further word. An unexpected rush of warmth overwhelmed me. Deep in the heart's core, I knew I had come home. I had found my place and understood for certain, like never before, that I had a new sense of purpose and a deep connection to others.

I sensed that I had Mamá's unconditional approval as I determined to become such as I truly was, now that I'd discovered who that is—someone clear-sighted and unstoppable—and I realised that without Mamá, I would have become no more than a shadow of myself.

I looked searchingly at Annie as vivid recollections of the day I spent with Tía Ariché at Cerocahui when I was five flooded my mind, as if I'd breached the wall between then and now, as if confirming I was irrevocably bound to the challenges chance and coincidence had arranged for me ever since.

'My mother, Suré, died on 10 May 1960, a month after I was born,' I began. 'Although I have no memory of her, I've spent my life trying to recall her particular smell, her comforting touch, the beating of her heart against my own. I have a tinted photograph showing me feeding at her right breast, taken a week before she died. I carry it with me everywhere.'

Gently releasing Annie's hands, I took the leather wallet from my breast pocket and handed it across to her with the photograph face up. 'She held me in her arms for those thirty days' I said, 'and I treasure every moment of our imagined closeness. The day she died is Mother's Day, of all days. Can you believe it?'

Acknowledgements

THIS NOVEL COMPLETES THE Truth & Reconciliation trilogy, which includes *The Glass Cenotaph* and *The Life and Times of Gerrit De Waal*. It wouldn't have seen the light of day in its current form without the cooperation and advice of others. I owe them my deepest thanks.

Lynne Stringer, my reliable and brilliant editor who has devoted so much time to correcting and tweaking all my work over the years. Lynne's changes are always spot on. They never fail to improve the word choice, plot sequences and storylines. I owe you my heartfelt thanks.

Tireless James Munro of Australian e-book publishing, whose extensive technical skills I have tested many times. Thank you for your creativity in preparing my work for publication to the highest standards and for your persistence and timeliness.

Many thanks also to my pre-publication researchers, readers and advisers whose guidance and interest I value: Mike and Jenny Purchase, Karen, Kaylee and Elly Monaco, Gill Bennett, De Kropach, Bruce and Inka Hutton, Cam and Jae, Jessica Lee, Dayna Norris and Kay Stehn. Without you none of my work would have reached the reading public.

About the Author

Born in Tanzania, from the age of six I was fortunate to grow up in Mombasa on the Kenya coast. One of my goals in life was to research the Arab, Chinese, Portuguese and Dutch explorers who sailed along the East African Swahili coast for centuries.

I migrated to Perth, Western Australia, in 1963. After a 7-year stint as a High School teacher, I transferred to Human Resources and worked on remote mine sites in the Pilbara, Northern Territory and Papua New Guinea. This brought me into close contact with local Indigenous people. I found their culture, deep rooted love of country, resilience and unfailing sense of humour inspirational.

I retired in 2008 and since then have dedicated myself to writing fictional novels based on historical themes. 3 of these comprise the Truth and Reconciliation Trilogy. They draw on 20 years of archival research undertaken in Australia and the Netherlands (Zeeland), and an appreciation of Australia's First Nations people, who have survived the effects of European settlement and colonialism. The trilogy gives you a fresh look at Australia's colonial history and reflects the current dialogue between the Aboriginal First Nation people and the rest of Australia.

I have also written a number of short stories, most of them included in my collection, including some drawn from sections of the trilogy. I trust you enjoy reading the novels and short stories as much as I enjoyed writing them.